China's African Challenges

Sarah Raine

CHINA'S AFRICAN CHALLENGES

SARAH RAINE

China's African Challenges

Sarah Raine

IISS The International Institute for Strategic Studies

The International Institute for Strategic Studies

Arundel House | 13–15 Arundel Street | Temple Place | London | WC2R 3DX | UK

First published May 2009 by **Routledge**
4 Park Square, Milton Park, Abingdon, Oxon, OX14 4RN

for **The International Institute for Strategic Studies**
Arundel House, 13–15 Arundel Street, Temple Place, London, WC2R 3DX, UK
www.iiss.org

Simultaneously published in the USA and Canada by **Routledge**
270 Madison Ave., New York, NY 10016

Routledge is an imprint of Taylor & Francis, an Informa Business

© 2009 The International Institute for Strategic Studies

DIRECTOR-GENERAL AND CHIEF EXECUTIVE John Chipman
EDITOR Tim Huxley
MANAGER FOR EDITORIAL SERVICES Ayse Abdullah
ASSISTANT EDITOR Katharine Fletcher
COVER/PRODUCTION John Buck
COVER ILLUSTRATION Steve Dell

The International Institute for Strategic Studies is an independent centre for research, information and debate on the problems of conflict, however caused, that have, or potentially have, an important military content. The Council and Staff of the Institute are international and its membership is drawn from almost 100 countries. The Institute is independent and it alone decides what activities to conduct. It owes no allegiance to any government, any group of governments or any political or other organisation. The IISS stresses rigorous research with a forward-looking policy orientation and places particular emphasis on bringing new perspectives to the strategic debate.

The Institute's publications are designed to meet the needs of a wider audience than its own membership and are available on subscription, by mail order and in good bookshops. Further details at www.iiss.org.

Printed and bound in Great Britain by Bell & Bain Ltd, Thornliebank, Glasgow

British Library Cataloguing in Publication Data
A catalogue record for this book is available from the British Library

Library of Congress Cataloging in Publication Data

ISBN 978-0-415-55693-4
ISSN 0567-932X

ADELPHI 404–405

Contents

The author gratefully acknowledges the support of John McLaren, chairman of the Barchester Group, in the conduct of research for this book. She would also like to thank all those experts, officials and colleagues who gave so generously of their time, help and hospitality, and who offered thought-provoking discussions.

GLOSSARY

APEC	Asia-Pacific Economic Cooperation forum
AFRICOM	Africa Command (US)
AGOA	African Growth and Opportunity Act
ASEAN	Association of Southeast Asian Nations
AU	African Union
CABC	China–Africa Business Council
CADF	China–Africa Development Fund
CAITEC	Chinese Academy of International Trade and Economic Cooperation
CASS	Chinese Academy of Social Sciences
CCP	Chinese Communist Party
CDB	China Development Bank
CIC	China Investment Corporation
CMEC	China National Machinery and Equipment Import and Export Corporation
CNOOC	China National Offshore Oil Corporation
CNPC	China National Petroleum Corporation
CPA	North–South Comprehensive Peace Agreement (Sudan)
CPCC	China Petroleum and Chemical Corporation
CSR	corporate social responsibility
DRC	Democratic Republic of the Congo
EBA	Everything but Arms
ECOWAS	Economic Community of West African States
ECZ	Trade and Economic Cooperation Zone
EITI	Extractive Industries Transparency Initiative
ExIm	Export–Import (bank)
FOCAC	Forum on China–Africa Cooperation
ICBC	Industrial and Commercial Bank of China

IFC	International Finance Corporation
IMF	International Monetary Fund
KMT	Kuomintang
KOAFEC	Korea–Africa Economic Cooperation Conference
MEND	Movement for the Emancipation of the Niger Delta
MONUC	UN Mission in the DRC
NDRC	National Development and Reform Commission
NEPAD	New Partnership for Africa's Development
NGO	non-governmental organisation
NOC	national oil company
OAU	Organisation of African Unity
OECD	Organisation for Economic Cooperation and Development
PEPFAR	Presidential Emergency Plan for AIDS Relief
PLA	People's Liberation Army
PRC	People's Republic of China
P5	Permanent 5 (members of the UN Security Council)
RMB	renminbi (currency of China)
SADC	Southern African Development Community
SAFE	State Administration of Foreign Exchange
SASAC	State-owned Assets Supervision and Administration Commission
SME	small or medium-sized enterprise
SOE	state-owned enterprise
SPLA/M	Sudan People's Liberation Army/Movement
TICAD	Tokyo International Conference on African Development
UNSCR	United Nations Security Council Resolution
ZTE	Zongxing Telecom Equipment

Africa

At the end of the Second Boer War in 1902, the operators of the gold-producing Rand Mines in the Transvaal in modern-day South Africa were faced with shortages in the supply of African labour. In 1904, in the face of fierce Boer opposition, the Legislative Council of the Transvaal, which was now a British colony, finally conceded to the passage of a Labour Importation Ordinance. This provided for the introduction of indentured Chinese labourers under strict conditions, and was intended as a temporary measure to hasten the release of the promised riches for which the costly war had, at least in part, been fought. In the years that followed, as many as 63,000 Chinese labourers were imported into the Transvaal, adding dramatically to the estimated 2,000 Chinese already resident there and in the Cape Colony.[1] The ordinance was controversial in the Crown colony, where it brought further tension to an already racially charged political environment, as well as in London. Questions were raised in Parliament about the cost, ethics and possible social impact of importing Chinese labour into the Transvaal; two debates in February and July 1905 focused on the issue in detail. It even became a theme of the 1906 British general-election campaign – a contest that the Liberal Party, which wanted to see the imported labourers repatriated, proceeded to win in a landslide.[2] In a parliamentary debate in 1907, Under-Secretary of State for the Colonies Winston Churchill remarked that 'the presence of 50,000 Chinese on the Rand was an element which added to the general insecurity of the country'.[3]

In the late 1950s and early 1960s, amid the complex politics of the Cold War, the West was once again fretting over Chinese ties to Africa, for different reasons. Could China's revolutionary attentions pull Africa into its orbit, shrinking or even ending the West's traditional sphere of influence on the continent?

Another half-century later, in 2006, it was China's 'Year of Africa'. Chinese Foreign Minister Li Zhaoxing had, as usual, begun the year with a trip to Africa, taking in six countries. In April, President Hu Jintao visited a further three African states. In June, it was the turn of Premier Wen Jiabao; he called on another seven countries on the continent. In November, in a triumph of choreography and ambition, China entertained high-level representatives from 48 African states in Beijing at a summit meeting of the Forum on China–Africa Cooperation (FOCAC). International interest in burgeoning Sino-African relations, already gathering some momentum, now went into overdrive. Western commentators quickly developed some pet themes, along with a vocabulary for their exposition. Was China's 'trade safari' a case of the dragon plundering while the ostrich buried its head in the sand? Was China, with its 'insatiable appetite' for resources pursued through neo-mercantilist trade policies, undermining any progress the West was making on preaching and then leveraging the virtues of democracy, good governance and transparency in Africa? Poles were quickly defined. For many observers it seemed either that China was engaged in a colonialist project of resource exploitation, undermining the West's influence with its own rival 'model' for development, or that China was simply offering Africa an opportunity to focus on trade rather than aid, and to break free from the clutches of the West's overpaid, dogmatic consultants who persisted in viewing the continent as 'hopeless'.[4]

Thankfully, greater moderation in the debate over Sino-African relations is now beginning to emerge. Conspiracy-minded questions about Chinese covert and provocative agendas on the continent are diminishing, along with any dreams that China might provide a single-entity panacea for the challenges of Africa's development. While Africa's fortunes have changed considerably over the past decade, serious challenges remain. Although more than $500 billion in aid has been disbursed on the continent over the last half-century, around 380 million people in sub-Saharan Africa still live on less than $1.25 a day.[5] In the resource superpower that is the Democratic Republic of the Congo (DRC), more than 70% of the population continues to live below the poverty line.[6] Against this background, the touted compatibility of China's interests with Africa's products and markets looks like a good opportunity for the further development of stability and prosperity in both Africa and China. In recent years, Angola and Equatorial Guinea have consistently ranked in the top ten fastest growing economies in the world, based on real growth rates of GDP. Between 2000 and 2006, sub-Saharan Africa's annual growth rate averaged 4.7%, in contrast to a 2.5% average rate between 1990 and 2000.[7] In 2007, the growth rate for the entire African continent reached 6.5%.[8] China has played no small part in the development of such trends. Although African growth rates will be damaged by the fall in commodity prices and the global economic turmoil that began in 2007–08, China's role in determining the level of this damage in Africa and the speed of the continent's recovery will be similarly significant.[9]

Yet even when the hyperbole has been removed, fundamental questions remain. Is China, in its extension of loans to secure resources, really negotiating a fair price with its often weaker counterparts, or is it instead encouraging this generation of African leaders to take on yet more debt that future generations will struggle to pay off, thereby counteracting the effects of current debt-cancellation schemes? What does China's 'no conditions' aid mean for the future of good governance and democracy in Africa? Can China find ways to secure its interests in the continent without becoming the partner of choice for pariah states, and even recognise that its growing investments in the continent deserve to be safeguarded by a parallel growth in its role in conflict prevention and resolution? At a time when fears about an increase in competition for resources are in danger of becoming self-fulfilling, how can all those involved, African nations included, develop and respect agreed standards of behaviour and avoid a 'race to the bottom'?

Sino-African relations deserve the attention they are receiving because of the importance of the issues at stake. If commentators on all sides agree that, handled properly, China's interests in Africa present an opportunity for African development, it is only right that those interested in Africa's development concern themselves with the question of how these relations might be 'handled properly'. But these relations also matter because they offer clues as to how China may be changing the international system within which we all live, as well as how the West's quest to ensure that China becomes a stakeholder within this system, and thus broadly a 'status-quo' power, is progressing. In seeking to develop this theme, this book moves the focus on Chinese engagement in Africa away from that continent and back onto China, considering what challenges China is encountering in these engagements and how it is responding to them. It argues for thinking about Sino-

African relations not just in the light of Africa's development, but in the light of China's as well. If Africa has become something of a commercial training ground for Chinese enterprises that are globalising their operations, it is also a training ground for a Chinese government going global, as well as for Western powers interested in helping to direct this process towards an end state of cooperation and partnership. The book therefore seeks to complement the important and growing body of literature examining African and Western reactions to Chinese interests and their effects by looking at early indications of Chinese counter-reactions and considering what these might herald for all those involved.

Be they state-level or regional, focused on business or on diplomacy, are China's institutions able to listen and control and adapt their engagements in Africa so as to ensure the development of sustainable relations? Rapid, geographically expansive engagements are not always deep or sustainable. Inventories of developing Sino-African engagements in the early years of the twenty-first century may look impressive, but business contracts can be reallocated and political alliances require upkeep. As courtships have led to engagements, and as relations now begin to mature, what will be the future of these relationships? How solid are their foundations? Cracks in some relationships are already appearing. Although mutual self-interest should ensure that these contacts will survive in some form or other, they will not necessarily prosper, especially if China fails to pay sufficient attention to the reasons behind the emergence of these cracks, which have the potential to jeopardise the stability and sustainability of its engagements.

The People's Republic of China (PRC) remains a relatively young nation. The year 2009 marks its 60th anniversary; its fifth generation of leaders will not take the helm until 2012. During its time in power, the Chinese Communist Party (CCP) has adapted to considerable changes in the international environment many times over, demonstrating impressive survival skills. As China increases its interactions in Africa and elsewhere, new adjustments to the CCP's strategies of international engagement are already in evidence. In politics, these adjustments include greater participation in multilateral attempts to tackle key transnational issues. In business, they cover the increased use of smaller stakes and passive investments, aimed at alleviating concerns about CCP-controlled capital in the international economic system.

But what do these adjustments look like in the context of China's African ventures? Concerns to ensure stability and further development at home, and possibly also to develop increased authority abroad, have brought the Chinese government to Africa. Yet in its initial handling of its engagements on the continent, China has too often played for short-term advantage, storing up challenges that will need tackling further down the line. In the medium term, will China's institutions be able to handle these challenges and develop better working practices in order to protect their investments and the progress they have made in Africa? A Chinese saying speaks of 'groping for stones to cross a river'. As China goes about groping for policies to support its increasing involvement with Africa, the question remains open as to how swift and smooth the crossing to a sustainable and positive Sino-African dynamic will be.

Naturally, the renewal of China's interest in Africa is not taking place in isolation from the country's engagements elsewhere. China has also become noticeably more active in other parts of the developing world. Chinese commercial and political relations with Latin America, Southeast Asia, Central Asia and the Pacific islands have all burgeoned over the past decade. These are parts of the world which, like Africa, tend to be resource rich and which, again like Africa, tend to be home to developing countries with which China seeks to establish a common bond. Some of China's approaches to the developing world are generic, such as the use of high-level state visits to cultivate personal relationships between the ruling elites. In February 2009, President Hu Jintao toured Mali, Senegal, Tanzania, Mauritius and Saudi Arabia, while Vice President Xi Jinping visited Brazil, Mexico, Colombia, Venezuela and Jamaica and Vice Premier Hui Liangyu went to Argentina, Ecuador, the Bahamas and Barbados. Many approaches, however, are more differentiated, varying according to China's priorities and its relationship with the partner in question. In Southeast Asia, China's burden of history is heavy, thanks to its past sponsorship of communist revolutionary movements and interference in domestic affairs through local ethnic Chinese communities. Here, therefore, China pursues its resource and trade interests with a careful eye on a wider strategic interest in building an 'amicable, tranquil and prosperous neighbourhood'.[10] In Central Asia, resource interests are paralleled by strategic and political interests of a different kind – for example, the concern to manage the potential for unrest in the Muslim Uighur population in China's northwestern province of Xinjiang, which borders to its west Kazakhstan, Kyrgyzstan, Tajikistan, Afghanistan and Pakistan-administered Kashmir. As China's trade with Africa has expanded rapidly, so has Sino-Latin American trade, which surpassed $100bn in 2007, a year before Sino-African trade broke the same barrier.[11] As in Africa, bilateral relations here have diverse foundations, from China's long-standing if complicated socialist ties with Cuba to its trading ties with Mexico. The global diplomatic struggle to secure Taiwan's recognition as a province of the PRC also endures, particularly in China's dealings with Central and Latin America and with Africa and the Pacific islands.

Some of the problems that have been created by China's African engagements have parallels elsewhere, as do some of the resultant adaptations in approaches. The antagonism that Chinese interests have faced from local workers, communities and media on a number of occasions in Africa – perhaps most prominently at the Chambishi copper mine in Zambia, but also elsewhere on the continent – has been mirrored in other developing countries. At Ramu nickel mine in Papua New Guinea, which has been run by the state-owned China Metallurgical Group Corporation since 2003, for example, there have been tensions with the local community and media, and even local state authorities, as witnessed by the arrest of 213 Chinese employees over visa irregularities in November 2008. Chinese authorities are responding here as they have in Africa and elsewhere, in part by increasing development aid, while the Ramu mine now has a community-affairs department that operates to the slogan 'One Ramu NiCo, One Community'.[12] Nevertheless, although it is important to remember the broader context in which China is developing its African relations, the ways in which China's interests are prosecuted under this 'developing world' banner and the priority that is given to particular interests vary considerably according to geography, economics, politics and history.

In discussions of China's relations with the African continent, the shorthand may be 'China–Africa', but the subtext is invariably 'China, Africa and the West'. As African countries develop and their economic and political suitors increase in number – be they traditional powers refocusing their attentions, or new powers emerging – sub-Saharan Africa is becoming one of the first significant regional testing grounds for multipolarity, or even 'nonpolarity'.[13] It is here that established powers from the West and developing economic powers from the East are increasingly rubbing up against each other, and it is here that the early dynamics are being set in motion that will help to determine how cooperative or competitive such a world will become. Africa is, to use the language of one 2007 academic dialogue between Africa, China and the US, 'in play' as never before.[14] The continent has become the arena in which the powers of Asia and the West can test each other's intentions and establish the opportunities and limits of cooperation, whether in the context of peacekeeping, the search for markets, or securing natural resources.

Of course, even the terms 'China' and 'Africa' present challenges of definition. Africa is a continent of 53 countries hosting more than 2,000 languages and cultures.[15] This book focuses its attentions on sub-Saharan Africa, which has a very different history and political–cultural orientation from the north of the continent. But even in the countries south of the Sahara, the diversity of ethnicities, cultures, styles of leadership, resource endowments and markets means that any generalisations remain precisely that. Likewise, despite the CCP's success in uniting the Chinese mainland under a single government, 'China' too remains a complicated host of different interests, institutions, cultures and ethnicities. To pick just one example, the sociological differences that exist within China are enormous, and the range and depth of these differences are mirrored in Chinese interactions in Africa. Even as a state, China has a dual identity. On the one hand, China is already a major player in the world in the fields of trade and economic power. In other respects, it remains a developing country, with more than 200m people continuing to live below the poverty line and a per-capita national income around one-eighteenth of that enjoyed by the population of the US.[16] It is both in deference to this plurality and as a reminder of it that plural forms such as 'engagements', 'relations' and the like are used here. Nevertheless, with all these caveats acknowledged, this analysis is intentionally and unapologetically broad-brush, in the firm belief that useful conclusions can still be drawn from such a perspective.

The motivation for China's African engagements is not unreasonable, and these engagements should come as no surprise to observers of these dynamics. Where China's leaders had previously judged the country's development best served by focusing inwards and keeping foreign engagements to a minimum, a new reality is emerging to which both China's leaders and the international community are having to adjust. China's ruling party needs foreign resources and markets to protect the country's impressive – and politically indispensable – rates of growth; it may also welcome the diplomatic influence these interactions can bring. Approaches based on Deng Xiaoping's exhortation that China 'never be the leader', or even on the later, more expansive, idea of the country's 'peaceful rise', are increasingly being challenged by the need to shift Chinese diplomacy onto a more active footing in the pursuit of a clearer set of interests that lie beyond China's borders.

The issue of how China is adapting in response to its African engagements is infused with political sensitivities. African leaders tend to repudiate the patronising viewpoint that sees them as requiring Western help in learning how to 'cope with' Chinese intentions. Meanwhile, Chinese leaders nod towards Western-originated proposals for trilateral cooperation but remain suspicious that this interest in Sino-African relations is in fact interference driven by jealousy and self-interested anxiety, and comes steeped in double standards. Headline-grabbing media reports of the 'threat' that China is posing to Africa and to Western interests there can make it awkward for Westerners to consider Sino-African relations without being seen as working to a patronising or interfering agenda. But this is neither fair nor helpful. The West's colonial impact on Africa was certainly tragic in many respects. The West may still not be as productive a friend to Africa as it might like to imagine. Yet this does not make Western interest in the future of China's relations with Africa illegitimate. It is not only a question of concern for Africa's future. If China succeeds in 'rising', then the West has an interest in the kind of world that China will help lead. If the West is concerned about the sort of international community with which the Chinese leadership would presently feel most at ease, then it has an interest in considering what opportunities and strategies might alleviate such anxieties, thereby allowing for peaceful and positive collaboration in the more multipolar world of the future.

CHAPTER ONE

Contextualising Today's Sino-African Relations

The invocation of a historical friendship underpinning contemporary Sino-African relations appears to be something of a preoccupation for Chinese scholars and officials. As they seek to establish their country's connections with Africa, scholars may draw attention to the discovery of ancient Chinese ceramics on the east coast of Africa, or to the trading ties begun under the Song dynasty (960–1279), while officials may approvingly recall the fifteenth-century adventures of Chinese explorer Zheng He. Under Emperor Zhu Di, the maritime expeditions of Admiral Zheng, a Muslim eunuch, helped temporarily to re-establish China as a key regional power and as the world's top naval power almost a century before Christopher Columbus began his well-documented explorations. At least two of Zheng's voyages reached the east coast of Africa where, Chinese officials and scholars like to remark, Zheng came, saw and never conquered. Despite the might of his naval fleet, Zheng's expeditions did not take advantage of the obvious asymmetry in power, seizing no slaves and leaving no colonisers. If they left a legacy, it was one of trade, stimulating a local market for Chinese silk and porcelain. China and Africa, Chinese leaders repeatedly observe today, are two great civilisations with impressive cultural heritages. China, as the world's largest developing country, is posited as a natural ally of Africa, the largest developing continent. The bonds between the two are presented as long-standing and deep-seated. During a 2009 visit to Tanzania, President Hu even remarked, 'Every time I come, it's like coming back home'.[1]

Anyone who has spent time in China will be aware of the official predilection for deploying historical references to account for present-day dynamics. In the case of Sino-African relations, the subtext of the referencing of history is clear: the intention is to be simultaneously assertive about the existence of a deep-seated bond between China and Africa and reassuring about what it signifies. China has been a great power before, and it has traded in Africa before. Despite having had opportunities to press home its advantages more forcefully, it has interacted commercially without further agenda and without detriment to Africa, or even to the West. The implicit contrast with the West's own sorry history on the continent is stark and deliberate.

Indeed, prior to 1949 and the establishment of the PRC, there was no specifically African element to Chinese foreign policy. Contact, when it came, came largely as a result of trade rather than from any conscious effort to engage. Perhaps ironically, Western colonialism also played a role in developing contact between the peoples of China and Africa. In the seventeenth century, African slaves were brought by their Dutch masters to the island the Dutch called Formosa (Taiwan). Some escaped and joined forces with the anti-Qing warrior Koxinga in his ultimately successful fight to expel the Dutch from Taiwan after only 38 years of colonial rule. Following the abolition of slavery in most of the British empire in 1833, and in the French empire in 1848, the practice of taking indentured Chinese (and Indian) workers to Africa in order to help meet the growing demand for labour there increased. Terms and conditions of employment were often harsh. In 1929, France enlisted 786 Chinese labourers to help to build a railway from Brazzaville to Pointe-Noire on the Atlantic coast of the modern-day Republic of the Congo. Riots soon followed, as Chinese labourers protested the conditions in which they were required to work. 190 purported rioters were soon returned to China.[2] At the start of the twentieth century, alongside the Chinese indentured labour brought to work in the gold mines at the southern tip of the continent, independent Chinese traders began arriving in Africa in greater numbers. Mauritius was a popular entry point; by the 1930s, there were as many as 20,000 Chinese on the island.[3] So it was that, when Chinese Premier Zhou Enlai visited Tanzania in 1965, he was able to follow the formula, referencing Zheng He's legacy, and proclaiming 'My colleagues and I do not find ourselves in a strange land. Intercourse between our countries dates back to 900 years ago'.[4]

The evolution of the PRC's African interests

Mao and revolution

In the years immediately following the establishment of the PRC, Mao's priority was to stabilise the country's borders and establish and legitimise the Communist Party's rule over all of China. In 1954, the first set of key principles for the conduct of the PRC's foreign relations was officially formulated. The 'Five Principles of Peaceful Coexistence' called for mutual respect for sovereignty, non-aggression, non-interference, equality and mutual benefit, and peaceful coexistence. These principles, which formally endure today, were originally devised as guidelines for China's dealings with India over Tibet. However, they soon took on a wider foreign-policy relevance when they were embraced by the 29 participating countries at the Asian–African Bandung Conference of April 1955.[5]

From the outset, China applied the principles with impressive pragmatism. Gaps between rhetoric and reality quickly emerged. It was in the political, military and economic support that the CCP leadership offered African countries in their struggles for independence, in the face of its rhetoric of non-interference and non-aggression, that the PRC's relations with Africa were first properly developed. Although it would not be until the early 1960s that China would really begin to emerge from the shadow of the USSR, already by the mid 1950s its foreign policy was increasingly assertive. At the eighth National Congress of the CCP in 1956, Mao declared 'We must render active support to the movements for national independence of the various countries in Asia, Africa and Latin America'.[6] In 1957, the first conference of the Afro-Asian Peoples' Solidarity Organisation was held. In 1960, China established the China–African People's Friendship Association. As African nations won their independence, the PRC began to win new diplomatic recognition. The PRC's quest for diplomatic partners was helped by its pragmatic offer of immediate recognition to newly independent countries on the basis of the Five Principles, regardless of the political orientation of their leadership.

It had not, however, been an easy start. When the CCP emerged victorious at the end of the Chinese civil war in 1949, none of Africa's three independent countries had recognised China's new government.[7] But once it had made the breakthrough of establishing diplomatic relations with Egypt in 1956, the PRC made good progress on the continent. New diplomatic partnerships offered useful support to a government increasingly in conflict with its supposed ideological partner, the USSR, and still fighting for recognition from the United Nations against the continuing claims of the Kuomintang (KMT) government, now in exile in Taiwan (the 'Republic of China'). Zhou Enlai, who as prime minister and foreign minister had headed the Chinese delegation to Bandung, worked hard to develop the 'Bandung spirit', conducting three major foreign tours to promote the PRC abroad. The third of these took him to Africa. Between December 1963 and February 1964, Zhou visited ten African countries.[8] It was on this tour that Zhou put forward 'Eight Principles Governing China's Economic and Technological Assistance to Foreign Countries', and 'Five Principles Governing Relations with African and Arab Countries'. These principles, along with the earlier 'Five Principles of Peaceful Coexistence', are among the small number of policy proclamations that continue to form the ideological backdrop for relations today. The 'Eight Principles' set out the requirement that, in the delivery of foreign assistance to a country, the sovereignty of the recipient government must be respected, meaning that there can be no accompanying conditions. They also establish the policy of supplying economic aid through interest-free or low-interest loans with long repayment periods, and promise personnel training and technology transfer. The 'Five Principles' reaffirm support for the struggle against colonialism and for non-alignment, self-determination, non-aggression and, once more, respect for sovereignty.

By the mid 1960s, the promise of the 1950 Sino-Soviet Treaty of Friendship, Alliance and Mutual Assistance was fading. The 1965 essay 'Long Live the Victory of People's War' by Defence Minister General Lin Biao revealed a China increasingly confident in its promotion of revolution, and competitive in its bid for Third World leadership. According to Lin, the developing world would seize power from the superpowers in a war of the rural areas against the cities, and a new order would be established, led of course by China. It was logical that Africa, along with Asia and Latin America, would take centre stage in this struggle.[9] From early on, Maoist theory had held that there was an 'intermediate zone' between capitalism and communism where the two systems would compete. The ground for revolution was most fertile here, where the contradictions between the two systems could be most strongly felt. Africa, as Zhou Enlai famously and controversially proclaimed in his 1963–64 tour of the continent, was just such a zone. By the end of the 1960s, with Soviet tanks rolling into Prague in 1968 and border skirmishes between Russia and China in 1969, the struggle to counter the influence of the USSR had become the primary strategic focus of China's interest in Africa. As Beijing's relations with the Soviets worsened, so a pragmatic understanding with the US developed. Perhaps the most controversial of the PRC's compromises on this front took place on the battlefields of Angola, where, in the mid 1970s, in an effort to combat the Soviet threat, the 'revolutionary' CCP supported the same side as the US and the apartheid regime of South Africa. Unsurprisingly, this proved to be something of an own goal for China's image on the continent.

Throughout the 1960s, the PRC continued its fight for recognition in the face of Taiwan's ongoing diplomatic efforts in Africa. By the end of the decade, Beijing had diplomatic relations with 18 African nations. It was still losing its annual battle for recognition at the UN, but the margin was shifting; in 1967, the scorecard showed 45 to 58, with 17 abstentions.

The turbulent years of the Cultural Revolution inevitably damaged China's foreign relations as well as its domestic development. Chinese ambassadors in every African post with the exception of Egypt were temporarily recalled. In the summer of 1967, Red Guards occupied the foreign ministry. Largely because most of the invitations predated the start of the upheaval, 116 foreign delegations still managed to visit China in 1966. But by 1967, this figure was down to 53 and, by 1968, to 12.[10] In many ways, however, relations with Africa proved impressively resilient. During the peak years of the

Cultural Revolution from 1967 to 1970, when many diplomats were reluctant to visit China, Tanzania sent 15 separate delegations, the Republic of the Congo sent 14, Mali 11, and Guinea and Zambia nine.[11] Presidents Kenneth Kaunda of Zambia and Julius Nyerere of Tanzania both made official visits. Nyerere even launched his own Green Guards and 'little green book'. China also sustained its military support for Africa. Arms, training, medicines and some financing were offered to a number of African liberation movements and their emergent armies. But China's revolutionary zeal was not uniformly welcomed by its African partners, some of whom worried about trading one foreign master for another and regarded Beijing's radical fervour as potentially subversive. Countries such as Burundi, the Central African Republic and Ghana went so far as to suspend diplomatic ties with the PRC. Even with China's African friends, there were some difficult times.

Still, the attention that China was giving to Africa paid off when, at the 26th UN General Assembly in 1971, the PRC's annual bid to take over China's permanent seat in the UN Security Council from the KMT-led Republic of China finally met with success. Twenty-six African states supported the motion recognising the PRC as the 'only lawful representative of China to the United Nations', comprising just over a third of the pro-PRC vote.[12] Of the 23 co-sponsors of the resolution, 11 were from Africa.

China's ambitions for leadership of the Third World saw further ideological crystallisation in 1974 in Mao's 'theory of three worlds', which grouped the US and the USSR on the same side, rather than the opposing sides of his earlier 'two camps' theory. Now, the US and the USSR together formed the exploitative and imperialistic First World. Their allies in the other developed countries became the Second World. The Third World was comprised of developing countries: all of

Africa, all of Latin America and all of Asia, apart from Japan. The PRC, a nation that claimed it was not and never would be a superpower, was in effect 'first among equals' in this Third World.[13] Meanwhile, in the world of realpolitik, Mao justified his 1973 meeting with Henry Kissinger and the subsequent development of Sino-US relations with his 'strategy of forming an alliance against an opponent'. In 1979, the US offered full diplomatic recognition to the PRC. As the Cold War continued to split allegiances in Africa and elsewhere, improved relations with the US brought strain to some of China's alliances in Africa, which had their origins in different, more anti-American times.

Some international-affairs analysts, such as Gerald Segal, have warned against exaggerating the PRC's influence in Africa during the Cold War. Segal used the examples of the defeat of the Chinese-backed National Front for the Liberation of Angola in the 1970s and China's failure to provide aid to post-independence Zimbabwe and Mozambique to argue that China was only ever a 'peripheral actor' in Africa, with an effective involvement confined largely to rhetoric.[14] Certainly Beijing was working within political, military and economic limitations that meant that its contributions tended to be modest by comparison to those of the two superpowers. But its efforts registered on the continent, and are repeatedly and deliberately invoked by Chinese officials as the backdrop for engagement today. Between 1950 and 1980, China gave aid for more than 800 diverse projects in Africa covering not only infrastructure, but also other areas such as agriculture and fishing. The US and the USSR may have been militarily and commercially stronger, but there were occasions when Chinese aid matched or even surpassed that provided by the superpowers. For example, from 1970 to 1976, China offered more in aid commitments to Africa than the USSR, which was temporarily preoccupied with domestic economic concerns.[15] By 1975, China had aid programmes in more African countries than the US.[16] Overall China's Cold War involvement in Africa was secondary to that of the USSR and the US but, by emphasising to Africans its status as a fellow developing country, China was able to build up significant diplomatic credits in return for its relatively minimal investments.

Deng and reform

Some momentum in Sino-African relations was maintained from Mao's death in 1976, through the power struggle that followed, and into the rise of Deng Xiaoping, with the Soviet challenge continuing for a period to attract Chinese attention to Africa. Vice Premier Li Xiannian toured Tanzania, Mozambique, Zambia and Zaire in 1979 and Vice Premier Ji Pengfei visited Kenya, Madagascar, Mauritius, the Seychelles and Djibouti in 1980, making them the most senior Chinese officials to tour Africa since Zhou Enlai in 1963–64. Meanwhile, however, the beginnings of a new direction also became evident following the adoption at the 1978 Party Congress of Deng's proposition to refocus attention away from 'revolutionary war' and towards domestic economic development.

With China's leadership focusing primarily on domestic goals for most of the 1980s, the decade is a little awkward for Chinese officials and scholars intent on depicting a continuous momentum of positive, active Sino-African relations from the inception of the PRC onwards. The re-evaluation in priorities that took place under Deng in the 1980s prompted something of a downgrading in relations between China and Africa. British scholar of Sino-African relations Ian Taylor goes so far as to label this time as representing a 'decade of neglect' in terms of China's Africa policy.[17] He notes that in the summer of 1986, African students at Chinese universities thought the neglect substantial enough to take to the streets with placards reading 'Remember the UN in 1971?'[18] As the rhetoric of Third World solidarity of the early 1970s was supplanted by an outlook that prioritised China's own development, such students faced growing racism in China. This culminated in the 'anti-African' demonstrations of 1988–89 that began in Nanjing and spread to other cities across the country.

Yet some positive contacts and interactions did continue through the 1980s. Between 1981 and 1989, African presidents managed 55 visits to China between them.[19] Premier Zhao Ziyang toured 11 African countries in December 1982 and January 1983. Aid projects, albeit refashioned in form and focus, also continued. Indeed, in 1984, China's announced aid commitments to Africa for the year exceeded the pledges each made by Japan, Norway and the United Kingdom.[20] Nevertheless, there is little doubt that substantial engagement with Africa receded somewhat during the decade, with China adopting a more critical, less empathetic, approach to the problems of development that Africa faced. The acknowledged paucity of Africa experts in Chinese government institutions even today tells something of a story about Beijing's relative disengagement from Africa during this time.

As China re-evaluated its relations with Africa in the 1980s, a new paradigm for engagement started to develop. Beijing began to invite African countries to cooperate commercially with China in the name of common development. Premier Zhao's 'Four Principles of Economic and Technical Cooperation with African Countries' offered a move away from Mao's costly aid programmes and asymmetric engagements. Zhao reiterated the importance of the pursuit of equality and mutual benefit in a spirit of non-interference and non-conditionality, as expressed by the 'Five Principles of Peaceful Coexistence', but he also added requirements for quick practical results, diversity of engagement – including cooperation with other countries involved in Africa – and the objective of enhancing the growth and self-reliance of both China and Africa. At least for a while, there would be no more prestige-driven big infrastructure projects. Instead, lower-profile collaborative projects, requiring smaller investments and offering quicker returns, were the order of the day. Aid, which had previously been primarily viewed as a means of encouraging ideological engagement to a revolutionary purpose, was now identified as a pragmatic means of stimulating trade. The basis for cooperation would be commercial. This more practical, less ideological engagement held some advantages for African nations. For one thing, it meant that African leaders no longer had to choose between China and the USSR or between China and the US. In 1983, for instance, China established diplomatic relations with the same Soviet-backed government in Angola whose influence it had spent much of the 1970s trying to curtail.

Jiang and the revitalisation of interest in Africa

In the 1990s, China's leadership began once again to pay closer attention to the country's African relationships, initiating in the late twentieth century the dynamic that is developing so rapidly at the start of the twenty-first. In 1995, three years before becoming premier, Vice Premier Zhu Rongji gave official notice of revitalised high-level interest in Africa with a trip to the continent. President Jiang Zemin followed suit the next year. During this visit, at the headquarters of the Organisation of African Unity (OAU) in Ethiopia, Jiang offered his 'five-point proposal' for the development of sustainable and cooperative relations between China and African countries into the twenty-first century. He also made some early soundings for a China–Africa summit.[21] These overtures resulted in the establishment of the FOCAC. Its first ministerial summit meeting took place in Beijing in 2000. It was the third such meeting, in 2006, which caught the attention of the international media with its eight major promises to Africa and which, arguably, established Sino-African relations as a favourite subject for Western policymakers and commentators interested in both African development and the global balance of power.

Policy pronouncements also returned. In January 1999, Vice President Hu Jintao visited Africa, where he reaffirmed the priority the party's leadership attached to developing relationships on the continent. In 2003, now-President Hu set out 'Six Pillars' to govern relations with Africa, adding in 2005 a further 'Three Principles' to a formula that broadly followed the outlines of Zhou Enlai's Five Principles, but which put greater emphasis on calling upon the international community to pay more attention to Africa and promote a fairer environment to aid its development. In January 2006, the Chinese government published its first White Paper on China–Africa relations, which set out the aim of 'establishing and developing a new type of strategic partnership with Africa'.[22] The establishment of this 'new type of partnership' was then swiftly declared achieved at the third FOCAC ministerial summit meeting later that year. Most recently, during his visit to Tanzania in February 2009, President Hu put forward a 'six-point proposal' on strengthening Sino-African ties, in preparation for the next FOCAC ministerial summit. The proposal updated CCP theory on Sino-African relations to prioritise the provision of mutual assistance in the context of the global financial crisis.[23]

Contemporary Sino-African relations

It is not easy to keep abreast of developments in China's increasingly multifaceted engagements with Africa, whether in terms of figures, geographical reach, or the nature of collaborative ventures. This is not helped by the paucity of official data

China's eight FOCAC 2006 promises

- To double development assistance to Africa by 2009
- To provide $3bn in preferential loans and $2bn in preferential buyer credits to Africa over the next three years
- To set up a China–Africa Development Fund to reach $5bn to encourage Chinese companies to invest in Africa and support firms investing there
- To build a conference centre for the African Union
- For the most indebted and least-developed African countries with diplomatic relations with China, to cancel all debt relating to interest-free government loans that matured at the end of 2005
- For the least-developed African countries with diplomatic relations with China, to increase from 190 to more than 440 the number of export items exempt from entry tariffs in China
- To establish between three and five trade and economic cooperation zones in Africa over the next three years
- Over the next three years, to train 15,000 African professionals; send 100 senior agricultural experts to Africa; set up ten agricultural-technology demonstration centres in Africa; build 30 hospitals in Africa and provide a 300m renminbi (RMB) grant to cover the provision of anti-malaria drug artemisinin and the construction of 30 malaria-prevention and treatment centres in Africa; dispatch 300 youth volunteers to Africa; build 100 rural schools in Africa; and increase the number of Chinese government scholarships to African students from 2,000 per year to 4,000 per year by 2009

coming from China. Statistics, where they are available, tend to be general and to cover a period of years. Chinese authorities carefully guard not only the details of China's activities in more diplomatically sensitive countries such as Sudan, but often also information about the most seemingly ordinary of ons. When challenged, officials argue that they are ᴜnable to reveal much about what their government is doing in individual African countries, even at a commercial level, because of the sensitivities of other African states over the relative strength of China's engagements. Yet, in the interests of transparency, other states with interests in Africa appear able to manage the supposed diplomatic difficulties of such declarations. China's reluctance to do the same understandably causes concern in the West over the nature of Chinese engagements, the intentions behind them and their possible consequences.

What is known about the extent of China's contemporary involvement in Africa? There are around 800 state-owned Chinese companies engaged in business on the African continent. Although precise figures remain elusive, the number of private businesses present on the continent alongside these state-owned businesses is growing as contacts and experience accumulate. The proportion of Chinese businesses in Africa that are private is also increasing. In 2007, state news agency Xinhua reported an estimated 750,000 Chinese nationals to be working or living for extended periods of time in Africa. Most scholars believe the real figure to be much higher, but estimates vary considerably. Informal local African estimates can tend to conflate Chinese and other Asian nationalities. Even where this confusion is taken into account, among African and non-African observers alike there is still limited differentiation between mainland Chinese, Taiwanese, people from Hong Kong and overseas Chinese. For the moment, it remains unclear how many mainland Chinese small traders and family businessmen have made Africa their home, how many are using it as a base before moving on to Europe or the US, and how many are working on contracts to remit money home, planning to leave once their contract is completed. Even if their total numbers remain small in comparison with, for example, the large Chinese diasporas in Southeast Asia or the US, the impact of Chinese workers is already noticeable across Africa.[24] Such workers include long-term residents such as market traders and small businessmen, shorter-term contracted unskilled labourers, and skilled professionals, including managers, government-sponsored specialists in areas such as health care and agriculture, and government representatives engaged in the promotion of diplomatic or trade ties. The development of new and more frequent air links between China and Africa reflect increased interactions.[25]

By 2008, China's Export–Import (ExIm) Bank was funding more than 300 projects in 36 countries in Africa. From $6.5bn in 1999, the value of bilateral trade between China and African countries rose to $73.3bn in 2007. In 2006, China's bilateral-trade target of $100bn by 2010 appeared ambitious, given that annual bilateral trade then amounted to $55.5bn. However, in 2008, two years ahead of schedule, this target was surpassed, with China's Ministry of Commerce announcing that the value of such trade had reached a historic peak of $106.8bn.[26] China is second only to the US in the table of Africa's single-country trading partners, with US–Africa trade recorded at $116bn in 2007, and also rising. In 2007, China registered either new loan agreements or economic and technical cooperation agreements with every country in Africa with which it had diplomatic relations apart from Angola, Equatorial Guinea, Mauritania and Lesotho (nevertheless, Angola, Equatorial Guinea and Mauritania had all enjoyed some form of new commitment in the previous year).[27] In 2008, China signed bilateral aid accords with 48 of Africa's 53 countries and loan agreements on favourable terms with 22.[28] China's concessional and non-concessional loans now offer African governments the prospect of access to considerable finance.

China's commercial engagements in Africa are strongly resource-focused. In 2008, China's biggest supplier of oil in Africa, Angola, was also its largest trading partner, with bilateral trade reaching a record $25.3bn.[29] The presence of China's national oil companies (NOCs) in Africa is set to grow, as some of their work on oil exploration matures into greater involvement in extraction leading to increased production, and as the NOCs further develop the confidence and expertise to build on their activities in some of Africa's remoter areas and establish a greater presence in traditionally lucrative countries, such as Nigeria. Indeed, as NOC involvement in Africa develops further, it is difficult to see big investments such as those in Sudan's Unity oilfields as anything other than a window on the future.

Massive resources-for-infrastructure deals, such as the contract for copper and cobalt extraction provisionally agreed by China and the DRC in early 2008, have already come to epitomise Chinese engagement in Africa. This agreement, originally worth around $9bn, was aimed at securing China's access to as much as ten million tonnes of copper and 600,000 tonnes of cobalt.[30] The precise composition and value of the deal remains unclear, but it evidently involves major infrastructural investment in the DRC, including the repair of transport links and the construction of hospitals, health centres, hydropower dams and airports. Although the details of the project will be adjusted in the light of the fall in commodity prices, the onset of the global economic downturn, and expressions of concern by the International Monetary Fund (IMF) and Western donors about the deal's impact on the DRC's finances, the scale of its initial intent still illustrates the magnitude of China's ambitions. Even before the agreement was made, 60 of the 75 processing plants in the DRC's Katanga province were owned by Chinese companies, with more than 90% of Katanga's excavated minerals being exported to China.[31] The DRC is just one, albeit somewhat extreme, example of a pattern of activity that is spreading across Africa. Complex and opaque package deals involving aid, investment, infrastructure, training and arms are frequently used by the Chinese government to entice African governments, particularly resource-rich ones, into business.

However, today, any suggestion that Sino-African relations can be viewed simply in terms of one giant resource grab is outdated at best. While resource exploitation remains central, relations are now increasingly multifaceted, with interactions developing in new economic areas, such as financial services, and in other spheres of cooperation, from agriculture to the development of information and communications technology. African experiences of Chinese engagement, already varied, are only growing more so. As these interactions become more diverse and complex, they increasingly belie simplistic labels of neo-mercantilism or colonialism, with or without 'Chinese characteristics'.[32]

In Namibia, China operates a space-tracking, telemetry and command station. For at least 18 months before it suffered an embarrassing technical failure in November 2008, Nigeria had its first geostationary communications satellite, having become the first foreign country to purchase both a Chinese satellite and its launching service. Chinese construction companies are helping to build entire new capital cities around Africa, such as Novo Luanda in Angola, Malabo II in Equatorial Guinea and Yamoussoukro in Côte d'Ivoire. The prestige projects of presidential palaces and party headquarters continue, but alongside them new schools, hospitals, airports, railways and hotels are all being built. The Chinese government has provided budgetary support to the civil services of the Central African Republic and Liberia.[33] In October 2008, the China National Petroleum

Corporation (CNPC) began the construction of Chad's and Niger's first oil refineries. Between September 1994 and June 2007, 283 Chinese enterprises focusing mainly on infrastructure and the health and security sectors registered with the Ghana Investment Promotion Centre, making China one of the largest foreign investors in Ghana. In late 2007, Chinese companies had either completed or were in the process of building, among other developments, a dam, two stadiums, offices for the Ministry of Defence and housing for the police, two hospitals and a youth cultural centre.[34]

By the end of the same year, China had committed $3.3bn to ten major hydropower projects that should see sub-Saharan Africa's hydropower capacity boosted by 30% upon completion.[35] Between 2001 and 2007, Chinese telecommunications firms supplied information and communications equipment worth almost $3bn to sub-Saharan Africa, mainly to Ethiopia, Sudan and Ghana.[36] Banking is also a growth sector, and one that points to China's longer-term aspirations for its African engagements. In early 2009, China's largest acquisition in Africa to date was the $5.5bn paid by the state-owned Industrial and Commercial Bank of China (ICBC) in 2007 for a 20% share in South Africa's Standard Bank, which operated more than 1,000 branches across 18 countries in sub-Saharan Africa at the time of the purchase. Although there have, unsurprisingly, been some initial tensions between the two new partners, the deal represents another step change in Sino-African relations, as Africa further opens up to Chinese financial services and support for areas in addition to the mining sector, including the development of power grids and telecommunications.

Chinese government officials remain acutely – and perhaps revealingly – sensitive to the charge that Chinese interests in Africa are excessively focused on resources, and that these interests are pursued aggressively without concern for their impact on China's partners. Thus, alongside attempts to stimulate the broadening of Chinese commercial interests on the continent, presentational steps are also being taken to encourage a new view of China's record in Africa. When President Hu made his February 2009 'journey of friendship and cooperation' to Africa, the choice of Senegal, Mali, Tanzania and Mauritius as his destinations was significant: none of these four countries are generally seen as major players in resource terms. During the visit, the president was at pains to emphasise the importance China attached to its ties with these countries, all of which are democratic states that have traditionally enjoyed friendly relations with China.[37]

Hu's 2009 Africa tour, his sixth since his first trip in 1999, was yet another instance of China's extensive use of personal, high-level, state-to-state diplomacy to develop bilateral relations and emphasise the equality of its engagements. Between 2000 and 2005, China hosted 15 presidents, three vice presidents, six prime ministers, ten parliamentary speakers and 14 foreign ministers from Africa.[38] Hu visited 17 African states in 2006 and 2007, more than any other world leader. Foreign Minister Li Zhaoxing visited the Comoros Islands in 2004 and Cape Verde in 2006, both states accustomed to receiving little attention from major powers.[39] China's top legislator, Wu Bangguo, called on Madagascar and the Seychelles during his five-nation tour of Africa in November 2008, following up on Hu's visit to the Seychelles during his 2007 tour. Hu's Seychelles visit had exacerbated concern in India over China's ambitions to increase its influence in the Indian Ocean, across which most of India's trade and almost all of its imported oil is shipped. Neither Wu's follow-up visit nor Hu's own return visit to the Indian Ocean, to Mauritius in February 2009, did anything to alleviate this concern.

Such high-level state visits serve not only political, but also commercial purposes. Premier Wen Jiabao's 2006 tour of Africa is a typical example. In Egypt, Wen signed 11 bilateral trade and cooperation deals, including an agreement on the production of wireless communication equipment between private company Huawei and Telecom Egypt. The premier agreed a further six deals in Ghana, some again relating to telecommunications, and seven in the Republic of the Congo, most of which were focused on natural-resource extraction. In Angola, Wen oversaw a new $2bn infrastructure loan from China ExIm Bank before proceeding to South Africa to sign 13 further agreements on agriculture, minerals and energy. Yet more accords followed during his visits to Tanzania and Uganda.[40]

Although China accompanies its commercial activities in Africa with declarations of its collegiate developing-world status and talk of 'South–South' allegiances, these notions probably play little role in attracting African leaders to China. It is China's seat among the permanent five (P5) members of the UN Security Council, and the power of veto that this brings, combined with China's non-judgemental approach and its resistance to closely scrutinising the behaviour of its partners that seems to provide a greater incentive for African leaders to strengthen their ties with Beijing. Furthermore, China's claims to developing-world status and its self-proclaimed role of advocate of developing-world interests in international institutions such as the UN will become increasingly tenuous as China's national interests, for example in world trade talks, evolve to reflect its continuing development.

At the start of 2009, the impact of the financial crisis on Sino-African trading figures was still to be documented, as the indirect effects of the crisis, among them falling demand for Chinese exports in the West and China's consequent need for fewer African exports to support its own export industries, worked their way through the system. In October 2008, the head of the West Asia and Africa Department of China's Ministry of Commerce, Zhou Yabin, warned that global financial problems would adversely affect China's trade with Africa, and stressed that sustaining existing high rates of growth would be difficult. Nevertheless, with just over 45% growth in bilateral trade from 2007 to 2008 and a year-on-year growth rate of more than 30% throughout the decade, a considerable cushion is in place.

The reality is that such rates of growth would probably not be sustainable even in benign economic conditions. The question is more about the sustainability of the general upward trend. A long and severe international economic crisis, as opposed to a shorter recession, would clearly impact on China's demand for Africa's raw materials, but even this scenario would be more likely to lead to hard-headed recalculations of the sums involved in any deals made than to a major strategic disengagement. China's domestic demand, augmented by infrastructure projects undertaken as part of the government's fiscal-stimulus efforts and by the continuing, albeit reduced, requirement for raw materials for its export industries, will perpetuate its commodity interests in Africa.[41] The larger state-owned companies will have the financial resources and support to continue working to a relatively stable medium-term resource agenda, whereas smaller, private firms are liable to be more affected by short-term interests and demands. In November and December 2008, more than 60 Chinese mining companies closed their operations in the DRC's Katanga province. By early 2009, similar evidence of the effects of the financial crisis on small mining operators could also be found in Zambia.[42] However, the reduction in capital inflows to Africa that will result from the recession are likely to hit Western businesses harder than Chinese ones, which are backed by their state's massive foreign-exchange reserves, while China's state-owned enterprises

(SOEs) are protected from having to respond to fluctuating shareholder priorities. Furthermore, the relative liquidity of the Chinese state could further enhance China's importance as a provider of loans to African governments – provision that is already closely linked to cooperation on resource exploitation, but which could yet become more so. A major economic downturn could, therefore, bolster China's relative importance on the continent.

In October 2008, the head of the Chinese Ministry of Commerce's Department for Foreign Economic Cooperation, Chen Lin, stated that China would continue to encourage domestic firms to increase their investments in Africa.[43] This reflected the approach of a well-funded government that, though temporarily more cautious about the deployment of its purchasing power, is focused on longer-term interests beyond short-term price trends. Although Sino-African trade will not escape the downturn, China's investment plans are likely to be more protected than most. In December 2008, Liberia's minister for investment announced the commitment of investment conglomerate China Union to inject $2.6bn into Liberia's main iron ore mine and establish within the year a refining plant at the mine with an annual capacity of a million tonnes, providing the country with its biggest-ever foreign investment.[44] When Premier Wen Jiabao greeted Angolan President Jose Eduardo dos Santos in Beijing in December 2008 and Wen's heir-designate, Li Keqiang, spoke in Egypt the same month, both men reiterated China's commitment to work together with African leaders to deal with an economic situation in which both Chinese and Africans perceive themselves as victims of unregulated Western profligacy. President Hu pledged to continue increasing Chinese assistance to Africa on his African tour a couple of months later.[45] If Africa has been slipping slightly in China's list of priorities since the financial crisis hit, there has been little sign of any downgrading of the diplomatic attention China is paying to the continent. Already between the New Year and Hu's February 2009 tour, Foreign Minister Yang Jiechi had visited Rwanda, Malawi and South Africa, while Commerce Minister Chen Deming had toured Kenya, Zambia and Angola.

It is clear, then, that China's interests in Africa have developed over the decades, with contemporary relations looking substantially different to previous periods of engagement. But why have these changes taken place? Why have China's recent leaders, beginning with Jiang Zemin, made such efforts to cultivate Sino-African relations?

Resource requirements

Like that of any country, China's foreign policy is intended to serve its domestic interests. China needs resources. While florid talk of 'dragons', 'insatiable appetites', even the 'great Chinese takeaway' may be wearing a little thin, it is difficult to argue with the figures. In 2005, sub-Saharan Africa had a $5.9bn trade surplus with China. If oil sales are subtracted from this figure, the region is left with a $7.3bn trade deficit.[46] One World Bank report suggests that petroleum accounted for as much as 80% of China's imports from sub-Saharan Africa in 2006.[47] Nine of China's top ten trading partners in Africa in 2008 were oil-producing states, the exception being the mineral treasure trove that is South Africa (see Table 1 overleaf).[48] Oil accounted for 99.9% of Angola's total exports to China in 2008 and unprocessed wood for 87.9% of Sierra Leone's exports to China in the same year.[49] At the start of 2008, Chinese companies were running mining operations in 13 African countries and were prospecting in more.[50]

China's continued economic growth, a key factor in the country's stability and the Communist Party's legitimacy,

Table 1: **China's top ten African trading partners in 2008**

Top two-way trade partners of China in Africa	Top African exporters to China	Top African importers from China
Angola	Angola	South Africa
South Africa	South Africa	Nigeria
Sudan	Sudan	Egypt
Nigeria	Republic of Congo	Algeria
Egypt	Libya	Angola
Algeria	Equatorial Guinea	Morocco
Republic of Congo	Gabon	Benin
Libya	DRC	Sudan
Morocco	Mauritania	Ghana
Equatorial Guinea	Algeria	Libya
Top ten as overall percentage		
78%	**93%**	**74%**

Source: Trade Law Centre for Southern Africa (Tralac), 'Africa's Trading Relationship with China'. 2009 spreadsheet, based on data from the Chinese version of the World Trade Atlas.

requires the import of substantial supplies of energy, minerals and other materials. China's leaders appear to have concluded that the stakes are sufficiently high that it is too risky simply to compete for these crucial resources on the global market. Diversifying the sources of its priority goods is seen as a sensible way for a country to limit its exposure to risk. Writing in 2005, analysts David Zweig and Bi Jinhai argued that an 'unprecedented need for resources [was] now driving China's foreign policy', with Beijing actively engaged in supporting Chinese companies in their efforts to secure these resources abroad.[51] The major policy review conducted in August 2006 by the Central Foreign Affairs Work Conference appeared to confirm this priority. Chinese academic Wang Jisi subsequently recorded its verdict: 'Foreign-affairs work must continue to be centred on economic construction'.[52] Whatever else it may do, the financial crisis that began in 2007–08 is unlikely to radically change this conclusion.

It is certainly difficult to see how China can continue its progress from the developing to the developed world without the considerable resources needed to power the manufacturing sector that has been responsible for so much of its recent wealth creation. China currently accounts for around 30% of the global market for copper concentrate and is the world's largest consumer of aluminium. In 2007, China imported 380m tonnes of iron ore, making it the world's largest consumer of that commodity, and helping to sustain it as the world's leading producer and exporter of steel. The country is the world's top importer of tropical woods, doing major business, legal and illegal, in Liberia, Gabon, Equatorial Guinea, Cameroon and Mozambique, among other countries.

Even if China manages to move up the value chain, away from a focus on a manufacturing sector fuelled by a vast and cheap labour pool and towards the production of more high-technology products, it will still need to import metals such as cobalt, tantalum and niobium for use in such products. It will also need to provide energy for its expanding, and increasingly wealthy, population. The state's energy-efficiency drive and its plans to rapidly expand China's nuclear-power capacity may alleviate the country's energy pressures, but they will not dispel them.

There is also a powerful commercial logic guiding the activities of the Chinese NOCs abroad. These companies have the choice of selling oil from their domestic reserves to the domestic market at state-enforced subsidised prices, depleting these reserves in the process, or expanding overseas to develop new sources of supply, which they can then sell on the international market at international market rates. Alongside the commercial agenda run the politics of energy supply. It is not something that tends to be discussed openly by officials in China or elsewhere, but the issue of access to energy reserves is not only about domestic energy security; it also has an international political dimension. China's 2003 National Energy Strategy and Policy, produced by the Development Research Centre of the State Council, remarked that 'oil is the key factor in the creation of public wealth, and also one kind of most important commodity influencing the global political pattern, economic order and military operations'.[53]

Why is Africa a key part of China's strategy for meeting its growing resource requirements? There are several reasons. Firstly, and most obviously, Africa has the resources. It currently supplies around 12% of the world's oil, and has vast unexplored oil reserves. (Between 2001 and 2004, 85% of the world's newly found oil reserves were located in West and Central Africa.[54]) The eight states on the West African coast around the Gulf of Guinea already produce some 5m barrels of oil a day and could yet be found to hold as much as 10% of the world's total oil reserves. The continent also has a large proportion of the world's reserves of key metals such as chromium, tantalum, cobalt and the platinum-group metals. China depends on Africa for 80% of its cobalt imports and 40% of its manganese imports.[55]

Secondly, China, like other powers, sees in Africa a region that is open for business with foreign-state and international oil companies in a world where 'resource nationalism' and protectionism appear to be on the rise. In August 2005, tempers were frayed by what China viewed as an example of US chauvinism and mistrust, when a last-minute all-cash bid for US oil company UNOCAL by China's biggest offshore oil producer, the China National Offshore Oil Corporation (CNOOC), was turned down on the grounds of US national security, and the contract awarded to US company Chevron. As well as causing consternation in China, the decision appears to have exacerbated concerns about the country's energy security. Reflecting on the incident, CNOOC's chairman, Fu Chenyu, concluded that 'if you can't do it somewhere, then you can always do it somewhere else. We're looking at opportunities in Africa.'[56]

Chinese thinking appears to be that African states are less likely to turn down foreign investment for political reasons.

Thirdly, Africa appeals in part because it is not the Middle East. In theory at least, Africa offers China broad-ranging opportunities to diversify its sources of oil while avoiding the political difficulties involved in pursuing resource interests in regions in which the US is already a major presence. As one analyst at the state-controlled China Institute for Contemporary International Relations has observed, 'Chinese companies must go places for oil where American and European companies are not present'.[57] From a Chinese perspective, Africa offers space to explore in the hunt for resources. This space is most obviously available in countries, such as Sudan, that have been the target of Western sanctions, but it can also be found in places that have been of limited interest to the major established international oil companies, which tend to avoid concerns that carry substantial risk and project low rates of return. Thus Sinopec Corporation, the listed arm of the China Petroleum and Chemical Corporation (CPCC), moved into wells in Gabon in 2004 that had previously been abandoned by international oil companies that had lost interest in the country's declining oil industry and its diminishing known reserves.[58]

Furthermore, Beijing has reasoned that Africa is somewhere China can go looking for resources without its activities incurring too much unwanted third-party political attention. If Chinese companies work in regions of limited interest to competing international oil companies, the reasoning goes, not only are they more likely to win contracts, they are also less likely to attract critical scrutiny from the Western countries importing their products. This has not, however, turned out to be the case to the extent that China might have hoped.

The willingness of Chinese companies to exploit difficult regions where competition is limited can be seen in the example of the remote Belinga province of Gabon, which hosts 500m tonnes of iron-ore deposits. Though they were first discovered in 1955, the Belinga deposits went unexploited for decades because of the hazards and difficulty of connecting the forest hills of Belinga with the Atlantic coast 560 kilometres away. In 2006, having initially been in a consortium with Chinese SOE Sinosteel and a Brazilian and a French firm, the China National Machinery and Equipment Import and Export Corporation (CMEC) won the sole right to develop the Belinga reserves, signing a formal contract with Gabon's government in May 2008. Chinese companies led by CMEC and financed by loans from China's ExIm Bank (to be repaid in iron ore) are not only offering investment in mining at Belinga, but are also building a hydropower dam to power the project, a railway line to connect Belinga to the coast and a deepwater port from which to export the ore.[59] This infrastructure will support the mining of up to 30m tonnes of iron ore a year, contributing substantially to China's efforts to diversify its sources of this vital mineral.[60] The protestations of both Gabonese and international civil-society groups about the possible environmental impact of the facilities under construction and questions about the distribution of rewards show that even the remoter African projects can incur the kind of foreign attention China had thought its African ventures might avoid.[61] Still, the Gabonese government continues to support the project, and the first shipments of ore are due to depart for China in 2011.

Though its African concerns have not been as insulated from criticism as it had perhaps initially hoped, China still appears to calculate that its engagements in Africa are less likely to meet political objections than, say, the pursuit of sensitive contracts with Western firms; in addition, there is a commercial and security logic for diversifying away from investment in the Middle East, for example, and increasing China's presence in Africa.

Furthermore, where domestic objections do arise in Africa, the appeal of China's deep pockets is thought likely to ensure that host governments will not allow such concerns to seriously inhibit China's activities.

China's attraction to Africa's energy and mineral resources is supplemented by its interest in another resource that Africa has in abundance – land. Although currently the world's biggest grain producer, China hosts more than 20% of the world's population but possesses only 7% of the world's arable land. Even before rising food prices caught the attention of governments around the world in 2007–08, making agriculture a priority issue, China's leaders were aware of their country's vulnerabilities in this area, which are compounded by the population's changing dietary demands, as well as the falling water table under the all-important northern plains.[62] With such concerns in mind, the state is now encouraging Chinese agricultural companies to buy farmland in Africa.[63] At FOCAC 2006, ten agricultural training centres were promised to Africa, with China seemingly certain to follow up these initiatives with further suggestions for broadening agricultural cooperation. At the senior-officials meeting of FOCAC held in 2008 in preparation for the 2009 ministerial conference, considerable attention was reportedly paid to the issues of agricultural cooperation and food security.[64] Rumours abound about Chinese firms expressing their interest in leasing and running 'megafarms' and cattle ranches in Africa, with vast tracts of land reportedly being sought free of charge or at nominal rents in return for infrastructural investment. Mozambique is among the countries China is reported to have approached for such deals.[65] Meanwhile, the Angolan government is said to be considering the revenue possibilities of its 35m hectares of arable land, and to be seeking a total foreign investment in agriculture of $6bn between 2008 and 2013.[66] Other countries, such as Ethiopia and

Sudan, are similarly courting Asian and Arab investment in their agricultural sectors.

China's exploitation of Africa's energy resources and its nascent interest in the continent's agricultural potential both raise a key issue: is China focused on the challenge of increasing global supply or, less cooperatively, on increasing its ownership of production facilities? The area of food security is fraught with complex diplomatic issues and potential problems such as, for example, the prospect of food being exported from one part of a country while another part faces severe shortages. Agricultural development can cause friction: if Ethiopia and Sudan were to increase their demand for water from the Blue Nile, Egypt would worry about the negative effects this demand would have on its own agricultural fertility downstream.[67] In such instances, managing relations within and between states would not be easy. Already the director general of the UN's Food and Agriculture Organisation has spoken of 'neo-colonial agriculture', and the risk of exploitation faced by poor but fertile countries.[68]

China's interest in securing access to Africa's multiple resources leads to commercial engagements of other kinds, such as construction contracts and the provision of communications-infrastructure support as part of package deals to win crucial resource contracts. This means that, at least initially, some of the apparent developing diversity of China's African engagements is rather illusory; although the activities may vary, the intent behind them does not. Take the field of infrastructure as an example. A 2008 World Bank report noted that 35 African countries had received Chinese infrastructure finance, with many projects costing under $50m, but with a handful worth more than $1bn.[69] This might appear to signal both a diversification away from straight resource exploitation and a focus beyond the main resource-rich countries. But a more detailed look at the figures reveals that an estimated 70% of China's infrastructure finance in Africa goes to only four countries: Nigeria, Angola, Sudan and Ethiopia. The bulk of China's infrastructure investment in Africa still appears to be directed either towards smoothing the transit of resources for export from source to the coast, or towards providing infrastructure in accordance with host-government agendas in return for licences for mines and oil blocks.

Nevertheless, limited in geographical scope though they may initially be, such deals do provide a platform for the Chinese companies they draw in to develop independent commercial interests, first in the country of operation, and then on the continent more generally. The result is that, as resource-focused engagements unfold, so a more mature array of interests develops. Furthermore, the inclusion of Ethiopia in this list of favoured countries is significant, as it is a major host of neither hydrocarbons nor strategically important minerals. Its presence on the list therefore hints at the presence of other rationales for China's African courtships.

The search for new markets
In addition to hosting the headquarters of the African Union (AU), Ethiopia is sub-Saharan Africa's second-largest market by population. As a result, like some other non-resource-rich African countries, it is the focus of substantial Chinese interest. Though Mozambique, for example, does have timber and agricultural resources, the extent of the increasing presence of Chinese companies there would appear to confirm a growing appreciation for the diversity of opportunities in Africa beyond the usual focus on oil, minerals and materials. According to the Mozambican Centre for Investment Protection, 41 Chinese companies were operating in Mozambique by May 2008, and were collectively responsible for the creation of more than

11,000 jobs.[70] China offered aid, concessional and non-concessional finance and commerce to its traditional ally Ghana before oil was discovered off its coast in 2007. Through the construction of the Bui Dam, China is helping Ghana tackle a chronic shortfall in energy capacity.

With and without accompanying resource interests, infrastructure, telecommunications and financial services are all growth areas in Sino-African commercial engagements, and it is not only SOEs that are involved. Private companies such as Huawei, one of China's top telecommunications providers, are establishing a strong market presence across the continent. The same goes for manufacturers of household goods, such as the Chunnan Consumer Electronics Group from China's eastern Jiangsu province.

China's government and Chinese companies, both state and private, appear to view Africa as a market with growth potential, recognising compatibility between Chinese manufactured products and the African market, with its one billion potential consumers. The low cost of Chinese products is particularly attractive to many African consumers. Africa can provide an outlet for Chinese companies facing a saturated domestic market and surplus production capacity. As well as providing new sources of revenue and employment, Africa also offers a good training ground and a springboard for Chinese companies with wider global ambitions. Such companies can, for example, seek joint ventures with Western companies already operating in Africa to gain experience, bring technology transfer, and speed their development towards international competitiveness.

Yet, in basic trading terms, it is still very early days. Africa's role as a provider of resources to China, in part to power the production of Chinese goods for export, still heavily outweighs its role as a market for these goods.[71] There are also problems associated with all kinds of Chinese commercial targeting of Africa, whether for trade in hydrocarbons, minerals, or manufactured goods. Perceived compatibility of producer and consumer are not the only motivators: Africa is a continent where regulations can be weak, and where state elites can sometimes be persuaded to take a relaxed approach to their enforcement. It is a place where reputations can be forged, but mistakes not always accounted for. A further concern from the point of view of African development is that big Chinese business in Africa tends to operate to one of two broad models. A business usually either handles African-mined, Chinese-processed products, or Chinese-manufactured products that are assembled and sold in Africa. If African nations are to reap substantial benefit from Chinese interests, they will need to break down the boundaries between these two models of engagement to ensure that African-mined products, whether financed and directed by Chinese or other foreign interests, can be African-processed or manufactured and, as appropriate, African-assembled and sold.

It can be tempting to dismiss the global significance of China's engagement with Africa by using the fact that China 'needs' Africa's resources, and to a far lesser extent, its markets, to argue that China comes to Africa in weakness and not in strength.[72] Chinese commentators and officials tend to emphasise this angle, with their self-deprecating refrain that 'Africa needs China, but China needs Africa more'.[73] However, those interested not only in Africa's development but also in China's should be wary of this line, particularly in view of China's interactions with weak regulatory and enforcement capacities on the continent. In identifying Africa as a benign environment for its business and resource needs, China has established a set of broadly asymmetric relations that help it to pursue its agenda in a part of the world where it thinks it can conduct its business quickest and with the fewest concessions.

Strategic considerations – the politics of developing-world alliances

The PRC's quest to win international support for its 'one China' policy, which recognises Taiwan only as a province of the PRC, has long formed a political backdrop to China's engagements in Africa. In the 1990s, Taiwan began to make some progress countering the PRC's diplomatic advances in Africa, winning back recognition from several countries at the expense of those countries' ties with Beijing. Diplomatic competition between China and Taiwan has led to what has disparagingly been termed 'dollar diplomacy', whereby Taiwan has supplemented its diplomatic overtures with private offers of financial support, which have proved particularly attractive to the poorer countries in Africa and Latin America. As China has grown richer and more confident, it too has adopted such techniques.

In refocusing its own attentions on Africa from the mid 1990s, China was in part motivated by Taiwan's diplomatic activities there. It made quick progress – between 1994 and 1998, five African countries recognised the PRC. Key among these was South Africa, with which diplomatic relations were established in 1998, after Beijing successfully thwarted President Nelson Mandela's attempts to promote the concept of 'dual recognition'. Malawi's switch to the PRC in 2008 was a major blow to Taiwan's diplomacy, as it came after 41 continuous years of recognition. The defection of Malawi left Taiwan enjoying diplomatic relations with only four countries in Africa, hosting a combined population of fewer than 17m people (Burkina Faso, Gambia, São Tomé and Principe and Swaziland).

By the end of 2008, with the onset of the global economic downturn and with relations with the mainland improving following the election of Taiwanese President Ma Ying-jeou, Taiwan appeared to be moving away from the use of dollar diplomacy in its battle for recognition in Africa and elsewhere.

More broadly, the general trend on the Taiwan issue seems clear. When Taiwan attempted to hold an inaugural Taiwan–Africa summit in September 2007, though the heads of state of the five nations maintaining diplomatic ties with Taiwan at the time attended, turnout from the other African states invited was poor. Taipei was quick to claim that Beijing had attempted to sabotage the summit, citing a number of rather suspect bureaucratic obstacles delegates had faced in trying to reach the meeting.[74] Nevertheless, the event served as an uncomfortable reminder of the progress the PRC had made on the international stage towards securing the recognition of Taiwan as a province of China.

Beyond the continuing tussle over Taiwan's status, there has been a broader political agenda behind China's African reawakening in the 1990s and its continued engagement today that it would be naive to discount. Resource requirements and the need to diversify supply sources would have led China's leadership back to Africa sooner or later, but politics has also played an important role. The late 1980s were a difficult time for China, with high inflation and domestic discontent eventually bringing large-scale demonstrations out onto the streets. In the aftermath of the massacre of protesters in Tiananmen Square in June 1989, China's leadership was sharply reminded of the need for allies, and it began to take a renewed interest in the potential for friendship that Africa offered.[75] As the Western world initiated sanctions against a regime that it temporarily labelled a pariah, Africa and Asia (with the exception of Japan) offered their support to Beijing. Between 1989 and 1992, Foreign Minister Qian Qichen visited 14 African countries. With his 1991 visit, Qian began the convention, still observed today, that Chinese foreign ministers start their year with a tour of Africa. Post-Tiananmen, the extension of invitations to African leaders and officials came back into vogue, with these leaders finding themselves courted for their continued favour and rewarded for their loyalty with considerable ceremony.

The dramatic collapse of communist regimes across Eastern Europe in 1989, 1990 and 1991 was also traumatic for the CCP. As US President George H.W. Bush declared the advent of a 'new world order' in 1990, Beijing was forced to consider its diplomatic options in the face of a sole hegemon with an expanded definition of its national security. In late 1989, in the name of the restoration of democracy, the US invaded Panama to arrest the sitting president, Manuel Noriega. In 1991, *Operation Desert Storm* in Kuwait offered an awe-inspiring demonstration of US technological and military might. Such events convinced the Chinese leadership of the advantages, indeed the necessity, of a foreign-policy framework that went beyond the Taiwan issue. Further reminders, if any were needed, of the importance of restructuring China's foreign engagements in the post-Cold War world came with the July 1996 US–Australian joint security declaration of a 'Strategic Partnership for the Twenty-First Century' and, even more unsettlingly for the Chinese, the approval in September 1997 of new guidelines on US–Japanese defence cooperation, following an April 1996 US–Japan joint security declaration of an 'Alliance for the Twenty-First Century'.[76] As security expert Bates Gill explains in his book *Rising Star*, China increasingly understood that the new dispensation necessitated a move towards greater diplomatic engagement, both in its region and beyond.[77]

Today, as China tries to maintain its old allegiances alongside broader engagements with newer partners, Chinese policymakers typically divide China's bilateral relationships into three categories. These were formally set out at the Central Foreign Affairs Work Conference in August 2006 in the phrase '*daguo shi guanjian, zhoubian shi shouyao, fazhanzhong guojie shi jichu*' ('big powers are the key, periphery [i.e. neighbouring] countries are the priority, and developing countries are the foundation'). The formula is deliberately vague, assigning all types of country an important status in China's foreign-policy thinking. The reality behind the diplomatic phraseology is that stable relations with the 'big powers' and 'periphery countries' are more immediately important to China's security than relations with the 'developing countries'. Nevertheless, China's relations with the countries of one category are inevitably affected by its ties with those of another – as evidenced by the impact of China's relations with Sudan, a developing country, on its relations with US, the leading 'big country'.

Within the developing-world category, relations with Africa are China's priority. Good relations with African nations serve several political purposes for China. Chinese analysts regularly cite the value of developing-world partnerships in defending China's sovereignty from a hegemonic US anxious to maintain an international order on its own terms. Chinese Academy of Social Sciences (CASS) scholar He Wenping has noted the effectiveness of Africa's support for China in the face of US efforts to 'foist [its] values on others' by tabling 11 motions condemning China's human-rights record before the UN Commission on Human Rights between 1990 and 2004. African support in these cases ensured that China was able to put through 'no action' motions that meant the US's draft resolutions were rejected before they could even be put to a vote. 'China', He observes, 'could not have defeated such proposals without the stalwart support of Africa'.[78] With the creation in 2006 of a council to replace the commission, a four-yearly 'Universal Periodic Review' of the human-rights records of all UN member states was established, somewhat diminishing the protection from censure on human-rights issues that could be afforded by sympathetic voting blocs. Nevertheless, with China's record under review in February 2009, China's African friends can still play a role, with 13 of the 47 members of the 2008–09 council coming from Africa. African support has also been crucial in thwarting repeated proposals put over the years to the General Committee of the UN General Assembly for a formal agenda item to consider allowing Taiwan to rejoin or otherwise participate in the UN.

As the need for China's African diplomacy to focus on the Taiwan issue lessens, China is increasingly concentrating on cultivating partnerships on the issue of the expansion of the permanent membership of the UN Security Council. Despite some improvements in Sino-Japanese relations following the departure of Japanese Prime Minister Junichiro Koizumi in 2006, including Chinese support for Japan's election as Asia's temporary member of the UN Security Council in October 2008, China continues to be concerned by Japan's interest in permanent Security Council membership, and it is discreetly exploring its concerns with its African friends. Africa is becoming one of the unspoken battlegrounds for votes on Security Council reform.

The issue of Security Council reform also has implications for Sino-African relations themselves. If China wants African support on the issue of Japan's promotion, it needs to recognise the interest of the likes of South Africa, Nigeria and Egypt in a similar promotion, and to navigate the diplomatic difficulties of maintaining neutrality between the likely rival candidates. China will also privately question whether its interests are in fact served by an African candidacy. If Africa has its own representative at the top table, will not that representative speak for Africa? What then will happen to China's own claim to speak for African concerns and interests?

African ties also serve a broader purpose for the PRC. China looks forward to the decline of US hegemony, and recognises in Africa 53 potential partners in what it hopes is becoming an increasingly multipolar world. The successful construction of political partnerships and intertwined commercial relationships in Africa will boost China's influence in global diplomacy and, therefore, in international institutions. Some have argued that China sees in Africa an opportunity to create 'a paradigm of globalization that favours China',[79] or that China seeks to use its influence in Africa to build 'alternative pockets of reality' – that is, to establish bilateral relationships according to its own rules in remote regions largely insulated from external scrutiny, with these pockets then being enlarged as China grows stronger.[80]

Such assertions are a step too far; it is not clear that Chinese leaders are bent on creating an entirely new global order. These theories in all likelihood credit Chinese diplomacy with a more proactive and coherent agenda than the country is currently capable of pursuing. Nevertheless, there does seem to be somewhere in the background of China's activities a continuing interest in at least significantly readjusting the existing order, which is perhaps unsurprising since China had little say in its original determination. He Wenping has remarked that 'strengthened Sino-African relations will help to raise China's own international influence and that of developing countries as a whole'.[81] Her choice of word order inadvertently reflects China's evident priorities.

How much do China's engagements in Africa matter?

Before going on to examine how China conducts its African engagements, the problems that it is facing in so doing, and the implications of these issues, it is important first to address the sceptics. In the face of considerable Western media coverage, some are asking whether China's role in Africa is receiving disproportionate attention. They argue that even if destructive competition between major powers for natural resources does come about in Africa – and it is far from certain that it will – at least for the time being, Western drilling and mining companies remain the biggest players in the African market, and continue to enjoy considerable technological advantages. Other Asian countries, they point out, have greater foreign direct investments in Africa than China does, yet these transactions attract relatively little attention.[82] Thus, they ask, is expressing interest in and concerns about China's commercial activities in Africa not simply a – somewhat disingenuous – way of expressing more general fears about a rising China?

If we look at resource and trade issues in isolation, the comparative statistics marshalled by the sceptics make some important points. Here are a sample few that should place the resource aspects of Sino-African engagement, and the challenges these pose to other players in Africa, in perspective:

- 16% of Africa's oil exports went to China in 2006, while 55% went to the US and the EU combined.[83]
- In 2006, the total output from Africa of Chinese NOCs was around 267,000 barrels of oil per day (b/d). In contrast, ExxonMobil, then the largest foreign oil company in Africa measured by output, pumped around 780,000 b/d. The continent's largest producer, Algerian oil company Sonnatrach, pumped 4.1bn b/d.[84]
- The commercial value of Chinese oil-company investment in Africa amounts to 8% of international oil-company investment in the continent, and only 3% of total oil-company investment there.[85]
- In 2008, Sino-African bilateral trade broke the $100bn barrier. However, in 2007, China's bilateral trade with South Korea alone (population 49m) already stood at $160bn.[86]
- According to a 2007 UN report, only 3% of China's total foreign direct investment went to Africa in 2005.[87]

However, these points do not address the question of the effect of China's engagements on Africa's development, or their potential impact on the political environment on the continent and beyond. Furthermore, even if the focus is kept purely on resource requirements, the statistics change somewhat when we move from noting the current situation to looking at developing trends:

- Having first become a net oil importer in 1993, in 2003, the PRC became the second-largest consumer of petroleum products in the world after the US, and its requirements are projected to surpass those of the US by 2015. By 2030, China's primary energy demand will have doubled from its 2005 level, and its demand for oil will have quadrupled. The proportion of its oil that China will need to import will rise from around 50% to around 80%.[88]
- China receives around 33% of its imported crude oil from Africa. In March 2008, one senior Chinese official said that China aimed to increase this figure to 40% in the next five to ten years.[89] Meanwhile, the US may increase the proportion of its oil that it imports from Africa, from more than 15% currently to around 25% by 2015.[90]
- Trade between China and Africa increased by 700% in the 1990s.[91] Between 2000 and 2005, Africa's exports to China increased at an annual rate of 48%, two-and-a-half times as fast as its exports to the US and four times as fast as its exports to the EU.[92]

These trends confirm the Chinese government's declared commitment to dramatically increase its commercial engagements with Africa, a commitment on which it has been making remarkable early progress. In a speech in 2007, Foreign Minister Yang Jiechi declared that there could be no letting up: 'We should increase high-level contacts, conduct strategic dialogue, enhance mutual understanding and trust, build new consensus and create new impetus for growing our relations'.[93] Although the financial crisis may dampen Chinese enthusiasm a little, China is a marginal player in Africa no more. It is a contractor, a financier, a deliverer of a variety of goods and services, a donor and an investor on the continent. Already Africa's second-largest single-country trading partner, it is probably also its leading single-country lender and its leading single-country infrastructure investor.

China's attraction to Africa's resources is entirely to be expected and, clearly, the country cannot and should not be denied its right to compete commercially in new areas and pursue its own development. Similarly, it is quite natural that, as a rising power and following a period of relative isolation, China should be seeking to bolster its diplomatic relationships and its influence on the international stage. Furthermore, some of the logic behind the developing interplay between China and Africa has little to do with either the compatibility of China's material requirements with Africa's resources and markets, or the interest in cultivating diplomatic partnerships. Modern-day China offers one of the best examples of poverty alleviation in history. Between 1981 and 2005, more than 600m Chinese were pulled out of poverty. Meanwhile, the number of Africans living below the poverty line grew by 180m.[94] Lessons clearly need to be learned, and China will have ideas and experiences to contribute. In May 2005, the International Poverty Reduction Centre in China was established in Beijing by the Chinese government in cooperation with the United Nations Development Programme and other international aid organisations, to support international exchanges on poverty reduction and improve international cooperation in this area.[95] In July 2007, China hosted a seminar on 'Development-

Oriented Poverty-Reduction Policies and Practices' attended by 32 government officials from 18 African countries.[96]

It is thus important to retain a sense of proportion about developing Sino-African relationships. But China's engagements in Africa do matter. They matter for African nations because Chinese interests offer them a major opportunity. Handled well, that opportunity will be for faster development. Handled badly, the only things to grow will be corruption and autocracy. They matter for China because African nations possess what the PRC needs to fuel its growth, in terms both of resources and of potential political support. They matter to other new aspirant powers looking at increasing their own African engagements, who will be seeking to learn lessons about the rules of the game: will it be a ruthless competition, a 'race to the bottom' in which anything goes, or will certain standards be maintained and responsibilities accepted? They matter to the West because how China adapts to the challenges it faces in Africa will help to determine Africa's development, peace and security. Finally, they matter because they will help to determine China's own development, the degree to which China perceives its interests as best served within, rather than in opposition to, the current international system, and the effects China's calculations will have on relations between East and West.

The PRC has changed considerably since the days of Mao, and its relations with Africa reflect this. The language of brotherhood remains, but the ends to which the rhetoric is directed have altered. A more diverse, flexible and differentiated foreign policy has emerged. However, determining the extent of this flexibility and differentiation will continue to challenge China's foreign-policy establishment, operating as it does to both a more consensual and a more confused model of leadership than it did under the charismatic personal leaderships of

Mao and Deng. Can the PRC continue to adapt its African strategies in order to meet its needs on a sustainable basis? History may well turn out to be on its side, but the challenges that are already emerging should not be underestimated.

The Great Tazara Railway Project: China's largest-ever foreign aid project

The idea of building a railway from the town of Kapiri Mposhi in the Zambian copper belt to the Tanzanian shores of the Indian Ocean at Dar es Salaam was first sparked in the late nineteenth century, by Cecil Rhodes's vision of a 'Cape to Cairo' railway that would link together Britain's African colonies. After a long interval, the idea was revived in the 1960s, this time with the purpose of freeing landlocked Zambia from its trading dependence on transport routes through white-ruled Rhodesia and South Africa. A loan application for the project was rejected by the World Bank in 1964. When the presidents of newly independent Zambia and Tanzania lobbied Western countries for help with funding following the bank's refusal, they met with little interest. Then, on 5 September 1967, with the Cultural Revolution in full flow, an agreement was signed with China, which committed itself to financing and constructing the line. By 1970, work had begun, with more than 20,000 Chinese labourers employed to help build Africa's longest railway, covering 1,860 kilometres of track and serviced by 147 railway stations. Despite the scale and technical demands of the project, construction was completed in 1975, two years ahead of schedule. China provided an initial rolling stock of 85 locomotives, 2,100 freight wagons and 100 passenger coaches for use on the line.[97]

The scale of the commitment China had shown in delivering the railway, when Western countries and the World Bank had dismissed the project, was highlighted by the Chinese government as a symbol of their friendship with Africa. There was certainly no doubting the commitment China had demonstrated, but it soon became clear that the focus of the rhetoric had to be kept on the good intentions behind the scheme, rather than on the reality of its delivery. The last Chinese engineers working on the track left Africa in July 1976. By October 1978, Zambian copper exports were once more being sent through Rhodesia as maintenance of the railway became a growing problem. Shortfalls in technology transfer and capacity-building severely limited the usefulness of the line to the Zambians. There were also problems with quality. Five years after the railway's completion, only 30 of the original 85 locomotives remained in regular service.

The railway's problems have been a source of some discomfort to the Chinese authorities. In 1999, China called upon the Tanzanian and Zambian governments to overhaul the line in order to save it from total collapse. In September 2008, the Zambian minister for communications and transport said that the railway required an immediate investment of between $70m and $100m. With only 300 of the 2,000 wagons required for the railway to be commercially viable still in service, the line has reportedly been operating at around 40% capacity for the past decade.[98] In 2008, Tanzanian media reports spoke of accumulated debts of around $45m and of workers unpaid for three months.[99] Discussions over Tazara's future continue; talks are reportedly under way to grant the concession for the task of overhauling the railway to a Chinese firm.

CHAPTER TWO

Managing China's African Relations

While there can be no equivalence between one country, however large, and a continent of 53 countries, shorthand references to 'China' and 'Africa' can prove useful for the purposes of broad explanation and discussion. Particularly for as long as Chinese engagement in the African continent was either minimal (pre-1949), ideologically driven (1960 and 1970s), or restricted (1980s), the notion of 'China' in 'Africa' was a convenient shorthand. However, in seeking to understand contemporary, more pragmatic Chinese engagements in Africa, the danger of such a shorthand is that it hides the multiple interests, structures and outlooks within both China and African nations that combine to form 'Sino-African' relations. As the Chinese government seeks to deepen relations for its own strategic reasons, and as Chinese commercial interests accumulate, tensions and differences in priorities within Chinese interests and approaches are becoming increasingly apparent. Similarly, if the Chinese actors nominated to prosecute their country's interests in Africa are to succeed in the longer-term development of Chinese interests across the continent, they will need a better appreciation of the disparities both within and between their partner countries in Africa. It is time for Chinese actors in Africa to start recalling how they feel when Westerners talk of 'Asia' in anything other than geographical terms. As much as the Chinese authorities might sometimes appear to wish it otherwise, 'China' is in a series of relationships with 'Africa' that run not just from state to state, or from citizen to citizen, but between a multiplicity of interests and institutions within individual states at central, provincial and city levels, combined with overlapping regional and sub-regional interests and institutions.

China's engagements in Africa may be resource-focused, and these engagements may be supported by the CCP's medium-term thinking about China's strategic requirements, but there is a danger that recognising these realities can lead to the misguided identification of a uniform and linear 'Africa strategy', whereby Beijing issues demands in accordance with its thinking and Chinese companies go forth and deliver. Turning to consider the challenges of coordination and cooperation (both internal and external) faced by Chinese institutions operating overseas, two factors become clear. Beijing has developed an impressive array of mechanisms for advancing Sino-African relations at continental, regional and national levels. Yet those deploying these mechanisms do not always work well together, and their aims are not always complementary. Even from the brief overview offered here, it is apparent that any notions of a kind of 'China Ltd' 'Africa policy' are ill-founded. The difficulties of coordinating any overarching strategy in Africa are evident. Indeed, the tensions that have emerged within China over how to prosecute and develop the country's multifaceted engagements in sub-Saharan Africa's diverse environments have formed a key backdrop to the sometimes painful evolution of China's African diplomacy.

As China's engagements with African countries increase, so does the anxiety of the Chinese state about managing the developing array of actors involved. The state has two basic, interlinked concerns. Firstly, it seeks the development of sustainable engagements that deliver results against key strategic requirements. Secondly, it seeks to retain sufficient control over these engagements to be able successfully to balance its interest in advancing them against the country's broader international interests, including, for example, the preservation of stable relations with the US. The idea is that success in securing China's key domestic strategic requirements does not come at the price of unnecessary damage to its key international strategic relationships.

It is with these concerns in mind that the Chinese state has worked at least as hard as any other power to restructure and adapt its approach to the African continent over the past decade and cultivate positive relations there. Just as the state was in the vanguard of China's earlier, ideologically inspired engagement with Africa, so it has similarly positioned itself at the front of this more pragmatic foray.

State support for Chinese business abroad

Chinese government institutions have long played the key role in determining which Chinese companies operate abroad and how. In 1979, China's State Council for the first time permitted certain companies to operate overseas independently of government-directed and supported projects. As the authority of the Ministry of Foreign Economic Relations and Trade, established in 1982, grew over the course of the 1980s, Chinese companies began to be encouraged to consider opportunities abroad, and to receive practical support to do so. In the early 1990s, the oil company CNPC, which had been created from the disbanded Ministry of Petroleum in 1988, began to invest abroad and establish a presence in the international oil market.[1] The commercial logic behind the move abroad – which the state went on to co-opt as official government policy – was powerful then as it is now. For companies such as CNPC, the appeal of investment abroad lies not only in the opportunities it presents for access to new sources of supply, but also in the greater profit potential of international markets, with energy-company profits limited in domestic markets by the state-enforced requirement to meet demand at lower prices.

During his 1992 'southern tour', in which he travelled through China's southern provinces reasserting his reform-ist economic agenda in response to his opponents within the party, Deng Xiaoping reaffirmed his support for an 'open-door' economic policy, confirming that there would be no turning back from his reformist platform, even in the face of hostile Western actions following the Tiananmen Square massacre. In 1993, the Ministry of Foreign Trade and Economic Cooperation drafted a report identifying Africa as a key market for Chinese manufactured products.[2] At the CCP's 15th Party Congress in 1997, the concept of 'grasping the large, while releasing the small' was formally promulgated. Key strategically important companies were consolidated and kept under the control of the state, while the rest were privatised. The policy of Chinese companies 'going global' was then developed during China's tenth Five Year Plan from 2001 to 2005. By the time the plan began in 2001, Africa was already provoking strong interest in China: at the end of the 1990s, China had some 480 joint ventures in 47 African countries worth a total of $820m.[3]

During the 1980s, three major NOCs emerged as a result of the government's restructuring of the management of its petro-leum and chemical industries. CNPC, CPCC and (to a lesser extent) CNOOC were then further developed into 'vertically integrated' corporations, active at each level of the process –

in exploration, production, refining and distribution – with boards appointed by the CCP's Organisations Department and presidents enjoying ministerial status.[4] The state's project to develop Chinese enterprises into leading international companies soon yielded results. Following its initial public offering on the Shanghai Stock Exchange in late 2007, PetroChina Ltd, the publicly listed subsidiary of CNPC, surpassed ExxonMobil to become the world's largest listed company by market value.[5] The 2008 *Forbes* 'Asia's Fabulous Fifty Companies' list, which ranks firms according to factors such as long-term profitability, sales and earnings growth and stock-price appreciation, included 13 Chinese companies, with China's second-largest steel maker, Angang Steel, ranked second.[6] Having previously had only a modest presence in international markets, in 2008, Huawei became the world's fifth-largest telecommunications-equipment supplier; in 2007, the company ranked fourth in the world for quantity of international patent applications filed, indicating important progress in developing research-and-development capacity (and probably also in observance of patent law).[7] Having also had a limited international presence earlier this decade, another Chinese telecoms provider, Zongxing Telecom Equipment (ZTE), similarly now enjoys more international than domestic sales. In 2007, ZTE turned a profit of RMB11.4bn, employing 8,000 staff in around 100 offices abroad.[8]

State institutions (controlled by the government, which is in turn controlled by the party) perform the political and commercial groundwork for Chinese companies operating abroad, acting as facilitators and often guarantors to create a favourable environment for companies to enter. The 2006 Africa White Paper notes how the government 'encourages and supports competent Chinese enterprises to cooperate with African nations in various ways ... to develop and rationally exploit their resources'.[9] A 2007 report of the secretariat of the FOCAC Follow-up Committee reminds readers that 'the Chinese government actively encourages Chinese enterprises to carry out economic and trade operations in Africa'.[10] The National Development and Reform Commission (NDRC),[11] the country's top planning and policymaking agency responsible for formulating national-development strategies, maintains a list of countries in which investment is particularly encouraged, which it updates to reflect current priorities, although the criteria for selection are opaque. Additionally, any Chinese company wishing to invest more than $30m abroad requires prior clearance from the NDRC, or from the State Council if the investment is more than $200m.[12] The leading role played by the government in China's African enterprises reflects the CCP's continuing efforts to preserve elements of state control and direction alongside a market economy and an increasing interest in the generation of profit. The state encourages and then attempts to direct Chinese activities in Africa in furtherance of its own aims. Yet even the briefest conversations with officials engaged in such tasks leave an impression of a Chinese government in the strange situation of operating something akin to a containment policy in relation to its own 'go global' instructions: it is simultaneously desirous of African engagements and nervous of their consequences.

In 2003, the State-owned Assets Supervision and Administration Commission of the State Council (SASAC) was formed to restructure, reform and supervise the work of China's largest SOEs, including the three NOCs. By the end of 2008, SASAC had reduced the number of these large, centrally supervised SOEs from 196 in 2003 to 150, with numbers intended to fall further to around 50 over the next three years. This restructuring and consolidating is intended to develop 'national champions' in key strategic industries.[13] The SASAC structure reaches down from national to regional and city level in a government effort to coordinate and oversee the operation of provincial SOEs. The intention is that under the supervision of SASAC, which is either the sole owner or the largest shareholder in the SOEs that have gone public, these firms can develop their commercial interests while still playing their part in implementing strategies devised by Beijing on the ground in Africa and elsewhere.

Of course, reality is rarely as neat as theory. Problems with command and control quickly appeared. While SASAC nominally supervises China's SOEs, the informal *'guanxi'* or personal connections of the most senior officials in many of these companies, in particular the three NOCs, mean that such individuals do not often feel obliged to conduct their business with the government through the administrative channels offered by SASAC, preferring instead to deal directly with the relevant senior officials. Informal networks also offer ways for companies to bypass the prior approval from the NDRC or the State Council officially needed for sizeable investments abroad. The lengthy processes involved in securing this approval can be a source of frustration to company bosses, who complain that cumbersome bureaucracy means that they miss out on contracts, and who are increasingly finding ways to circumvent the formal approval system. There are similar problems associated with monitoring projects once they have begun.

One of the most obvious ways in which the state supports expanding Chinese commercial interests is by gaining market entry through providing and packaging aid. The China State Construction Engineering Corporation is one example of a Chinese business whose initial entry into the African continent came through aid projects.[14] Grant aid, interest-free loans and concessional loans are all deployed, as are non-monetary forms of aid, such as technical assistance and training, and other stimulative tools, such as debt relief and tariff exemptions, that fall somewhere between monetary and non-monetary aid. These are packaged by the state along with, for example, infrastructure investment or arms sales, to help secure targeted and often lucrative commercial contracts in Africa. The 2006 annual report of China's ExIm Bank noted how concessional loans 'facilitated Chinese companies' entry into the markets of developing countries' and how they had also 'enhanced the international competitiveness of Chinese companies'.[15]

The location of the Department for Foreign Assistance within the Ministry of Commerce is a clear reminder of the agenda to which Chinese aid operates, and is increasingly a source of frustration to a Ministry of Foreign Affairs that would like to play a greater role in the design and delivery of aid projects. The department is, furthermore, reported to severely lack capacity, a particular problem given that around 15 separate ministries are involved in one way or another in the delivery of foreign assistance.[16] The problem this poses for Chinese aid to Africa – and, indeed, for any benefits such aid might have for China's own commercial and political interests on the continent – is that such personnel shortages, when combined with confusions resulting from the mixed political and commercial motivations behind aid projects, can make Chinese projects less effective than might be expected from what are often impressive original investments of money, materials or human resources. Lacking the capacity to plan projects properly and monitor their implementation, and without a requirement to verify that a project is self-sustainable after the initial donations have been made and the short-term political and commercial rewards reaped, China is not always offering African aid recipients the benefits that it initially appears to be. The fact that China is far from being the only country to face such challenges will not protect it from the consequences of the frustrations that could develop as a result.

As China's delivery of development assistance increases – with 2009 set to witness a 200% increase in the value of aid agreements with Africa over 2006 – the argument for the creation of a Chinese ministry for foreign assistance becomes more powerful.[17] Such a body would be particularly welcomed by some of the more established foreign donors, as it would be expected to increase transparency and facilitate greater partnership and coordination. But for a country insistent on its developing-world status and scornful of donor vocabulary (preferring for example to provide 'assistance' to 'partners', rather than 'aid' to 'recipients'), the fear is that its creation would bring presentational and political complications.[18]

In addition to state-sponsored aid and trade, there is evidence to suggest that Chinese companies are sometimes deployed to Africa to work on projects with more straightforwardly political ends. The practice is difficult to prove, and it is unlikely to be very widespread, given the main focus on profit-making enterprises, but anecdotal evidence indicates that commercial compromises are sometimes made for political ends. In 2005, *Wall Street Journal* reporter Karby Leggett documented how $4m in Chinese aid was funnelled to a Chinese state-owned construction company to build new homes for hundreds of Ethiopians left homeless following severe flooding. Leggett discovered that the homeless families had never moved into the new homes that had been built for them. Instead, the apartments had been commandeered by the Ethiopian defence ministry for their personnel. A senior executive of the construction company that had delivered the project remarked, 'We don't really care who uses it … It was a political task for us and so long as Ethiopia officials are happy, our goal is fulfilled.'[19]

The role of the Chinese state in the decisions of major Chinese companies to develop operations in Africa is partly sustained by the web of well-financed supportive institutions that the state puts at the companies' disposal. Scholars James Reilly and Wu Na have described this mass of institutions as a 'policy juggernaut'.[20] Financial support is available from exploration to exploitation. There are export credits for feasibility studies, government guarantees for the bank loans that are required next, further export credits to cover operational costs, and more credit lines for capital goods and machinery. And in case it all goes wrong and customers default, there is also cheap insurance.[21]

As impressive as it is, however, this state support focuses primarily on large-scale companies. Companies operating to key national priorities such as resource exploitation will tend to benefit (and suffer) more from state interest than those operating in less sensitive areas, such as light industry. Such firms attracting state interest tend to be SOEs, but large private companies, particularly those focused on resource extraction, do not escape this interest. The CCP has mechanisms for influence, with party branches operating inside major companies. As a McKinsey report on China's SOEs commented, 'Most Chinese companies large enough to pursue global aspirations have some connection to the government in its capacity as financier, customer, or tax authority.'[22]

Meanwhile, private small or medium-sized enterprises (SMEs) operating in Africa tend to do so with limited state support. One government official interviewed on the subject indicated that some of these companies saw advantages in operating independently of state support, and at times even deliberately sought this distance.[23] But it seems clear that, while benefit can no doubt be derived from a clear separation of commercial interests from the interests of the state, SMEs could still profit from greater access to information, expertise and financial resources. This was reflected in the SMEs' cautious response to FOCAC's appeal for greater SME participation in Sino-African activities.[24] Of course, these enterprises can profit indirectly from state efforts to develop environments favourable to Chinese business, but such efforts are unlikely to have been made primarily on their behalf. The participation of SMEs in the Sino-African dynamic remains largely a spin-off of China's official, SOE-focused, top-heavy engagement.

Key party and state elements involved in China's African engagements

Over the period in which the CCP has been cultivating China's relations with Africa, myriad institutions and agents of the party, central and local government and commerce and even civil-society and cultural bodies have been created for or otherwise become involved in the development of China's African relations. The individual agencies and institutions involved do not always have a clear sense of the limits of their remit in Africa, or of their priorities within this remit. Amid China's fast-evolving engagements, such uncertainties are magnified as institutions try to work together to mould their diverse array of interests into something approaching a coordinated agenda. Even within the party and the state alone, the picture is a complex one.

The CCP, with the nine-member Politburo Standing Committee at its apex, remains the central decision-maker in all China's affairs, domestic and foreign. Within the party, consideration of African issues is mainly undertaken by the Leading Group on Foreign Affairs, chaired since 2003 by President Hu Jintao, but these issues are also discussed in other leading groups, including the Leading Group on Finance and Economy. Below these broad-ranging leading groups and further into the central party apparatus come other departments and organs, working to more focused mandates and reporting to the party's Central Committee, the key chokepoint for policy papers moving upwards to the Politburo and the Politburo Standing Committee. Many of these departments consider or influence foreign policy in some way, including, most obviously, the Foreign Affairs Office of the Central Committee. One particularly influential department is the International Department, which is tasked with maintaining the party's contacts with political parties and movements overseas, and which has its own bureau for sub-Saharan Africa, Bureau IV. The International Department is also one of the party's key sources of policy analysis and advice. By contrast, the government's Ministry of Foreign Affairs plays a less analytical, more executive role, focused on responding to events than on formulating policy. Among its other activities, the International Department directs the visits of 'friendship delegations', such as that which visited Malawi, Zambia and Tunisia in July 2008, headed by the vice minister of the department, Li Jinjun.[25] Though the department's role involves developing foreign contacts across the political board, its officials appear to be more comfortable in dialogue with their counterparts in government, and wary of risking upsetting these relations by seriously engaging with those in opposition. This excessive focus on those in power is a particular weakness in the politically dynamic landscape of Africa, where governments can come and go, and not always on predictable electoral cycles.

The United Front Work Department, which is responsible among other things for maintaining relations with Chinese communities overseas, also plays a prominent role in African affairs. Other party departments, such as the Organisations Department and the Propaganda Department, have roles to play as well, as do organs such as the Central Party School and the Party Research Centre.

At a nationwide state level, the State Council (which itself has a Development Research Centre including an Asia–Africa

Development Research Institute) oversees a multitude of ministries, and departments within ministries, involved in Sino-African relations. Foreign Affairs and Commerce are the key government ministries, with the importance of commercial interests in Africa meaning that the ministry of commerce tends to prevail in the event of any policy dispute. The Ministry of Defence and the People's Liberation Army (PLA) have their own interests in military training and exchanges. China's defence industries continue to search for markets in Africa, though Chinese military exports declined after the appeal of the simplicity of Chinese weaponry faded somewhat in the wake of the US display of high-tech prowess in the First Gulf War.[26] The Education, Health and Agriculture Ministries are also involved in Africa. The FOCAC Follow-up Committee, whose secretariat is located in the Ministry of Foreign Affairs, is responsible for coordinating implementation of Chinese promises made to Africa through as many as 27 separate ministries and organisations.[27] It has the mammoth task of monitoring and supervising the timely fulfilment of the ambitious pledges made by China at FOCAC's 2006 summit. Among the other state institutions involved in China's African affairs is the NDRC, which considers issues such as energy procurement.

At a regional level, both provincial and city governments maintain foreign contacts, as do provincial SASAC offices. There are also Provincial Chinese Foreign Affairs Offices and Provincial Bureaus for Foreign Trade and Economic Cooperation.[28] The provinces are the engine of China's economic development, with provincial SOEs constituting almost 90% of all Chinese firms investing abroad.[29] In 2006, South Africa received delegations from Guangdong, Hebei, Jiangsu, Shaanxi, Shandong and Zhejiang provinces.[30] China's centre will always struggle to supervise all the bilateral dealings of its 23 provinces, five autonomous regions, four municipalities (including Beijing) and the two special administrative regions of Hong Kong and Macao. Beijing can design policies to protect its interests and retain control over the country's economic development, but it is the provincial authorities that will implement the policies. A tension therefore develops, as Beijing has to balance its interest in pursuing the implementation of its favoured policies against its – ultimately greater – interest in maintaining its informal pact with the provinces, whereby they provide employment and tax revenue to help maintain Beijing's control, in return for some devolution of responsibility on policy details.[31] The centre's need to carefully steward close relations with the provinces is likely to increase as China suffers the effects of the global economic downturn and seeks to limit its domestic social and political consequences.

Key entities involved in China's commercial engagements with Africa

China ExIm Bank

Established in 1994 to promote the expansion of Chinese business overseas, China ExIm is a state-owned, policy-oriented financial institution offering products such as export credits, foreign-exchange guarantees and loans for overseas investments.[32] It is the only Chinese institution offering concessional loans to foreign governments. ExIm's credits reached a total of $20bn in 2005, making it one of the world's largest credit-export agencies.[33] The bank explains on its website that it is mandated to 'implement state policies in industry, foreign trade, diplomacy, economy and finance … to support Chinese companies with comparative advantage … to develop and strengthen relations with foreign countries and to enhance Sino-foreign economic and technological cooperation and exchanges'.[34] The terms of ExIm's loans – which can be non-concessional or concessional – vary and are rarely made public, making the bank vulnerable to charges of indulging corruption and encouraging debt accumulation.

ExIm's focus is firmly on providing support to big companies engaged in major projects. According to its 2006 credit report, 90% of the export credits provided that year went to SOEs and projects worth more than RMB100m each.[35] ExIm is China's largest Africa-related lending institution and a major player in the extension of loans to Africa among single-country lenders, and even among multilateral lending institutions such as the World Bank and the IMF. In May 2007, the bank pledged $20bn in loans to Africa over the following three years.[36] ExIm's Africa projects are heavily concentrated on expanding power, infrastructure and transport capacities. It is engaged, for example, in developing oil facilities (Sudan, Nigeria), copper mines (DRC), dams (Sudan, Ghana, Mozambique) and railways (Sudan, Angola, Nigeria).

The China Development Bank (CDB)

One of the world's largest banks in asset terms, CDB has expanded its scope from an original focus on China's domestic infrastructure to engagement overseas, including in Africa. With $1bn of outstanding loans to Africa and involved in 30 projects worth a total of $3bn by March 2007, CDB remains quite some way behind ExIm in African financing.[37] Yet its engagements are increasing. In August 2008, for instance, the bank agreed to extend a $50m credit line for telecommunications infrastructure and other projects to the Eastern and Southern African Trade and Development Bank (PTA Bank), headquartered in Burundi.[38] CDB has sought to combine commercial interests with broader political and economic requirements. Though the bank is currently undergoing conversion from being a policy bank to commercial status with the help of $20bn from the China Investment Corporation (CIC), ties to the state will remain close.[39] In 2008, the bank's president was Chen Yuan, an alternate (reserve) member of the CCP's 17th Central Committee and the son of influential revolutionary and top CCP official Chen Yun.

The China–Africa Development Fund (CADF)

Established in June 2007 and funded and managed by CDB, the CADF has an anticipated lifespan of 50 years. Initially financed with $1bn, to be expanded to $5bn, the CADF is intended to support Chinese firms venturing into Africa through single-project loans worth between $5m and $50m, with repayment periods of five to eight years.[40] The fund will not take a controlling stake in any project and is in theory not restricted to supporting specific industries, although some, such as natural-resource exploitation, infrastructure and agriculture, are prioritised. The CADF's debut deal in Africa, announced in January 2008, saw it invest $90m in four major projects in construction, mining and energy.[41] By the end of the year, the fund had invested around $400m in 20 African projects.[42]

Though it is allegedly commercially oriented, the fund's investment criteria remain opaque. Its chairman, Gao Jian, has said that 'profits are not the fund's first priority. The China–Africa Fund first seeks to advance economic, political, and societal development.'[43] Projects that attract CADF support tend to tie a sound business strategy into broader Chinese strategic aims or interests in Africa. Anecdotal evidence suggests that the fund is finding it a little difficult to identify appropriate projects, and would like to see a larger body of applications from which to choose. The evolving investment activities of the CADF should make it an interesting case study as new ways are sought to encourage, guide and regulate the interests and activities of targeted Chinese companies in Africa.

The China Investment Corporation (CIC)

Founded in September 2007 with an initial capitalisation of $200bn and more in the pipeline, CIC manages part of China's foreign-exchange reserves and is one of the world's largest sovereign wealth funds. Just under half its capital is reported to be apportioned for deployment abroad, with the focus on private-equity investment.[44] The fund also functions as a source of support for Chinese SOEs expanding overseas. CIC is one example of a broadly commercial institution reported to come under pressure to support Chinese companies 'going global' in accordance with the state's strategic priorities. As a result of this pressure, the fund's investment strategies can lack some coherence. CIC's progress has also been undermined by an ongoing debate over the kinds of investment the fund should be making. Traditionally, it has tended to focus on the high-technology sector, investing in projects that will increase Chinese access to technological expertise. However, some – including former Chinese Vice Premier Zeng Peiyan – have suggested that the fund should instead prioritise investment in energy and mineral reserves. This view appears to have gained support following the onset of the financial crisis and losses incurred through the fund's US investments.

The China–Africa Business Council (CABC)

When it was established in 2004, the CABC was welcomed as a unique public–private partnership between its three founding members, the UN Development Programme, the Chinese Ministry of Commerce and a private organisation, the China Society for the Promotion of the Guangcai Programme. The council's purpose is to inform and connect interested investors, in particular those from the private sector, and help them find partners in China and Africa to advance their investment interests. To this end, it holds 'road shows' and seminars in both China and Africa. The CABC is another Chinese institution that is influenced by the political and strategic calculations of the state, with its private-sector element, the Guangcai Programme, enjoying close links with the party and its 'princelings', the sons and daughters of former top CCP officials. Until mid 2008, the council's chairman, Hu Deping, was also the deputy head of the Party's United Front Work Department. Other United Front Work Department officials continue to use the CABC to progress party interests. The CABC has been criticised for seeming to pay considerably more attention to developing the Chinese capacity to do business in Africa than to developing the African capacity to do business in China.

Chinese embassies

Present in all but one of the 49 African countries recognising the PRC in early 2009, China's embassies in Africa have an important role to play in cultivating local political contacts, identifying commercial opportunities and preparing the ground for the arrival of Chinese companies.[45] Representatives of the Ministries of Foreign Affairs and Commerce work from the embassies in support of China's strategic ambitions, albeit often in the context of substantial interdepartmental rivalries. Of course, the impact a diplomatic mission has on initiatives in a given country is to some extent determined by the skill of the individuals involved. Some of the more dynamic Chinese diplomats have worked to improve cooperation and experience-sharing among local Chinese businesses. The Association of Chinese Corporations in Zambia, for example, which was established in 2005 by the Chinese commercial counsellor at the embassy in Lusaka, offers its members a business network, regular meetings and support with administrative issues associated with trade and investment regulations.[46] In early 2008, the Chinese embassy in Pretoria was promoting a campaign for Chinese businessmen in Africa to learn local languages, including English.[47] However, diplomatic oversight of the activities of Chinese companies is not always straightforward, or even feasible. Some companies will choose to register with the embassy and seek access to its expertise, or simply invitations to its parties. Others will not bother, or will actively choose not to do so. As Chinese companies often enter Africa through intermediate territories, such as semi-autonomous Hong Kong, their presence is not always easy for their embassies to detect should they forget to register or opt to avoid contact. Sometimes, relations between businesses and embassies can be uncomfortable, with embassy officials having been known on occasion to be embarrassed by some of their fellow citizens, even dismissing them as members of a less 'civilised' class.[48]

The SOEs, including the NOCs

While China's state-owned businesses certainly have their own commercial agendas to pursue, their party and government ties also make them powerful influences on and agents of Chinese foreign policy. In particular, the three NOCs – CNPC, CPCC and CNOOC – exert a major influence on Sino-African relations, both in Beijing and on the ground in Africa. As their activities have become more integrated, the traditional boundaries between the commercial focuses of these companies have broken down. As a result, an often fierce rivalry between them has developed, as they compete to win contracts for new reserves and boost productivity and profits. One consequence of this competition has been bid undercutting, which has forced down prices and, inevitably, put pressure on winning contractors to identify cost-cutting opportunities.

Trade and Economic Cooperation Zones (ECZs)

At FOCAC 2006, the Chinese government pledged to establish between three and five 'trade and economic cooperation
zones' in Africa as a means of attracting more Chinese business
and investment to the continent. The Zambia–China Economic
and Trade Zone in the copper-rich region of Chambishi was
the first to come into operation. In early 2009, some confusion
remained as to which other zones currently under consideration by a range of Chinese companies would be adopted as
the official evidence of China's fulfilment of its FOCAC 2006
promises at FOCAC 2009. Commerce Minister Chen Deming
suggested that further zones had been earmarked for development in Nigeria, Egypt and Ethiopia.[49] But Chinese companies
are also engaged in discussions over other zones. For instance,
in late 2006, Mauritius secured an agreement with Shanxi
province's Tianli Enterprise Group to build an ECZ, although
by February 2009, despite some impressive models on display
at the site, construction had yet to begin.[50] In August 2008,
Chinese firm Paradise International Investment Ltd signed a
memorandum of understanding to invest $1.5bn in the devel-
opment of a Lake Victoria Free Trade Zone in Uganda's Rakai
district, to be known as Sseesamirembe Eco-City, setting a
new record for the largest single private investment in East
Africa.[51]

China Nonferrous Metal Mining (Group) Company, which
owns the Chambishi copper mine, is overseeing development
of the ECZ in Chambishi, in which Chinese companies have
pledged to invest more than $700m. In addition to some 3,000
houses that Chinese construction companies plan to build
there, the Zambian government has claimed that 6,000 new jobs
for local workers will be created within the Chambishi zone.
By late 2008, around ten of the 50 Chinese firms ultimately
expected to invest in the zone were already operating there

and, in January 2009, a 'sub-zone' in Zambia's capital Lusaka was inaugurated during a visit by Commerce Minister Chen.

Uncertainty persists over some of the operational details of the planned ECZs, in particular over the issue of whether other foreign or host-country companies will be welcome in them. Similarly, their impact on the local business environment remains to be seen. The history of special economic zones in Africa is chequered; the zones will need to be carefully harmonised with host-country interests if they are to make as substantial a contribution to African development as China's 'win–win' rhetoric currently promises.

There are of course other actors and institutions involved in China's commercial engagements. For example, the various types of insurance offered by the China Export and Credit Insurance Corporation (Sinosure) offer a valuable safety net to exporters as they explore new markets. Sinosure's guarantees to CNPC, CPCC and CNOOC provide valuable support to those companies' operations in difficult areas. There are other lines of credit too – for example, the Hong Kong-based China International Fund is one of the main lenders of Chinese finance to Angola alongside China ExIm. As commercial relations develop further, banks such as the Industrial and Commercial Bank of China will also have an increasingly important role to play.

Key agents supporting China's political engagements in Africa

FOCAC

Since the inaugural meeting in 2000, the triennial FOCAC meetings between Chinese and African leaders have set the bar high in terms of both substance and pageantry. The third FOCAC ministerial meeting, in 2006, saw Beijing hosting high-level representatives from 48 countries, joined by 1,500 businessmen. The array of commitments announced at the meeting was undoubtedly impressive (see box on p. 25), though perhaps not quite as impressive as it initially appeared. For instance, it is difficult to accurately judge implementation of the pledge to double assistance to Africa by 2009 when the 2006 figure remains to be clarified. Several of the pledges announced at the summit were, in effect, compilations of commitments already made in existing bilateral agreements. Furthermore, fulfilling such an array of promises within a three-year period – including such pledges as the construction of 30 hospitals and 100 rural schools – has unsurprisingly proved challenging. The Chinese institutions charged with implementing the plans, already experiencing difficulties coordinating among them- selves, face a tight timetable as they try to coordinate with their bureaucratic counterparts across Africa. Even before the onset of the financial crisis, it appeared that, in recognition of the challenges posed by the FOCAC 2006 pledges, Beijing was recalibrating its approach in preparation for FOCAC 2009. While there will no doubt be some headline-grabbing moments at the 2009 summit, China's attentions seem likely to focus on deepening cooperation in targeted areas such as infra- structure and agriculture, rather than on broadening it through another vast range of commitments. Where it might have been inferred from earlier Chinese pronouncements that China saw its commitment to Africa as being largely measurable in terms of the quantity of its pledges to Africa, it seems that attention may now be shifting to the quality of these pledges, and their fulfilment.

Part of the proclaimed role of FOCAC is that it should offer a mechanism for dealing with the challenges and difficulties that will inevitably arise as China's relations with Africa mature. Delegates to the 2006 meeting were assured that FOCAC would 'properly handle issues and challenges that may arise in the course of cooperation through friendly consultation in keeping with China–Africa friendship and the long-term interests of the two sides'.[52] In a similar vein, China's state councillor with responsibility for foreign affairs, Tang Jiaxuan, remarked shortly before the 2006 meeting that 'It is hardly avoidable that some problems [will] occur in the process of the continuous expansion of China–Africa cooperation. These problems are limited in nature and can be resolved through cooperation and consultation in accordance with the principles of equality and mutual accommodation.'[53]

One important flaw in the generally impressive conduit for Sino-African relationships that FOCAC represents is that China very obviously continues to drive the FOCAC process. This is partly a consequence of the absence of a formal African counterpart to the forum's Beijing-based, Chinese-staffed Follow-up Committee. By the end of 2008, the closest approximation to such a body that existed was a group of African ambassadors in Beijing informally coordinating to provide input for the FOCAC process and feed back from it. This lack can make it difficult for China to coordinate its offers of largesse with host-government priorities on economic development and poverty alleviation. Budgets tend to be allocated to individual countries in accordance with priorities determined in Beijing, which often bear little relation to needs and economic realities on the ground. Some Chinese officials also worry that the forum needs to broaden out from its focus on economic issues and provide a wider platform for engagement in spheres such as culture, technology and politics.[54] The fear is that by focusing on economic engagements, especially on those carrying the self-imposed requirement of being 'win–win', China is putting itself under excessive pressure and, as African partners do gradually become more engaged, is risking raising expectations to a point where it can no longer realistically expect to satisfy all its partners.

Other multilateral channels

Established in 2003, the triennial Forum for Economic and Trade Cooperation between Chinese and Portuguese-speaking Countries offers China another channel for strengthening its relations with Angola (its largest African trading partner), Mozambique, Guinea–Bissau and Cape Verde (with São Tomé and Principe absent due to its ties to Taiwan). In April 2004, the forum set up a permanent secretariat in Macao, staffed from Macao's executive government and China's Ministry of Commerce. All the African countries involved have since established resident representation in the secretariat in order to influence the forum's development.[55]

China rarely misses an opportunity to initiate contacts with Africa on broader international issues. In 2007, in accordance with an agreement made at FOCAC 2006, the foreign ministers of China and 48 African countries met for the first time on the margins of the annual UN General Assembly to discuss major international issues of mutual interest.[56] In May 2008, a Beijing symposium organised by the Chinese Ministry of Finance, the Ministry of Commerce and the State Council Leading Group Office of Poverty Alleviation and Development considered the challenge of poverty reduction. It was attended by 60 senior government officials and experts from 17 eastern and southern African countries.[57] In February 2005, a Conference on China–Africa Cooperation in Environmental Protection was convened in Nairobi, and in October 2004, Beijing even hosted a 'Symposium on Sino-African Human Rights'.[58]

The media

The Chinese media not only provides coverage of Sino-African relations; it will also play a role, for better or worse, in their development. The party's Propaganda Department plays the principal role in controlling the messages that are transmitted.

Inside China, the state-controlled media is an important tool for ensuring a positive view of the developing commercial and cultural relations with Africa. Blanket coverage of FOCAC 2006 left few Chinese in doubt about the importance their government attached to this event. The media also aims to influence international audiences. In June 2008, President Hu visited the headquarters of the *People's Daily* newspaper, reminding the assembled journalists that 'news and public opinion are at the forefront of the ideological field … The struggle in the field of news and public opinion is getting more intense and more complicated.'[59] The multiple potential functions of journalists as reporters of news, agents of influence and, further, collectors of information are well understood by the state. China's state news agency, Xinhua, has more than 100 branches worldwide, with an African regional bureau based in Nairobi. These offices act as centres not only for the overt collection and dissemination of information, but also for the covert collection of tactical and strategic information on behalf of the government, far removed from any journalistic purposes.

As with the entities supporting China's commercial engagements in Africa, there are of course other institutions that play a role in China's political relationships on the continent that cannot be examined in detail here. One organisation that does not yet appear to have played a political role in Africa, but which may have an interesting potential to do so in future is the State Administration of Foreign Exchange (SAFE). SAFE is China's foreign-exchange regulation agency, and it has responsibility for managing the country's foreign-exchange reserves. Its Hong Kong-based subsidiary SAFE Investment Company Ltd, which is officially a private company, has made several overseas investments. Although most of these appear to have been small-stake investments in Western companies such as BP and Total, some of the company's investments have also served political purposes. In 2007, SAFE agreed to the purchase of $300m in US-denominated Costa Rican government bonds as part of a deal whereby Costa Rica cut its 63-year-old ties with Taiwan in favour of the PRC.[60] With four African countries yet to establish diplomatic relations with China (as at early 2009), SAFE's substantial access to foreign exchange could yet be deployed to political ends in Africa as well.

Key agents supporting China's cultural engagements in Africa

Cultural interchange remains by far the least developed aspect of Sino-African relations. While it is of course natural for cultural contacts to take time to follow in the footsteps of commercial and political contacts, initiatives to increase cross-cultural exchange across music, art and literature have only recently begun, and many are understandably sceptical about the level of China's commitment here. With the state in the vanguard of developing commercial and political engagements, the relative lack of Chinese state engagement on cultural interactions with Africa has served to highlight both the strategic thrust of much of China's approach to Africa and the need for greater popular involvement in the primarily state-to-state, elite-to-elite relationships currently being cultivated.

Some official recognition of China's weaknesses here may be emerging. Hu Jintao's February 2009 Africa tour showed a greater focus on cultural issues, with a visit to the refurbished Chinese cultural centre in Mauritius and the specific inclusion of the goals of increasing 'people-to–people' exchanges and deepening cultural interchange in the president's six-point proposal for strengthening Sino-African relations.[61] While it is clear that the promotion of cultural relations will remain far from a priority element of China's pragmatic engagements in Africa, the growing preoccupation of the Chinese state with developing China's 'soft power' in the early years of the twenty-first century has, along with its concern to emphasise the notion of Chinese brotherhood with Africa, forced some limited attention to be paid to these issues. 'Confucius Institutes' have led the way in the cultural marketing of China through the promotion of the study of Chinese language and culture abroad. In 2004, a target was set of 100 Confucius Institutes by 2010. In 2007, this was dramatically increased to 500. By November 2008, 307 institutes had been established in 78 countries.[62] Seventy institutes had been established before the first was opened in Africa (in Nairobi in December 2005, just over a year after the first institute was opened, in Seoul).[63] By February 2009, 16 Confucius Institutes and four associated 'classrooms' had been established in 13 African countries.[64] The fact that in Africa there are fewer educational establishments offering the opportunity to study Chinese than there are in Europe, for example, may mean that the relative impact of the Confucius Institutes in Africa will be greater than the simple numbers of institutes established might indicate. Nevertheless, the institutes' impact has been somewhat undermined in Africa, as it has elsewhere, by a focus on establishing them quickly over the coordination and standardisation of activities. Curriculums have been largely uncontrolled, and institutes often have little in common beyond the Confucius Institute name.

Other cultural initiatives include the FOCAC pledge of 300 youth volunteers for Africa by 2009 and the November 2008 exhibition of African art in Shenzhen province sponsored by the Chinese Ministry of Culture. However, on the whole, cultural ties between China and Africa remain weak, in terms of interactions of Chinese with Africans in both Africa and China. Unless this changes, in the longer term, there will be limits to what cultural initiatives can achieve in building partnerships at a popular level.

Competing interests and policy coordination

There is, then, a wide assortment of Chinese institutions and actors involved in developing Sino-African relationships. Though each has its weaknesses, collectively they represent an impressive diversity of interactions. The sheer multiplicity of Chinese institutions and actors in Africa could perhaps lead one to imagine an intimidatingly polymorphous yet coherent Chinese entity, unified and coordinated in its intentions towards Africa and working to a consistent strategy for realising its interests on the continent. But the truth is that the assorted institutions described above have little holistic effect on China's African relations – the lack of a clear, established agenda binding them together impairs the impact that they can collectively have beyond their individual functions. Indeed, there are at least three important sets of fissures in the Chinese presence in Africa that negatively affect its overall efficiency and effectiveness. These are the fissures between the interests of the Chinese state and those of Chinese commerce; between the institutions of the Chinese state itself; and between the major Chinese businesses.

The interests of the Chinese state and Chinese commerce diverge as businesses develop their own approaches to their engagements in Africa, on occasion moving ahead of and even sometimes away from the government agenda. SOEs do not always respond positively to government promptings towards particular opportunities if the commercial appeal of those opportunities appears limited. For example, during a visit to Nigeria in April 2006, President Hu agreed a deal with the Nigerian government whereby CNPC would commit $2bn to the country's Kaduna refinery in return for four oil-exploration licences. When the Bureau of Public Enterprises in Nigeria initiated the bidding process for the refinery, and duly gave CNPC right of first refusal, the company raised concerns over the quality of the assets on offer and submitted a bid below the bureau's reserve price. For CNPC, the deal simply did not make commercial sense. No other bidders stepped forward, and the Kaduna refinery reverted to the Nigerian National Petroleum Corporation in July 2007.[65] Conversely, if SOEs spot a good commercial opportunity, they are not always eager to coordinate with government to ensure such involvement is in accordance with China's broader strategic interests. For example, an equity presence in Sudanese oil production may make good commercial sense for CNPC, and can even be presented by the company as beneficial to national energy security. But with events in Sudan intensifying third-party scrutiny of China's engagements both in Sudan and elsewhere in Africa, it is clear that China's commercial engagements do not always serve the state's immediate interests.

It seems that the state is aware of the problems associated with the command and control of the enterprises it owns, and of the extent to which the very nature of this relationship can render the state vulnerable. Already in September 2005, Vice President Zeng Qinghong was calling for better coordination of the foreign investments of Chinese companies, and for broader consideration on the part of business for China's national interests.[66] The Chinese state has worked hard to keep some control over Chinese commercial activities in Africa, and it does not intend to let up. In a speech to the African Development Bank in 2007, Premier Wen Jiabao reaffirmed his belief that business cooperation should be combined with 'government assistance', calling on his government to 'provide more guidance' to businesses.[67]

Rivalry and tensions among state institutions also hamper the effectiveness of the policy web that China has developed to support its African relations. Institutional mandates are often poorly delineated and have a tendency to overlap, causing inefficiency; organisationally, there is much scope for personal and institutional rivalry, and for individual and institutional evasion and impunity when things go wrong. These problems of coordination are long-standing, and hardly unique to the country's African concerns. British China analyst Kerry Brown has recalled how, when he was serving as a diplomat in Beijing in the early 2000s, it was a popular joke that Chinese ministries would use visiting diplomats to carry messages to rival departments.[68] Furthermore, decision-making systems tend to be convoluted, and corrupted by the exploitation of high-level *guanxi*, or personal connections, by key individuals both within and outside government, notably directors of the key SOEs. These unofficial personal ties, so prevalent in China yet so impenetrable to outsiders, can be particularly influential in areas, such as arms exports, that are dominated by princelings. The interests of the NOCs, for example, are well-protected by networks of *guanxi* between the oil companies and the upper reaches of government, connections that are reinforced by the habitual interchange of personnel between government, party and the oil industry. Zhou Yongkang, for instance, was president of CNPC when, in 1997, the company became the largest stakeholder in Sudan's Greater Nile Petroleum Operating Company. Zhou went on to become vice minister for oil and in 2007 became a member of the most powerful decision-making body in China when he was nominated to join the CCP Politburo's 17th Standing Committee.[69]

Some of these difficulties, particularly those relating to vested interests, are illustrated by the faltering and somewhat stunted development of China's energy policy. In 2006, the Central Foreign Affairs Work Conference identified the need for a more coherent energy strategy. The revival of a single energy ministry with real responsibility for coordinating policy across the board has been seen as a possible way of supplying the coherence that is currently lacking. However, government institutions such as the NDRC and the Ministry of Commerce have an interest in retaining their current close engagement in the politically and commercially influential business of energy policy. The NOCs, too, have been resisting moves to create a single energy ministry, which they fear might give them less opportunity to influence policy and insist on taking more control for itself than is held by government departments in the existing, more fragmented structure. To make matters more complicated, it is not only the current, fourth generation of CCP leaders whose personal interests in energy issues must be taken into account, but also Jiang Zemin's third generation, some of whom retain personal financial stakes in the energy business, either directly or through their offspring.[70] Consequently, progress on streamlining the coordination of energy policy is sporadic at best. When the March 2008 National People's Congress established a National Energy Commission and its administrative executive, the National Energy Administration, few saw the move as anything more than a small step on the long road towards improving efficiency in the face of the vested interests that currently riddle the system. Flaws in what is widely understood to be a short-term measure were immediately evident. For example, responsibility for oil pricing remained outside the National Energy Administration, within the NDRC, which also succeeded in ensuring supervisory control over the new administration, shared with the State Council.

The manipulation of *guanxi* and the use of corrupt practices to win lucrative contracts can bring a toxic element into the competition between Chinese businesses themselves in Africa. While progress towards international competitiveness is normally hastened by healthy domestic competition between firms, the competition between China's SOEs is not always healthy, often involving the vicious bid undercutting that forces bids downwards and lowers operating standards in the process. Furthermore, companies have a habit of briefing against one another, bringing confusion to policymaking.

Frustrated by the damaging effects of these fissures on China's progress abroad, and confronted by the tension between statism and profit-oriented business, the Chinese state has made some attempts to address issues of coordination and control. Perhaps unsurprisingly, these have largely focused on the activities of Chinese companies in Africa and their implications for the wider interests of the Chinese state, rather than on improving coordination between different elements of government itself. In October 2007, the State Council produced 'Nine Principles on Encouraging and Standardising Foreign Investment', aimed at developing a common understanding between the state and Chinese companies operating overseas. These called upon the government to improve and standardise policy guidance to 'prevent disorderly competition and safeguard national interests', improve policymaking mechanisms and better supervise state-owned assets overseas. There have also been some ad hoc initiatives bringing together key Chinese stakeholders in Africa. In July 2007, China ExIm Bank hosted a Symposium on Financing and Project Cooperation, which was attended by assorted government departments, commercial associations and Chinese companies with investment interests in Africa.[71] Efforts to improve coordination within, if not yet between, government ministries are also in evidence. In January 2008, the Ministry of Foreign Affairs convened a conference in Nairobi attended by 43 of China's ambassadors to Africa intended to improve coordination and communication between diplomats in Africa. Nevertheless, in spite of isolated efforts, the fissures within and between foreign-policymaking establishments and between state institutions and Chinese companies remain.

Of course, administrative and strategic coordination is a problem for any government. Most governments are not the unified, coherent decision-makers and actors they might aspire to be. For instance, there are around 26 different government agencies involved in the dispersal of US aid. Furthermore, such is the pace of China's engagement with Africa that any government would struggle to stay ahead of the game. One Chinese diplomat has likened China to a fast-growing, gangly schoolboy, still unsure of the size, stretch and weight of his limbs, lacking in coordination, and occasionally sending things flying more by accident than intent.[72] It will take Chinese institutions time to catch up with the pace of growth.

Recognising the practical difficulties China has in coordinating its African engagements can help outsiders to appreciate the extent of the challenges faced by the Chinese government as it negotiates strategies for Africa. Not only are there 53 different African countries for 'China' to deal with, each with different development priorities, trading interests and political perspectives, as well as bureaucracies and institutions, there is also a variety of different sets of Chinese actors involved, each with its own intramural tensions. Just as there is no singular, coherent and agreed China strategy for Africa, neither is there one for any individual African country. There are not even agendas for individual countries agreed among key Chinese institutions of state, such as the Ministry of Foreign Affairs and the Ministry of Commerce. China may be an authoritarian state, and the CCP may be in ultimate control, but this control is not absolute. Particularly on the ground in Africa, where relations are complicated by the interactions of private and state-owned commerce, the reality of 'China's Africa policy' is far more multidimensional than is often assumed.

An understanding of these internal dynamics is important for China's African partners and interested observers alike.

For African governments and societies, an appreciation of the diversity of their Chinese interlocutors and the nuances of intra-Chinese relations can help them to discern who the important decision-makers are and where power lies, enabling them to be tactical in choosing negotiating partners and building relationships. Both Africa and the West would do well to remember that China's institutions are still at a learning stage in their African relations, official rhetoric about a long history of continuous engagement notwithstanding. As one CASS academic has observed, 'at the moment, there is only response diplomacy'.[73] It will take time for China's African diplomacy to evolve and, for as long as basic lessons are still being learnt, this diplomacy is likely to remain more reactive than proactive. If this is well understood, both African and Western actors should be able to calibrate their approaches to China sensitively on issues of concern and importance such that the pressure that is needed to elicit a response from China comes within a context of engagement and partnership.

Another issue of direct relevance to China's African partners is that poor communication within and between Chinese ministries and major Chinese businesses can impede the ability of the Chinese government to identify the broader diplomatic implications of a policy decision in one area for their engagements in other areas. In 2007, for example, the PLA launched an anti-satellite test apparently without communicating with other state institutions, which then appeared unprepared to deal with international protest over the unprecedented amount of space debris that the test created. China's African relationships are similarly being conducted in a context of poor communication and coordination of decision-making, with all the pitfalls this entails. To stay with the military example, while it profits China's defence establishment to sell arms in Africa, should not the PLA and the country's leadership be viewing this trade in the wider context of the knock-on effects of these sales on China's longer-term interests in Africa?

However, all this being the case, the temptation to over-correct the false image of a singular and unified China in Africa also needs to be avoided. The network of actors involved in developing Sino-African relations may not be as tightly coor-dinated as the Chinese leadership might like, and it may indeed be difficult for interested parties to act in harmony, but a network of sorts does nevertheless exist. Moreover, it is generally well funded, well staffed and increasingly sophisti-cated in the pursuit of its goals. The CCP and its institutions have recognised the importance of delivering on promises, and are working hard to ensure success here. Furthermore, in spite of the undeniable problems outlined here, there is little doubt that the party and the state have the capacity to effect substantial change; if nothing else, the dramatic development of China over the past 30 years is testament to this. If the party was determined to alter China's regulatory environment so as to improve the effects of China's commercial activities on the development of host communities in Africa, it could ensure that its government made the necessary statutory changes. Given that Chinese firms already need state approval for major investments overseas, if the Chinese state wished to demand, for example, additional qualifications from companies hoping to invest abroad, including a commitment to behave according to certain standards, it could do so. Of course, questions about the capacity of central government to monitor the implementa-tion of any new regulations would be likely to remain.

While it is important to recognise the weak points in China's coordination of its African affairs, the presence of diverse inter-ests and the coordination challenges these create do not mean that the Chinese state cannot answer concerns of Africans and outsiders that may arise over China's African activities. China may face difficult challenges as it goes about its African operations – some faced by many other governments, some more particular to China – but these challenges do not exempt the Chinese state or its companies from the responsibility to demonstrate, at the least, respect for minimum international standards of behaviour in their numerous African engagements.

CHAPTER THREE

Adapting to the Challenges of Maturing Commercial Relations

The factors drawing China to Africa are unlikely to radically alter or disappear soon. Furthermore, the institutions are in place to develop Sino-African relationships, and these institutions know what their tasks are, if not always how to coordinate with each other effectively in carrying them out. But what can we expect from the next phase, as relationships mature, bringing greater familiarity, expectations and demand for accountability? If, as some have said, FOCAC 2006 can be seen as marking the end of the beginning, how sustainable will China's African relationships prove to be as they move into their next stage?[1] What are the issues that might yet threaten complications? As other powers, both traditional and newly interested, refocus their attentions on Africa, how confident can Chinese policymakers and businessmen be of protecting the investments they have made in their African relationships?

Much will depend on China's collective ability to recognise and address the challenges that such relations bring, be they commercial, political, or cultural. Many challenges are already in evidence, but the Chinese response to them continues to evade much serious scrutiny, at least in Africa. While some of Africa's established foreign partners may be honestly concerned about the continent's relations with China, many African leaders reject such concerns, seeing them as patronising and interfering, even self-serving.[2] Nevertheless, as African nations become more confident and demanding in their dealings with China, there will be closer African scrutiny of how China responds to the concerns raised about its African interests. China cannot afford to be complacent. It will need to take into consideration not just its own perspectives on the relations that are developing, but also the perspectives of its African partners, who will increasingly – and reasonably – expect to see 'win–win' returns in reality as well as rhetoric.

Both African elites and ordinary citizens have made many positive statements about Sino-African relations. Such statements anticipate the opportunities that engagement with China appears to offer. Yet they also reflect some of the successes of China's African policies to date. Senegalese President Abdoulaye Wade has been one of the more outspoken of Africa's leaders in his contention that China's approach to Africa is already 'better adapted' than those of Western countries. He argues that 'with direct aid, credit lines, and reasonable contracts, China has helped African nations build infrastructure projects in record time'.[3] Ethiopia's Meles Zenawi, a member of former British Prime Minister Tony Blair's Africa Commission, has said that 'we [African countries] are very comfortable to see China's increasing influence in Africa'.[4] A comment posted by a Nigerian citizen on the blog site of British magazine *Prospect* reflects some of the popular appreciation among Africans of China's interest in their continent:

> The only thing America and Britain need from my
> nation is oil. Americans and British are not interested
> in our banking sector, telecommunications sector,

food sector, building and construction or transport sector … no Western bank would invest US$5bn in a Nigerian bank … no Western government is interested in building economic processing zones in Tanzania.[5]

As we turn to focus on the commercial and political challenges China is confronting in Africa, the intention is not to deny China's real achievement in winning friends and admirers among diverse communities in many African countries, largely through the benefits of its infrastructure projects and cheap consumer goods. Rather, the aim is to examine the sustainability of these relationships as they mature, and to look for clues as to how readily Chinese institutions are able to adapt to overcome some of the difficulties that they face. Foreign observers frequently comment on the pace of change within China. Take a walk around the Pudong commercial district of Shanghai, or talk to different generations of Chinese about their extraordinarily contrasting lives, and it is difficult not to marvel. Yet what can be said about the pace of change in Chinese diplomacy and other activities abroad? Put more bluntly, can the CCP-controlled institutions directing Chinese engagements in Africa prove as adaptable in protecting the Party's interests here as they have so far proved themselves to be at home?

The challenges of commerce: 'business is business'

In 2005, Zhou Wenzhong, then China's deputy foreign minister, made the now-infamous 'business is business' remark when challenged on China's relations with Sudan in the context of the Darfur crisis.[6] Even if the remark can be dismissed as the faux pas of one rather naive and defensive minister, the briefest examination of Sino-African commercial engagements quickly reveals a multitude of concerns in the arena of Chinese business that, for many Western observers, gives Zhou's phrase a certain symbolic power. Many of these problems will need to be resolved through political action. Several, if left unaddressed, threaten political consequences. Bill Clinton famously ran his 1992 US presidential campaign on the slogan 'It's the economy, stupid'. The danger for China is that, even accepting that business is business, the slogan of many campaigning African politicians could yet become 'It's the Chinese, stupid'.

The charges laid against Chinese business operations in Africa are many and serious. Concerns have been raised by African workers as well as by international and African observers over the safety of working conditions, standards of worker pay, respect for human rights and the quality of Chinese products. There have been stories of environmental degradation and disrespect for host-country laws. The proportion of imported Chinese labour to local labour in Chinese projects and the issue of the integration of Chinese labourers into host societies have also attracted attention in Africa and beyond. Rival companies operating in Africa have accused Chinese firms of both underbidding for contracts and overbidding for access to resources, enabled in this by unparalleled levels of state support. Standards of transparency are seen to be low; allegations of corruption and bribery abound. Broader concerns have also arisen. Which African countries and communities really profit from these 'mutually beneficial' relations? Is it in fact only a small elite in a few resource-rich African countries that benefits, while other Africans, with little access to resources, markets or political influence, must settle for the occasional handout?

Some of these concerns inform the view, held by a number of Western businesspeople and politicians, that China is simply not respecting the rules of commercial competition. In 2006, President of the European Investment Bank Philippe Maystadt complained that Chinese banks operated to different standards, giving them a competitive advantage: 'They don't bother about social or human-rights conditions'. Interestingly from the point of view of the possible effects of increased competition in Africa on ethical and other standards, Maystadt went on to suggest that Western donors meet to discuss the removal of 'excessive conditions' from the bank's loans.[7] It is not just China's Western competitors highlighting these problems. In 2005, a study by the International Labour Organisation of 11 construction sites in Tanzania found that four of the sites surveyed displayed 'exceptionally low standards, with long working hours, low pay, low-standard occupational safety and health and a poor record on workers' rights'. Three of the four sites were operated by Chinese contractors.[8] The African workers repeatedly striking over pay and conditions of service at the Chambishi mine and smelter in Zambia raise similar concerns.[9]

Whatever the realities behind them, the mere existence of such allegations and concerns presents problems for China. Firstly, even if not all the charges are ultimately found to be fair, the sustainability of China's maturing bilateral relationships in Africa will still be undermined if genuine problems that are identified are allowed to go uncorrected. This is especially the case in the more democratically inclined countries, where evidence of genuinely mutually beneficial relations is more likely to be required. Secondly, Sino-African relations are already indirectly affecting China's developing relations with the West. If China is seen as a generally positive force in Africa's development, African engagement can become a driver for broader cooperation and communication between China and the West. A broadly neutral effect on African development, even with some glitches along the way, would be unlikely to damage these relations, especially as there are few in the West who would claim that their own African-development policies have always produced positive results. Increased commercial competition on the continent will inevitably create some tension, but this should be manageable. The problem will come if Chinese engagements are confirmed as undermining the West's liberal-democratic development agenda in Africa. The issue is not so much one of spheres of influence, but spheres of stability. As long as the West continues to view the liberal-democratic path as the one most likely to lead not only to sustainable African economic development, but also to political stability on the continent, it will look askance at any competitor whose activities undermine this agenda, even if unintentionally and indirectly. For the sake of Sino-US relations, China would do well to avoid furnishing those in the US and elsewhere in the West already apprehensive about its rise with any further reason to view its engagements with unease.

It is, therefore, important for China as well as Africa that China can develop a sustainable position that enables it to be seen by the West as a responsible, if not always attractive, partner in African development. China will need to listen to the charges that are made against it, consider them rationally and respond accordingly. Action now can prevent problems from accumulating, and obviate the danger that the worst of these charges comes to epitomise Sino-African relations.

The Chinese state considers the commercial challenges

International media scrutiny and Western-state-led diplomatic lobbying do appear to have precipitated a growing recognition of these issues within the party and the government in China, where concerns have been voiced and steps taken to tackle the poor commercial practices of particular Chinese companies in Africa and elsewhere. When unease around the standards associated with Chinese business activities in the developing world emerged in the first few years of this decade, China's diplomacy was too often clumsy, and its default position defensive. Chinese government officials would intimate that it was hypocritical of the Western industrialised world to accuse Chinese companies of malpractice and irresponsibility, and that such accusations were indications of the West's determination to inhibit China's rise. Bribery and corruption were facts of life in Africa; if the West had a problem with them, it should talk to Africa. However, official statements on these issues soon became more nuanced and at least a little less defensive. As the Chinese state adjusted in response to increased foreign interest in Sino-African relations, the official approach shifted towards taking the line that Chinese companies would respect the laws of the countries in which they operated, but that it was the responsibility of the host country, African or otherwise, to ensure that it secured and distributed the benefits from Chinese investment appropriately. Chinese companies could not reasonably be expected to ensure that the opportunities their activities brought for Africa were indeed harnessed by Africa. It was enough that they were presenting these opportunities.

As the decade has progressed, the initial knee-jerk response that critical scrutiny must necessarily be motivated by a Western desire to limit and disrupt Chinese commercial interests has been replaced by a more considered approach, partly as a result of the growing body of evidence about dubious commercial practices on the ground in Africa. The discourse has even begun to move tentatively in the direction of self-regulation. Recognising that it risks laying itself open to charges of colonial-style exploitation if it takes excessive advantage of the weak regulatory environments that exist in some African countries, and that this could have a damaging effect on China's longer-term relations with both Africa and the West, the Chinese state can now be seen to encourage self-regulation on the part of Chinese companies operating in Africa. The response has been more activist than mere proclamations of China's willingness to see African nations become stronger and more self-confident in regulating the operations of foreign companies on their territories. For instance, it appears that one of the reasons the CADF has been relatively slow to identify projects for investment is that the fund's managers are concerned about investing in projects that might attract negative attention over poor working conditions and standards. Representatives of the CADF have expressed a desire to fund projects that go beyond abiding by the laws of host countries to ensure that the companies involved operate to similar standards as those set out in the 'Guidelines for Multinational Enterprises' published by the Organisation for Economic Cooperation and Development (OECD).[10]

Spurred on by outside scrutiny, in September 2005, China's Commerce Ministry began talking to the OECD about promoting corporate social responsibility (CSR), asking for help in explaining the organisation's guidelines to Chinese companies.[11] The following year, the ministry published recommendations for Chinese companies operating overseas requesting that they behave responsibly, for example by working to international safety standards and hiring more local labour.[12] In early 2007, the vice chairman of the Standing Committee of the National People's Congress, Cheng Siwei, criticised the 'irresponsible practices' of Chinese companies that pursued profit abroad at the expense of their social responsibilities, and called for such companies to face legal sanction. Their behaviour, he said, damaged both their own and China's interests: 'Even in developing countries, foreign companies that turn a blind eye to their social responsibilities will be kicked out of the market.'[13] The Nine Principles on Encouraging and Standardising Foreign Investment issued by the State Council in October 2007, in addition to calling for improved policy coordination and better supervision of the activities of SOEs, also specified that firms should comply with local laws, protect the environment, accelerate personnel training and improve safety training, and preserve a good corporate image and reputation. In early 2008, SASAC formulated its own guidelines on SOE social responsibility. Inadvertently reflecting the difficulties the state was having bringing the SOEs into line, the SASAC guidelines again reminded the SOEs to obey laws on environmental protection, safety standards and employee rights. Companies were instructed to learn from foreign companies' good practice and their experiences with CSR.[14] Also in 2008, the CABC produced a handbook designed to explain and extol the virtues of CSR to its members. Meanwhile, a number of semi-official Chinese delegations visited Chinese enterprises in several African countries, including Sudan, to witness operations on the ground and consider opportunities for improving engagement. On his 2009 Africa tour, Hu Jintao kept up the state's lobbying for more responsible commercial engagements, calling on Chinese companies in Africa to 'shoulder more responsibilities and forge amicable relations with the local communities'.[15] The fact that he made similar calls during his 2007 tour reveals something of the difficulty the state continues to experience as it tries to persuade companies to take up this challenge. In April 2009, the Ministry of Commerce released guidelines on overseas investment and cooperation in relation to 20 countries to advise Chinese enterprises on fostering positive relations with local communities and handling the problems that may arise.

Thus, while the problems associated with China's commercial engagements appear to be gaining recognition as, one by one, the assorted institutions involved in policymaking begin to consider them, it is clear that recognising problems is not the same as solving them. In opting for non-binding guidelines, China lays itself open to the charge that its responses are more presentational than substantive, designed to promote a positive image of adherence to the rules without impacting on any company's bottom line. Certainly, although there can be long-term commercial advantages to being good corporate citizens, there are tensions between the drive to maximise profits in the short term and considerations of corporate social responsibility. But while concerns about profits and access to resources undoubtedly set limits on the levels of regulation to which Chinese businesses are subject, it is bureaucratic inertia, vested interests and the complex relations between the state and its SOEs that are more likely to be key impediments to bolder, more binding, regulatory Chinese policymaking.

Developing companies in developing countries

There are some signs of Chinese companies engaging in voluntary initiatives to address the social and environmental impacts of their activities overseas. By November 2008, 193 Chinese companies and business associations had signed up to the UN's Global Compact, a set of voluntary principles for businesses covering issues such as human rights, labour rights, the environment and the prevention of corruption. Membership of the compact commits participants to publicly advocating these principles and reporting annually on their own progress. All three Chinese NOCs are members, with CNOOC the last to sign up in June 2008.[16] Other Chinese enterprises in Africa that have signed the compact include the state-owned China Railway Engineering Corporation, the China Development Bank and private telecoms company Huawei. While hardly offering a comprehensive answer to the challenges faced by Chinese companies operating overseas in weak regulatory environments, this kind of voluntary arrangement to observe non-statutory guidelines signals the beginnings of progress on responsible engagement, and creates a skeleton framework of accountability for the businesses involved.

In an effort to clarify the challenges that China now faces in Africa, seven major charges that have been levelled against Chinese commercial concerns in Africa and which threaten the development of 'win–win' sustainable relations are now examined in more detail, along with Chinese responses to them.

Charge 1: An unreasonable preference for Chinese labour and materials

Chinese companies operating in Africa are hardly the first foreign companies to stand accused of providing too few employment opportunities for locals, or of failing to engage with the local economy by using local materials. Yet whereas developed-world companies have the benefit of long experience of such issues, and have adapted accordingly over time, Chinese companies 'going global' in Africa over the past decade or so have often been faced with resentment and criticism of their practices in this area for the first time, with the eyes of the world upon them.

When Chinese businessmen, usually attached to SOEs, began developing their business interests in Africa in the 1990s, they generally responded to a dearth of trained and incentivised local workers with whom they could easily communicate by importing workers from China. A focus on fast profits meant that investment in learning local languages and building indigenous capacity through the provision of training schemes and better wages received limited consideration, despite the fact that, in addition to winning the support of local communities, such measures would be likely to represent a saving in the medium term, as the import of labour would no longer be needed. Likewise, in order to keep costs down, materials needed for construction projects, for example, tended to be imported from China, further limiting the opportunities for businesses to engage with local economies and communities.

Perhaps unsurprisingly, when Chinese labourers arrived in Africa in the 1990s and were housed in specially constructed compounds largely segregated from the societies in which they were working, disparaging stories would often begin to circulate. There were rumours that the workers were prisoners sent to Africa to serve out their time as slave labourers.[17] Similar allegations had been made when Chinese labourers had arrived in the 1970s to help construct the Tazara railway. Such rumours reveal something of the isolation in which Chinese workers in Africa initially operated. Suspicion and resentment can also be seen in the tendency of some host communities to overestimate the proportion of Chinese to local labourers employed on projects, partly as a consequence of the visibility of the Chinese workers' compounds and the sense of mystery that their isolation creates. Any popular belief that a strong Chinese investment presence does not contribute much to local employment and empowerment is further reinforced by China's focus on resource extraction – an industry that is not known for creating jobs, tending to be capital- rather than labour-intensive.[18]

Even when policies change, past behaviour often continues to influence the perceptions of local communities, and China's poor reputation on the use of local labour and materials can unfairly precede it. There can also be a tendency to generalise from the experience of some of the more fragile African countries, such as Sierra Leone, where a high proportion of imported Chinese labour and materials is a consequence of a genuine shortage of local skilled labour and building materials aside from cement. The most extreme cases of dependence on Chinese labour and materials, important as they are to address, should not be taken as reflecting broader Chinese practice in Africa. Following a tour of Africa in 2007, former US diplomat David Shinn recorded an 'enormous difference' between the employment practices of Chinese concerns in different African countries. In Ethiopia, for example, Chinese infrastructure projects were being built mainly by Ethiopians; in Sudan, Chinese labour predominated.[19] Researchers from the University of Stellenbosch in South Africa have argued that low rates of local employment by Chinese firms tend to be found in recovering post-war economies, such as Angola and Sierra Leone.[20] With nearly half of its population under the age of 15 and only 16% of its government employees having completed secondary school, Angola has sometimes struggled to meet even the 30% local-labour quota guaranteed under the credit terms negotiated with China's ExIm Bank.[21] By contrast, in South Africa, where the skills picture is very different, it is easy to find counter-examples, such as the Jiuquan Iron and Steel Company's Buffelsfontein project, which in mid 2008 employed only five Chinese out of a total workforce of 1,000.[22]

In addition, outside scrutiny of Chinese practice on the procurement of labour and materials appears to have had positive effects over the past few years, with progress quickest where skilled workers and facilities for producing materials are most in evidence and the host government most assertive. Major Chinese companies with long-term interests in Africa are beginning to identify the advantages to be had from investing in local capacity-building projects. Since 2007, telecoms firm ZTE has promoted itself in Uganda and Zambia as a locally focused company, delivering local jobs and serving local markets.[23] By 2008, ZTE's rival Huawei had established three regional training centres in sub-Saharan Africa, in Nigeria, Kenya and South Africa. It had also developed pilot programmes for new recruitment approaches, including competitive pay schemes and job rotation, while advertising its contributions to promoting local information-technology projects, including in rural areas.[24] The commercial rewards of these kinds of policy can be seen in the continued successful expansion of both companies across the continent.[25]

These days, agreements about the ratio of local to foreign workers and the source of materials are often written into contracts or otherwise agreed for large-scale government-contracted projects. However, on materials, reform is limited by the reality that part of a Chinese contractor's appeal will often be its low bid, which makes it difficult for the contracting government to dictate product sourcing. Indeed, not only have Chinese companies often been permitted by host governments to use Chinese materials, their import has often been facilitated by considerable tax breaks. Though greater sensitivity about procurement chains has developed over the past few years in both Africa and China, rumours continue to abound of Chinese companies abusing these tax breaks to smuggle in other Chinese goods, including electronics and textiles, for sale locally.[26]

While Chinese companies have made reasonable progress, at least on local employment, relations with local communities could still be improved by the better integration of Chinese workforces. Even where Chinese workers are not housed in a compound, linguistic and cultural barriers have meant that Chinese communities in Africa have often remained largely self-contained. This has lead to the creation of prominent symbols of separateness in the form of Chinatowns. While such enclaves may be seen as offering welcome cultural variety, and can even be tourist attractions in times of prosperity, their existence can also magnify the Chinese presence in a given area, and provide lightning rods for local resentment.

Of course outsiders arouse suspicion all over the world, especially in times of economic hardship, but the pattern of engagement favoured by Chinese companies in Africa can make Chinese workers there particularly vulnerable to hostility. World Bank economist Harry Broadman has summarised the problem as follows:

> Chinese firms tend to enter new markets in Africa by building new facilities, creating business entities that are vertically integrated, buying supplies from China rather than local markets, and selling in Africa mostly to government entities. They rarely facilitate the integration of their workers into the African socio-economic fabric.[27]

Charge 2: Poor employment practices
The process of localising hiring patterns is complicated by the fact that Chinese firms are accustomed to paying low wages. A 2006 study of Chinese activities in Africa's construction sector found some Chinese engineers in Angola being paid $130 per month, a sixth of the salary European companies were paying Angolan engineers.[28] With host communities often in desperate need of employment, a buyer's market thus emerges in which Chinese salaries can be low even in relation to the most basic living costs, thereby removing one of the normal benefits of working for large foreign companies. The managing director of a Western mining company with interests in Zambia has estimated that his Chinese competitors pay their local workforce as little as 30% of the salary that his local workers receive. Thus the standards set by Chinese-branded and run companies impact directly on the lives of their employees, their employees' families and the broader communities in which they operate. Though they may bring employment, the difference this employment makes to local lives may not be what was originally hoped for.

Child labour remains a serious problem in many parts of Africa, and one to which Chinese companies are not immune.

The complexity of supply chains in the minerals industry, whereby various middlemen purchase ores at source, including from children, enables the companies that own the furnaces and smelters to deny knowledge of child labour and other practices. However, this does not prevent negative consequences for the international reputation of the companies and countries involved, including China.

The default goal of delivering quick returns at the lowest possible prices means that practical moves to remedy problems such as low wages and child labour are not much in evidence on the ground, despite some rhetorical flourishes at state level. In October 2006, the governments of China and Zambia signed a memorandum of understanding aimed at harmonising labour relations and promoting cooperation on the prevention of labour-law infringements.[29] Despite optimistic forecasts made at the signing ceremony, problems continue. With minimal experience of organised labour, Chinese employers are having difficulty managing both threatened and actual organised protest. The demonstrations, strikes and occasional riots over wages and working conditions in Chambishi in Zambia, for example, have rumbled on for several years. As the death of more than 50 workers in an explosion at the plant in 2005 demonstrated, the regulation of health and safety is a serious issue at Chambishi, as it is elsewhere in Africa. In January 2008, hundreds of workers blocked the roads to the Chambishi smelter once more, demanding better salaries and benefits. Two months later, in March, riots broke out in response to rumours that the plant's Chinese managers were about to go on holiday, thereby further delaying the conclusion of ongoing negotiations over working conditions. One Chinese manager needed hospital treatment after the riots.[30] Five hundred Zambian workers were initially sacked following the incident, but were later reinstated.[31] It is not only indigenous workers who have protested over wages and conditions. In

Equatorial Guinea in April 2008, two Chinese contract labourers were killed and four injured in confrontations with police over a strike that was illegal under local laws.[32]

African civil-society organisations, and sometimes even members of local governing elites, have drawn attention to the attempts of some Chinese companies to circumvent regulations aimed at protecting local labour. A standard technique is to use casual labour wherever possible, including on big projects such as Chambishi, in order to evade statutory responsibilities associated with employing full-time staff. There have been other kinds of evasions, too. Since 1998, Namibia has had affirmative-action legislation in place, which stipulates that companies with more than a certain number of employees (25 since 2007) are obliged to present affirmative-action plans to the newly created Employment Equity Commission. In mid 2008, Chinese companies operating in Namibia stood accused of a general failure to report on their affirmative-action activities. Companies such as China Nanjing International, Ziangsu Zhentai Construction and China State Construction were revealed to have somehow arranged exemptions from the requirements through individual arrangements with the Employment Equity Commission. Other firms had released themselves from reporting requirements through the use of subcontractors.[33] Meanwhile, in Katanga province in the DRC, the local governor claimed to have expelled around 600 Chinese nationals between March 2007 and summer 2008 for violating labour and environmental laws.[34]

An East African diplomat has described how attempts to attach employment-related conditions to investments, for instance local-labour quotas, could be strongly resisted by the Chinese government and its companies when negotiating market entry. The Chinese negotiators' default position appeared to be that if a country seriously wanted Chinese investment, it would make it easy for Chinese companies to invest, and not unduly restrict their operations with rules and regulations about sourcing materials and hiring labour. If it was easier for Chinese companies to go elsewhere, so the implied threat ran, then they would.[35] This comparative bargaining weakness means that African countries need to work together more effectively to build a regional negotiating platform.

Examples of more responsible approaches to local labour law are mostly to be found among the bigger, usually state-owned Chinese companies – such as, for example, the China National Overseas Engineering Corporation and the China Road and Bridge Corporation – where government influence is greatest. While the Chinese government may be a ruthless negotiator of agreements involving Chinese enterprises, it is also sensitive to the consequences for China's image in Africa of incidents such as mining accidents and severe local dissatisfaction over employment policies. It is well aware that such dissatisfaction can have political as well as commercial consequences, especially in times of particular economic hardship locally, when the problematic aspects of China's African engagements are likely to be more keenly felt.

Charge 3: Bribery and lack of transparency

As the stronger partner in what it nevertheless insists are equal commercial relationships, it is important that China uses its deep pockets responsibly. The willingness of Chinese companies to pay bribes to secure contracts and to ensure blind eyes are turned where necessary has been documented by corruption monitor Transparency International. In the organisation's 2008 Bribe Payers Index, which ranks 22 of the world's most economically influential countries according to the propensity of their firms to pay bribes abroad (with the companies of the 22nd country listed being the most likely to bribe), China came

21st.[36] In Africa, Chinese firms did marginally better than they did overall, but still ranked third from bottom, above India and South Africa.[37] However, the survey is also a useful reminder of the widespread nature of the problem – it is only fair to note, for instance, that in a table on bribery in Africa and the Middle East, on a scale of zero to ten where the higher the score the lower the likelihood that the country is engaging in bribery, Italy scored 8.1 and France 8.3, both only a little above China's 7.8. Some Chinese businessmen – apparently forgetting the official rhetoric about a long historic friendship – have also argued that China's relative inexperience in Africa means that its firms are less likely to know their way around the system, and are therefore more likely than their more experienced counterparts from other countries both to get tapped for bribes and to get caught paying them.[38] Whatever the precise causes of China's poor showing on bribery, mistrust in this area is only exacerbated by the country's weak record on transparency in its African transactions, an important issue for Western observers trying to understand China's intentions on the continent.

The industrial sectors in which China is most heavily involved in Africa – namely, public works and construction, and oil and gas extraction – are also those where bribery is most prevalent.[39] With China some way behind several other economically influential countries on improving its practice on transparency, it can at times seem as if there is little will to make progress, with Chinese firms appearing reluctant to make concessions to Western concerns on the issue. Director of China's ExIm Bank Li Ruogu has remarked that 'transparency and good governance are good terminologies, but achieving them is not a precondition of development; it is rather the result of it'.[40] The international Extractive Industries Transparency Initiative (EITI), which encourages companies in this sector to publish what they pay and governments to publish what they receive, continues to try to engage Chinese officialdom. China is beginning to make some gestures towards the initiative that may in due course be developed into concrete measures. When G8 energy ministers met for their 2008 summit in Japan, they were joined by their counterparts from China, India and South Korea. Although these countries have yet to offer their support to the initiative, the joint declaration issued at the summit still included the G8's usual endorsement of the EITI, offering some hope that the three countries might show greater inclination to support the initiative in future.[41] However, it seems clear that substantive engagement with the EITI is still some way off.

Charge 4: Poor workmanship and the dumping of poor-quality products and fakes

Chinese manufacturers have developed a reputation for producing cheap but low-quality products. With African markets particularly receptive to cheap and affordable goods, Chinese-traded and manufactured products have developed significant customer bases in many parts of Africa, usually at the expense of local manufacturers, who find themselves unable to compete with the low prices of mass-produced Chinese products 'dumped' in Africa. China's critics claim that Chinese involvement in Africa consists simply of buying up Africa's raw materials for processing in China and destroying Africa's fledging attempts to develop its own manufacturing base. While such criticism is fair to a point, the goods issue should be viewed from the point of view of local consumers, as well as producers. In Africa, a key element of the appeal of Chinese products, from consumer goods to big public-works projects, is that they are cheap. Complaints that Chinese Tiger batteries may not last as long as more expensive Duracell batteries are largely beside the point.[42] Products quickly acquire reputations for reliability or otherwise, and the rest is up to the consumer. 'You get what you pay for' is generally a reliable guide to variations in the quality of workmanship. It may well be the case that the cheaper Chinese products do not always represent good value, but it is unfair to view the provision of more affordable, lower-quality products as intrinsically exploitative.

However, the practice of dumping fake or officially substandard goods such as factory rejects on a market is exploitative, and it arouses strong resentment among African traders and consumers. Helped by pressure from African and international media, unionised labour and civil-society organisations, this issue has been attracting attention at senior levels. In October 2008, Nigerian Minister of Commerce and Industry Charles Ugwu used the opportunity of a visit from a delegation from the Chinese business community in Nigeria to protest the dumping of low-quality products.[43] In January 2009, the director general of the Standards Organisation of Nigeria informed the Nigerian media that an agreement between the Chinese and Nigerian governments aimed at the influx of substandard goods from China was soon to be signed. The agreement would insist that Chinese products imported into Nigeria conformed to the Nigerian Industrial Standard.[44]

There are other examples of African governments engaging with China to try to protect domestic industries and consumers from the problems that cheap Chinese imports can bring. However, the challenges associated with such agreements are manifold, and include the considerable practical difficulties of monitoring and enforcement. At street level, if one Chinese trader is caught selling fake or substandard goods illegally and is barred from trading, there will be others who will quickly take his place. In the Nigerian case, the limited capacity of regulators and enforcers to monitor activities in the country's heavily congested ports is one example of the multiple domestic structural problems that are likely to restrict the effectiveness of any agreement reached.

Quality can also be a concern in the context of major infrastructure and other public-works projects. Questions are already being raised about the durability of a number of Chinese projects in Africa. For example, some new Chinese-built roads in Angola have been reported as suffering severely from heavy rains because of poor drainage, resulting in premature ageing and, in places, near-disintegration.[45] In 2007, China launched a Chinese-made communications satellite on behalf of the Nigerian government. The satellite, for which the Nigerian government had paid 40bn naira ($336m), had an intended lifespan of 15 years. However, a serious fault developed following the launch, and it had to be shut down after 18 months.[46]

Sometimes, poor quality makes products unsafe. The 2008 scandal of Chinese milk tainted with the toxic chemical melamine touched Africa when, according to one report, only bureaucratic inefficiency ensured that contaminated supplies of dried milk had not already been delivered to the children of HIV/AIDS sufferers in Gabon by the time the scandal broke.[47] In April 2007, China's deputy minister for water resources, Jiao Yong, labelled thousands of dams in China 'time bombs'.[48] The June 2008 earthquake in Sichuan province in China tragically exposed the frailties of poor-quality buildings, and gave unusual oxygen in China to allegations of corruption and underspending. Africa is, fortunately, not particularly prone to earthquakes, but concerns remain that the quality of Chinese construction there, whether dams or buildings, could be similarly poor, with similarly grave potential consequences. The political fallout of the Sichuan earthquake required deft handling by the Chinese authorities, even though the disaster happened on home soil, within their sphere of control.

A comparable disaster in Africa – for example involving the controversial Chinese-financed Mphanda Nkuwa Dam on the Zambezi in Mozambique, where there are doubts about whether building plans have taken sufficient account of seismic activity – could have serious repercussions for China's reputation in Africa and beyond.[49]

Charge 5: Lack of respect for the environment
The reputation of Chinese businesses as responsible stakeholders is not helped by the fact that many of their engagements are in areas such as oil extraction, mining, logging and hydroelectric power, where environmental degradation is a perennial problem. In addition, environmental problems are often magnified in Chinese engagements by the relative willingness of the Chinese state to fund and Chinese companies to engage in projects that have been of limited interest to other foreign investors because of their likely environmental impacts. Chinese companies are also more likely than many others to deploy cheaper technology and cost-cutting techniques in pursuit of rapid and substantial returns on their investments at the expense of the host environment. In September 2006, Sinopec was forced to suspend oil prospecting in Loango National Park in southern Gabon following pressure from conservation groups on the Gabonese government to protect the country's new national parks from dynamiting and pollution.[50] In May 2007, the Zambian government closed a Chinese-run manganese mine at Kabwe, already one of the most polluted places in the world, citing concerns over air pollution.[51]

Illegal logging is a prime example of environmentally damaging Chinese activity in Africa. Though the practice is certainly not exclusive to Chinese companies, their involvement in it is substantial. When logging regulations were tightened in China in 1998 following devastating flooding of the Yangtze River caused by deforestation, Chinese timber companies were prompted to look abroad. China is now the world's biggest importer of timber and, according to the non-governmental organistion (NGO) Global Timber, in 2006, it was probably also the leading importer of illegal timber.[52] Allegations abound of illegal Chinese logging across Africa, in Liberia, Equatorial Guinea, Mozambique and elsewhere.[53] In January 2008, faced with heavy deforestation in the north of the country, the government of Sierra Leone imposed a six-month ban on timber exports in an attempt to stop the 'indiscriminate destruction' of its forests through illegal logging by foreign companies, with the forestry minister explicitly citing Chinese companies as being among the perpetrators.[54] While illegal logging is supported by companies from countries other than China, the over-exploitation of South African abalone and shark fin, enjoyed as delicacies in restaurants across China, is more easily attributable to Chinese or Chinese-financed poachers.[55] Likewise, the illegal trade in rhino horn and other protected-animal parts is well supported by the market for Chinese health products.

As China is not a member of the OECD and has not agreed to observe the guidelines for export-credit agencies laid out in the organisation's Recommendation on Common Approaches to the Environment, banks such as China ExIm can and do lend to projects that have been refused funding by OECD countries on environmental grounds. Examples include the Bui Dam in Ghana, the Lower Kafue Gorge Dam in Zambia and the Merowe Dam in Sudan. But external guidelines on environmental issues are slowly beginning to be taken up by China. In November 2004, ExIm Bank adopted its first environmental policy, the details of which were not made public until 2007. ExIm now requires the submission of environmental assessments of the projects it funds before, during and after a project is undertaken. The bank claims that it will withhold funding in the event of non-compliance or failure to act on negative findings. In May 2007, ExIm signed a memorandum of understanding with the World Bank's International Finance Corporation (IFC) aimed at supporting environmentally sound Chinese investments in emerging markets, particularly in Africa. The IFC has since sponsored workshops introducing its Environmental and Social Investment Standards and familiarising Chinese banks with its standards and procedures.[56] In January 2008, the IFC signed a cooperation agreement with China's State Environmental Protection Agency to provide similar guidance on international environmental initiatives.[57] In October 2008, the Industrial Bank of China became the first of the country's banks officially to adopt the Equator Principles, a set of voluntary guidelines on environmental and social risk management in international project financing.[58] The assumption is that other banks will follow the Industrial Bank's lead. It will, however, take time for it to become clear how this commitment by organisations in Beijing will affect the financing of Chinese activities in Africa and elsewhere.

Inside China, measures are being adopted to try to safeguard the environment in the context of continuing rapid economic growth. New laws aim to tackle illegal logging and timber smuggling, and include the provision of transportation certificates for imported logs as proof of legitimate origin.[59] China has also worked hard to limit the trade in rhino horn and, to a lesser extent, ivory.[60] In August 2007, a 'green credit policy' was launched by the State Environmental Protection Agency (which was upgraded to ministry status in March 2008, in a further indication of increasing environmental engagement), in partnership with the People's Bank of China and the China Banking Regulatory Commission. The policy was intended to

stop banks lending to industries that caused excessive pollution or wasted large amounts of energy.[61] In November 2007,
the deputy chief of the NDRC announced that steps would be
taken against local officials who failed to meet environmental
targets.[62]

However, it is unclear to what extent increasing attention to
environmental regulation within China itself will be mirrored
by regulations – as opposed to recommendations and guidelines – for Chinese operations abroad. As pressure grows to
curb the activities of heavily polluting manufacturing inside
China, and African countries demand more processing of raw
materials prior to export, there is a danger that polluting industries, which have already been shifted inland from China's
seaboard, will simply be transplanted further westwards, to
Africa.

Charge 6: Unfair competition enabled by excessive state support
The Chinese state's extensive support for Chinese commercial enterprises in Africa is controversial, and the view, held
by Western companies in particular, that it results in unfair
competition for contracts creates tensions. State backing is
often viewed as unfair by companies that do not enjoy equivalent support – though of course some of those complaining
have an advantage of their own in the form of an established
presence in the market. Certainly, protected from responsibilities towards shareholders, and with a mandate from the state
to collect resources on its behalf, China's NOCs do enjoy more
freedom of manoeuvre than many of their competitors. State
support and funding mean that Chinese companies can overbid
on purchases in cases where the state sees a strategic interest in
spending the extra money, and underbid for contracts in cases
where strategic interests override the company's impetus to
maximise profits.

Charges of overbidding for access to resources can be difficult to prove. For example, the price of copper quintupled between 2001 and mid 2008; deals that may once have looked questionable look very different in times of soaring commodity prices. Furthermore, those making such charges are very often interested parties such as bidders that have lost out to Chinese firms. But there is little doubt that overbidding does occur, and objections to it are not confined to established developed-world companies. India's Oil and Natural Gas Corporation can testify to Chinese gazumping practices in countries including Angola, Nigeria and Sudan.[63]

At the other end of the scale, Chinese companies in Africa are able to operate to profit margins below 10%, in contrast to the 15% to 25% preferred by their Western competitors.[64] Ian Taylor cites the General Manager of the China Road and Bridge Corporation, Deng Guoping, to illustrate the extent of the Chinese competitive edge here, and the reasons for it. In 2005, Deng reported that the company's operating instructions for its activities in Ethiopia were to work to a profit margin of just 3%. This paltry target made losses almost inevitable. However, Deng noted, 'we are a government company, and the Chinese government wants us here building things'.[65]

As with overbidding, the issue of underbidding is tricky to assess. After all, it is difficult to complain about African countries having access to cheaper contractors. But local, as well as Western, competition suffers from these low margins. For example, in early 2006, South Africa's state-owned water-infrastructure firm TCTA confirmed the award of a contract relating to a water utility in Mpumalanga province to the China National Overseas Engineering Corporation after its bid undercut two local bids by 25%.[66] South African firms are increasingly losing out to Chinese firms across sub-Saharan Africa. It is one thing frustrating Western competitors, but relations with African competitors, particularly those from strategically important countries such as South Africa, might require some careful handling in the future.

A greater willingness to take risks in profitable areas such as oil exploration is another characteristic of Chinese firms that is in part a consequence of state encouragement. It too can excite resentment over unfair competition from firms that do not enjoy the same levels of government support. However, Chinese businesses' relatively high tolerance of political, economic and security risk is not always the subject of envy. In June 2007, CNOOC finalised a deal to explore for oil in Puntland in the severely unstable state of Somalia, a region with a particularly uncertain future in view of its claims to autonomous status. Although the deal was signed by the president of the Transitional Federal Government in Mogadishu, Abdullahi Yusuf Ahmed (himself a Puntlander), it was initially kept secret from the Mogadishu government, in what appears to have been an effort to circumvent the regulations being formulated by the government as it debated introducing a national hydrocarbon law. It can have come as little surprise to CNOOC when the deal's legitimacy was subsequently challenged by Mogadishu.[67]

In this case, China showed itself ready to take substantial risks exploring for oil under questionable legal and political conditions in a country which does not have proven oil reserves, but which does have a pitiable security environment.[68] However, even if most of CNOOC's rivals would have little desire to imitate its Puntland adventures, rival non-Chinese firms are keenly aware of the opportunities available to Chinese companies as a result of their openness to high-risk investments.[69] Generally speaking, if a firm is engaged in a region of strategic interest to the Chinese state, the normal restrictions placed on commercial activity – by shareholders and funding limitations, as well as by risk assessment – do not apply. Chinese SOEs are able to invest in places where large international companies are prevented from working by shareholder pressure over ethical or political issues, and where smaller foreign companies cannot operate because they lack financing or state support. In regions where other companies do operate, Chinese companies are aided in their often aggressive pursuit of major agreements by the Chinese state's cultivation of local officials. It is, therefore, perhaps unsurprising that rival firms complain that commercial competition is being corrupted by China's political support for its firms.

It is not always clear that the level of risk being incurred by a given Chinese investment is fully understood, either by the company concerned or by the Chinese state. With experience of significant investments and deployments of personnel in fragile environments overseas only now being accrued, formal risk-assessment structures remain seriously underdeveloped in China. The deficit is particularly acute when it comes to judging political risk. This is partly a consequence of China's rather wishful attachment to its non-conditional approach to investment, which it somewhat naively hopes will ensure that politics does not seep into its commercial concerns. The state's limitations when it comes to assessing political risk and developing strategies for managing it are compounded by poor communication between the various government agencies involved in handling overseas projects.

Thus, while some risks taken by Chinese companies are taken deliberately, calculated to be worthwhile for the potential national strategic gain, others are incurred largely by accident, by being misjudged or ignored. While China calculates that its deliberate risk-taking will play to its strategic advantage, misjudgements in this area too often rebound on China's image and reputation in a way that threatens to negate any advantages that might be gained from intrepid investing.

Charge 7: Exploitative relationships: the problem of trade imbalances
China's overall bilateral trade with Africa has been relatively
balanced in recent years, but this masks sharp contrasts between
China's trading relations with different African states.[70] China's
trade deficits lie with oil exporters such as Angola, Nigeria
and Sudan. It remains relatively uninterested in other African
exports – Chinese exports to Kenya, for example, exceed Kenyan
exports to China by a ratio of 19:1.[71] China's ongoing failure to
open its market to African imports is a key obstacle to realising its declared goal of contributing to Africa's development.
However, for those African countries that have found a market
in China for their raw materials, the narrowness of this bilateral
trading relationship is not necessarily immutable or, indeed,
a problem. The export of one product can be a starting point
for exporting more, bringing in valuable funding to support
export diversification in the medium term. In 1979, 40% of the
total value of Chinese exports to the US was accounted for by
one commodity: oil.[72]

Nevertheless, many African nations remain understandably concerned about the nature of bilateral trade with China.
Assuaging these concerns is not something that the Chinese
state or Chinese businesses can do easily or quickly. Chinese
manufacturing prowess is posing a considerable challenge
to African attempts to develop manufacturing capacity and
diversify export economies away from raw materials. The situation is raising awkward questions about the compatibility of
Chinese and African trading interests throughout Africa.[73] In
the 1980s, Nigeria's textile industry was the country's second-
largest employer, providing well over 250,000 jobs. By 2008, it
could barely offer 24,000 jobs. In early 2009, the Nigerian Senate
said that it would act to impose greater controls on Chinese
textile products, while the minister of commerce promised
to discuss with the Chinese government the large quantities

of smuggled and counterfeit goods arriving from China and their contribution to the severe decline of Nigerian manufacturing.[74] Manufacturing accounts for 4% of Nigeria's GDP; the equivalent figure in China is around 40%.[75] The Chinese state's undervaluation of the renminbi makes China's currency no friend to Africa's industries either, as it functions in effect as both an import tax and an export subsidy. However, it is not entirely China's fault that its industries are restricting opportunities for their less competitive African rivals. While China does have some natural advantages over individual African countries – most obviously a very large pool of cheap labour – at the same time, African nations have to an extent impeded their own industrial development through protectionist trade policies limiting African industries' ability to develop markets in neighbouring countries. But this does not mean that China should simply dismiss the problem as one not of its making. If it desires strong and stable relations with its African partners, the Chinese state needs at least to be seen as sympathetic to African concerns on this issue, interested in identifying Chinese markets for African products and open to some rebalancing of the books.

China has made some moves in this direction. Having made an initial commitment in 2003 to exempt the least-developed African countries with diplomatic ties with China from paying Chinese customs duties on 190 products, in July 2007, China removed tariffs on more than 450 commodity items entering China from these countries. However, a lack of widespread awareness of the arrangement in Africa combined with problems with production capacity and the quality of export products has so far limited the effectiveness of such gestures. Tariff exemptions for the period 2006 to 2008 amounted to $680m.[76] When Commerce Minister Chen Deming visited Kenya during his African tour in January 2009, Kenyan Deputy Prime Minister and Finance Minister

Uhru Kenyatta raised concerns about Kenya's trade imbalance with China.[77] Soon after, Chen declared his interest in 'further expanding' the tax-exemption programme.[78]

In all likelihood, the problem of trade imbalances will continue to nip at the heels of some of China's bilateral relationships in Africa. At a seminar to celebrate ten years of diplomatic relations between China and South Africa in Beijing in 2008, South African Foreign Minister Nkosazana Dlamini-Zuma identified as a 'central challenge' the need for trade relations to be put 'on a more suitable footing', and called for greater engagement with the problem by both governments.[79]

China is the world's third-largest and Asia's largest import market. There should be scope to receive more imports from Africa, but China needs to demonstrate that it is serious about engaging with the issue. Signs of problems that may lie ahead include the forced temporary closure of a Chinese-operated mine in the DRC's Katanga province after it broke a ban on exporting cobalt ore that had been designed to push companies to use local firms for processing in order to add value to DRC cobalt exports.[80] In addition to simple rule-breaking, there is also concern that, without strong enforcement capacity, any regulations designed to increase the export of processed, rather than raw, materials from Africa could backfire. For instance, the illegal trade in timber in Gabon, in which Chinese companies are thought to be heavily involved, appeared to receive an unintended spur in 2007, when new rules permitting only producers with operational local processing facilities to export a proportion of their log production drove foreign, including Chinese, timber businesses underground.

Questionably productive tariff exemptions apart, the burden of stimulating African exports to China currently falls heavily on the private sector, with Africans living in China representing a useful prospective tool for stimulating exports from Africa to China, and indeed from China to Africa. The traditional presence of African students on China's university campuses, dating back to Mao's time, has been supplemented and surpassed by the growing presence of African business-men and small traders. Businessmen are often used to smooth the passage of large-scale commercial transactions between Chinese and African companies – usually but not always involving export from China to Africa – while small traders have established a noticeable presence in many of China's east-coast manufacturing hubs. These small traders tend to mirror the activities of the businessmen, focusing on looking for cheap products to export to African markets, rather than on identifying and developing markets for African imports. More than 100,000 Africans live in Guangzhou, the capital of Guangdong province – the city even has its own 'Little Africa'.

As the African business presence develops within China, Sino-African relations might benefit from greater investment in this presence as part of the development of a two-way flow in China–African trading relations. The state might even play a role by leaning on institutions such as the CABC to develop projects to encourage African business in China, as well as Chinese business in Africa. Even if the state chooses not to help, it must beware of being seen to hinder, whether through continued resistance to opening up Chinese markets to African products or by allowing discrimination against or ill-treatment of African businessmen in China. Speaking in early 2009 about harassment by local officials of the African community in Guangzhou, one African trader commented, 'The Chinese make money from Africa, but they want to stop us doing the same here. To me, it doesn't make sense.'[81] China's relations with Africa would not be well served by any approach that made such feelings likely to fester and spread.

A further concern: debt accumulation

Each of the charges discussed above has been levelled at China by African communities and governments, as well as by Westerners. There is, however, another aspect of China's African engagements that is causing some apprehension in the West, if not yet in Africa. So far, it remains more of a concern than a charge. It relates to China's apparently generous extension of loans to Africa, most of which are non-concessional and many of which are secured against natural resources. As Western states write off tranches of previous generations of African debt and remain under pressure to forgive still more, there is some concern that through the sheer volume of its lending to selected, mainly resource-rich, African countries, China might be piling up more debt for future African generations. In spite of China's own debt-cancellation programme, which effectively converts some of its loans into grants, there is fear that China's lending policies may be doing more harm than good to attempts to break Africa's vicious cycle of debt. Instead of sponsoring African development and illustrating China's commitment to Africa, Chinese loans could in effect just be facilitating China's access to African resources, representing a cost to Africa that has yet to be appreciated and which Africa's governments and its citizens may come to regret. This is not to say that this is China's intent.

It would be easier to determine the probability of this emerging as a major problem if the precise terms and conditions of the major loans were readily available for scrutiny. But low levels of transparency in China's transactions mean that not enough is known about the substantial loans that China ExIm Bank and others have been extending to African governments over the past decade. However, some deals have simply been too large and too closely interlinked with debt-cancellation programmes to escape notice. For instance, soon after the details of China's

$9bn minerals-for-infrastructure deal with the DRC began to emerge in 2008, the IMF expressed concern about the terms of the loans associated with the deal, and said that it would seek clarification from the DRC about the expected impact on national finances before approving a new programme for the country.[82] By early 2009, the deal was under further pressure following Western donors' expression of reluctance to relieve the DRC's $11bn debt if the DRC agreed to Chinese financing on commercial terms that would also give Chinese firms involved state-backed financial guarantees.[83]

As China moves over time from being a novelty lender to being a more established debt collector, its loans to Africa may begin to cause difficulties for Sino-African relationships. This will, of course, be particularly the case if the fears outlined here are justified. However, for the time being, African governments appreciate the unprecedented quantities of credit China is offering. This leaves the West standing largely alone in its concern over their possible implications. It is important to be clear about what is and what is not causing concern. Even those who oppose the DRC deal, for instance, understand its value to the DRC, and the fact that the country is unlikely to gain access to such levels of badly needed financing elsewhere. It is not the sums in themselves that cause concern, rather the precise terms on which they are lent. The uncertainties surrounding this issue create mistrust. Such an atmosphere damages China's relations with the West, while China's ongoing opacity on the subject hardly encourages the West to view it as a responsible stakeholder in this context.

Facing the challenges ahead

The challenges brought by rapidly developing Chinese commercial activities in Africa over the past decade are wide-ranging, and they need to be addressed. Although underperformance on individual issues will probably have few serious consequences, a failure properly to address enough of these challenges will invite unwelcome attention and undermine prospects for sustainability in Sino-African engagements. There are clear signs of awareness of the problems at state level, and of early attempts to push for change in China's clumsy and complicated world of inefficient regulation and confused relations between state and business.

The early indications are that smaller Chinese businesses operating in Africa on a long-term basis are, perhaps necessarily, the most engaged with and sympathetic to the environments in which they operate, conscious of the rewards of cultivating good relations with the local community. The drive to engage at this level also reflects the fact that such businesses have little state-sponsored financial support, or relationships with established long-term clients to fall back on should relationships sour. Medium-sized enterprises will tend to impact more heavily on local communities, and the employment opportunities they provide give them greater power over these communities. Though by comparison with larger firms, medium-sized companies will tend to have limited access to state funding, they will usually also have a fair degree of operational leeway, with Beijing tending to be preoccupied with its complex dealings with larger firms. Medium-sized firms therefore operate in something of a twilight zone, bound neither by the social necessities observed by the small traders who depend on the goodwill of local communities for their businesses to survive, nor by the influence or directives of the authorities in Beijing.

As a result, as the state begins to take an interest in CSR and pushes Chinese companies to adopt CSR initiatives, it can reasonably be expected that medium-sized companies will tend to lag behind the larger companies in implementing any such strategies. Conversely, higher profiles and more direct state engagement should put larger state-owned and private companies at the forefront of CSR experimentation. In the case of some such companies, a combination of state direction and a maturing understanding of their own medium-term interests has meant the beginnings of progress towards adapting their African strategies to offer more favourable terms of engagement to local communities. But more work remains to be done. Certainly, many of the larger Chinese enterprises gain credit with local communities simply through their speedy completion of much-needed major projects at relatively low prices. Nevertheless, a more holistic, longer-term approach to business development is needed. Businesses that listen and respond to feedback, checking not just that the Chinese supplier is content with his sale but that the African consumer is content with his purchase, will stand China in good stead. This will be particularly true in difficult economic or political times for the host country, when appearing committed to the broader development of the country and its communities is an invaluable insurance policy for any outsider against possible damage to its interests.

Scrutiny and pressure from NGOs, some African states and a wary West have helped to push the Chinese government towards considering some of these issues. Where progress has been made, work is now needed to turn tactical concession into genuine enduring adaptation. But problems such as low pay and poor safety and environmental standards are problems in Chinese business operations at home as well as abroad. Even the State Administration of Work Safety has acknowledged that coal-mining accidents killed an average of nine workers daily in China in 2008.[84] Seventy per cent of China's lakes and rivers are badly polluted by industrial waste, and 16 of the world's 20 most polluted cities are in China. The practice of using casual labour to avoid incurring legal obligations to

contracted workers can be seen in the employment of an estimated 150m migrant workers in Chinese cities, often without
formal contracts, who sustain China's impressive rate of development. As academic Chris Alden puts it, 'China exports the
capitalism it knows'.[85]

As some change becomes apparent in China itself, for
instance with protection for workers being increased through
the Labour Contract Law of January 2008, to what extent
will these standards be transferred to Chinese operations
abroad? With China coming to appreciate the advantages of
more holistic business models, it is beginning to demand their
observance by foreign companies on Chinese soil. In August
2008, Ministry of Commerce subsidiary Chinese Academy
of International Trade and Economic Cooperation (CAITEC)
issued draft 'Guidelines on Corporate Social Responsibility
Compliance for Foreign Invested Enterprises'. These suggested
that a company should 'voluntarily practice acts that bear less
relevance to its business growth but are in the interest of social
progress, economic growth and environmental protection'.[86]
As China expects more from its foreign investors, so its own
companies, backed by a Ministry of Commerce increasingly
familiar with the concept of CSR, need to consider their own
activities abroad.[87] The CNPC is one of a growing number of
state-owned enterprises to have begun to produce annual CSR
reports, but with only fleeting reference to activities abroad.
In October 2008, Sinosteel, which has been active in Africa
for 12 years, became the first Chinese enterprise to release a
'sustainability report' on its African operations, outlining its
CSR contributions, stakeholder relations, and the measures
it has taken to ensure health, safety and environmental
protection. It also reported that 80% of its employees were
local.[88] The report followed the company's decision to join
the UN Global Compact earlier in the year. Although there

was an unfortunate irony in Sinosteel publishing a sustainability report just as the downturn in commodity prices and
demand prompted it to suspend operations at a major mine
in Zimbabwe that had been a large local employer, it is important to recognise the progress that the report represents. But
in spite of this encouraging example, the danger remains that
Chinese companies will continue to apply developing-world
practice to developing-world countries, replicating and sometimes even magnifying in Africa problems of development
that China itself suffers.

There are a number of questions surrounding China's
future commercial adjustments in Africa. As domestic demand
for resources to sustain growth and stability increases, will
China's behaviour in Africa deteriorate? Will competition
with other resource-hungry powers encourage more – or less –
responsible engagement? Might a temporary lessening of these
immediate pressures as a result of the financial crisis offer a
window of opportunity for China to make progress on the
quality of its commercial engagements? Or will increased pressure for profits in tough economic times and a relative shift
in power from producer to consumer result instead in stagna-
tion or even a decline in the standards of business practice?
Domestic evidence of the effect that increased pressure on
resources has on standards is not encouraging. In May 2008, as
China once again faced the prospect of an acute power shortage, the central government tried to ensure an increase in coal
output by speeding up the granting of licences to small mines
it had previously ordered closed while safety standards were
improved.[89] The closures had been sensible; small coal mines
in China are reported to be around eight times as deadly per
tonne of coal extracted as the larger mines. But demand for
resources meant that the rules were relaxed. In June 2008, 34
miners were killed in an explosion at a small coal mine in the

Luliang region of Shanxi province, just a month after its licence to reopen operations was granted.[90]

While China's official rhetoric of 'traditional friendship' might imply that the lessons of its African engagements need not be too taxing, the reality is that substantial knowledge of business and politics in Africa has only recently begun to be accumulated by Chinese actors on the continent. As one CASS researcher has put it, 'We are learning from doing, rather than learning first and acting later'.[91] On the commercial front, this can be seen in flawed market-entry strategies. Underbidding, for example, may sometimes be a consequence of ignorance of the local market, rather than government instruction. Unfamiliarity with local working practices, legal requirements, labour standards and expectations can all cause friction and complications. For example, Chinese firms arriving in South Africa initially found the comparatively high levels of regulation in the country and the existence of a relatively engaged civil society and powerful trade unions difficult to handle. As recently as 2005, the China Overseas Engineering Corporation won a civil-engineering contract from the South African government with an unrealistically low bid that failed to take into account the costs of doing business in South Africa. The firm quickly ran into trouble with the project as a result.[92] When Sinosteel partnered with the Limpopo Economic Development Enterprise to create the joint venture ASA Metals in 1997, it soon faced protests by workers (who at the time did not even have a personnel department to complain to) and problems with local government, including tensions over the country's 'black economic empowerment' policies.[93] In both cases, the companies learnt from their experiences and have gone on to prosper in the South African market.

It is of course natural that companies 'going global' find themselves facing unexpected challenges and making mistakes when entering new markets. What matters is how quickly companies can adapt to challenges and consolidate the competitive edge that brought them into the market in the first place. It is important in this context that China appreciates the advantages of dealing with relatively strong African partners, such as South Africa. Such partners might initially prove more demanding in bilateral negotiations and more taxing in the investment environment they offer than weaker, more compliant partners that invite China to do business in laxer regulatory environments. However, China needs to trust that the higher level of regulation and engagement offered by stronger partners will ultimately work to its advantage, by providing Chinese firms with greater support in identifying and adapting to the challenges of entering new markets, and offering protection against subsequent charges of commercial exploitation that might be made in the event that host communities' expectations of the benefits of Chinese investment are not fulfilled. Should the Chinese state mistakenly view enhancing the capacity of others to engage critically with it as a threat to Chinese interests, this would be damaging, not only to Africa's interests, but also to China's.

Within China itself, President Hu has been promoting the principle of 'scientific development' as the key to sustainable growth. Given the unspoken requirement that each CCP general secretary contribute at least one grand theory to the party's constitution, such principles often meet with wry smiles in the West. Yet, setting scepticism aside for the moment, Hu's notion of 'scientific development' is not without merit. The basic concept is that the people's interests are no longer best protected by focusing on all-out growth to the exclusion of all other considerations. Instead, the need for continued growth should be balanced against other concerns, such as environmental protection. By viewing the concept of development more holistically, the idea is to limit the potential damage wrought by social divisions sharpened by years of unrestricted growth. The challenges that Chinese business interests are facing in Africa suggest that a similar principle may be needed there and, as in China, not only voiced in theory but implemented in practice. The challenge for China in Africa as elsewhere is not simply to make money and acquire resources, but to do so in a way that is sustainable. If 'scientific development' within China means addressing issues such as workers' pay and conditions and environmental protection and working towards a broader social contract between the state and its citizens, then the concept surely has relevance for China's thinking about its commercial approaches to Africa too.

One major obstacle to the development of sustainable Sino-African relations remains. Increased regulation and enforcement capacity, wherever implemented and whether initiated by China or its African hosts, will mean nothing without the rule of law. As long as this remains weak, any new regulations and enforcement procedures, whether in China or in Africa, will be vulnerable. Respect for the rule of law is needed not just among the business community, but also among state institutions. One independent report on the mining sector in Zambia in 2007 described the disparity between the rules and reality as follows: 'the state seems to have developed political relationships with certain mining houses that mean that health, safety, labour, immigration, and environmental regulations can be ignored with impunity'.[94] The concern is that such problems are widespread on the continent.

All parties now face challenges, none of them easy. With China still equivocal at best in its responses to all but the most vehemently expressed Western concerns on these issues, the challenge for African civil societies is to focus attention on areas of concern. Among other beneficial effects, the raised voices of African civil society will offer a context in which Africa's governments can have the confidence to negotiate harder with their Chinese counterparts. For Western policymakers and analysts, the challenge is to ensure that negative Chinese and sometimes African reactions are not allowed to undermine their continued attention to Sino-African relations. Accusations of Western double standards should of course be heard out, and where such charges are fair, changes will need to be made before Western scrutiny of Chinese activities can be productive. However, it is better that the West stands accused of occasional hypocrisy than that it permanently disengages from such important issues. Finally, the challenge for China will be to balance two opposing processes: to regulate more tightly its companies' activities in some instances, while also learning to relinquish control in contexts where state involvement is bringing tension and confusion to the activities of Chinese businesses overseas. The Chinese government needs to develop a framework within which its companies can responsibly conduct their activities internationally, even in weak regulatory environments.

An awareness seems to be emerging within the government in Beijing that China's own perception of its activities in Africa is not always perfectly aligned with African perceptions, either at elite or popular levels. Cumbersome policymaking structures will delay the regulatory improvements needed, and rule-of-law deficiencies will continue to undermine those steps that are taken, but the rationale of good commercial practice should encourage Chinese businesses to cooperate with the state in making the adjustments necessary for sustainable relations.

Managing the challenges of commercial engagement
Case Study: Zambia

Since its birth as an independent country in 1964, Zambia has enjoyed some of the most stable and strong diplomatic relations with the PRC in sub-Saharan Africa. Thus, the tensions that arose over Chinese commercial engagements in the run-up to the Zambian presidential elections in 2006 appear to have caught the Chinese government somewhat by surprise.

Major Chinese commercial involvement in Zambia began in 1998, when the China Non-Ferrous Metal Mining (Group) Company bought the dilapidated Chambishi copper mine. In 2000, the restoration of what was to be China's first overseas non-ferrous-metal mine began. By 2006, China's 'Year of Africa', 160 Chinese companies had established operations in Zambia, investing $316m and providing employment to more than 10,000 Zambians.[95] Chinese investment became caught up in domestic politics in 2006 when the opposition in the presidential elections campaigned on a platform of limiting foreign ownership of mines and deporting foreign investors 'exploiting' the local workforce. Presidential candidate Michael Sata's populist campaign, in which he referred to foreign investors as 'infestors' and spoke of expelling Chinese traders, provoked much concern on the part of China. Rumours circulated that behind the scenes, Chinese coffers opened up to the campaign of the incumbent government in response. While President Levy Mwanawasa went on to win re-election by a clear margin, every urban seat in the copper belt, where China had invested so heavily, went to the opposition.

Though there have been many Chinese investments elsewhere in Zambia, it has been the ongoing problems at Chambishi, in the heart of the copper belt, that have come to symbolise the difficulties associated with Chinese investment in the country. Two incidents in particular stand out. April 2005 saw the explosion at the Chinese-owned explosives plant at the mine that killed more than 50 workers, the worst disaster in Zambia's mining history. In July 2006, several demonstrators were shot and wounded during protests over delayed wages by African workers at the mine. There have been problems elsewhere as well. In June 2006, the operations of private Chinese firm Collum Coal Mining Industries in southern Zambia were shut down following allegations that miners were working underground without safety equipment or even boots. With such events providing the backdrop to the 2006 elections, and with Zambians still suffering appalling poverty despite the new wave of investment that China's Chambishi project heralded, Michael Sata's campaign struck a chord in the most affected areas, as popular expectations about the improvements that new investments would bring were largely unmatched by reality.

In 2007, Hu Jintao visited Zambia with a package of measures aimed at improving China's image in the country. But when he arrived, the president's itinerary was changed in response to fears about possible embarrassing protests. A planned public lecture at the University of Zambia was cancelled, as was a visit to the opening ceremony of a $220m copper-smelting plant established as part of the Chambishi ECZ. This was particularly disappointing for the Chinese authorities as the ECZ, with its substantial opportunities for job creation and projected $450m annual boost to Zambian exports, is trumpeted by China as a prime example of its commitment to Zambian development.[96] Nevertheless, initiatives to court public and state favour in Zambia continued. China has cancelled a substantial quantity of Zambian debt, including $211m at FOCAC 2006.[97] By 2008, China was responsible for some $1bn of the $4bn worth of foreign investments in Zambia.[98] These levels of investment do appear to be bringing some softening of attitudes towards China, with the Zambia Congress of Trade Unions in June 2008 commending the establishment of the ECZ – support which was echoed by a Parliamentary Committee for Economic Affairs and Labour in the same month.[99] As well as hiring local labour, Chinese promoters of the ECZ have promised to conduct an environmental review and to work to International Organisation for Standardisation environmental standards.[100] In September 2008, the Zhonghui International Mining Group proposed a $2bn investment in Zambia, centred on new mines in Zambia's Luapula and Northwestern provinces, and featuring the creation of a new city with its own hydroelectric power station and water-supply system.[101] The project promises to be the largest investment by a private company in Zambia's history.

The global economic turmoil that emerged in 2008 brings its own challenges for bilateral relations, as China seeks to position itself as an all-weather friend to a country suffering from the collapse in commodity prices and a drop in demand for goods. At the end of 2008, in response to growing concern in Zambia about the impact of the financial crisis on the country, the Chinese chairman of the Chambishi ECZ was forced to offer explicit reassurance that the development of the Chambishi copper smelter would continue, despite the unfavourable international economic conditions.[102]

In comparison with the heated rhetoric of 2006, the tone of the election campaign that followed the death of President Mwanawasa in 2008 was noticeably less hostile towards China. This may have been partly the result of concern on Michael Sata's part not to give China unnecessary incentives for offering financial support to his opponents. Whatever the reason, Sata now claimed that his 2006 campaign had been misunderstood and that he welcomed Chinese investment, publishing an advertisement greeting the Asian community as genuine investors to prove it.[103] His aim, he argued, was simply to empower Zambian workers by protecting jobs in the country's parastatal companies and by ensuring that they received a fair wage. Sata's change of emphasis notwithstanding, the victory of Acting President Rupiah Banda in the October 2008 polls augurs well for state-level ties between Zambia and China.[104] It remains to be seen, however, whether China once again becomes the focus of popular resentment as the economic downturn works its way through the system.

Sporadic protests at Chambishi continue, and broader diplomatic and commercial engagements that go beyond state-to-state, elite-to-elite contact to cultivate more popular engagement with Chinese investment activities are advisable to prevent a resurgence of hostility towards the Chinese presence. A more sophisticated strategy for safeguarding growing engagements will need to be developed along these lines in order for China to avoid the unattractive alternative prospect of needing to rely on an increase of suppressive measures and tighter security. Meanwhile, Chinese firms investing in the Chambishi ECZ can expect considerable scrutiny of their practices there from both local and international civil-society groups. The Chinese government will need to find ways to monitor the behaviour of these firms and ensure they are held to account if it wishes to avoid further incident and, indeed, bring lingering discord to an end.

CHAPTER FOUR

Adapting to the Political Challenges of Commercial Relations

Given that approximately one-third of the world's civil wars take place in oil-producing countries, a state that needs to import oil, especially one that seeks equity stakes abroad, is likely to find itself embroiled in political issues overseas.[1] Often, simply being a foreign investor in a troubled country is enough to cause difficulties. Appealing to notions of developing-world fraternity or laying claim to a relatively benign historical relationship with African nations has failed to insulate China from attacks by the militant group Movement for the Emancipation of the Niger Delta (MEND) in Nigeria, for example. In April 2006, following a Chinese investment of $2.2bn in a Niger Delta oilfield, a warning came from MEND in the form of a car bomb and a declaration that 'the Chinese government, by investing in stolen crude, places its citizens in our line of fire'.[2] Kidnappings of Chinese workers duly followed. In Ethiopia in April 2007, nine Chinese oil workers were killed along with 65 Ethiopians in an attack by 200 masked gunmen on an oilfield in the Ogaden region. Seven more were taken hostage.[3] As instability in Sudan continues, China's engagement in that country faces similar problems. Following one rebel attack in South

Kordofan state in late 2007, a rebel spokesman declared: 'We are doing these attacks because China is trading petroleum for our blood'.[4] In October 2008, nine Chinese oil workers contracted to Sudan's Greater Nile Petroleum Operating Company were kidnapped in the same region.[5] Only four escaped with their lives. Other kinds of violence have also affected Chinese operations and personnel in Africa. In February 2008, a rebel siege of the Chadian capital of N'Djamena forced the Chinese embassy to evacuate more than 200 Chinese nationals to Cameroon. Chinese-owned ships and Chinese crew members have been among the many victims of pirate attacks off the coast of Somalia.[6]

Productive engagements between businesses and governments provide governments with crucial streams of revenue with which to pursue their agendas. This can give such transactions an uncomfortable political dimension. In Sudan, oil revenues generated largely by China's engagements have boosted the government's ability to finance arms purchases during a period in which some 300,000 people in Darfur have died as a result of conflict and a further 2.7m have been forced from their homes.[7]

It would be either naive or disingenuous to claim that business can be decoupled from politics, especially in Africa, where the burden of history remains heavy and where political environments are often fragile. In a globalised world, a country's peace and prosperity are more tied than ever to its protection of its key trading relationships. 'Geo-economics' is taking over from the geopolitics of the Cold War. Thus bilateral trading relationships have an important political value – one that has not gone unrecognised by China. China has shown an understanding of the symbiotic nature of the relationship between the political and economic worlds in its domestic affairs. The Chinese state does its best to ensure that a positive political relationship is key to doing productive business in China. When the US imposed trade sanctions on China in the 1990s following its transfer of military technology to Pakistan, the Chinese aviation authorities switched the allocation of a major contract from American-based Boeing to European-based Airbus.[8] Likewise, every time a foreign leader decides to meet with the Dalai Lama, Chinese officials are careful to impress on that leader's government the potential damage to bilateral relations, including business ones. Business can be politics, and the Chinese authorities know it as well as anyone.

The political challenges China is facing in Africa are various, and several are making major demands on the Chinese state. Finding answers to them is likely to be a more complex task that the comparatively straightforward regulatory developments that are needed to address commercial challenges.

Determining the meaning of 'energy security'

At the nexus of commercial and political interests sits the much-debated concept of 'energy security'. The Chinese government is of course not the only government struggling to determine the best way of securing the country's access to energy. But while all energy-importing states are conscious of the vulnerabilities of their supply routes to problems such as terrorism, piracy and natural disasters, China views such challenges through the prism of a historical suspicion of energy markets and an emphasis on self-sufficiency, and with a particular wariness about the response of other powers to its rise. Chinese energy insecurity dates back at least to the early years of the PRC, and Mao's concerns over the country's vulnerability in the wake of a wide-ranging trade embargo orchestrated by the US during and after the Korean War.[9] More recently, the memory of the 1993 interception by the US of a Chinese container ship, the *Yinhe*, which it mistakenly believed to be carrying chemical weapons bound for Iran, has also informed Chinese thinking on national energy security, sharpening fears about the vulnerability of China's energy supply lines to blockade. A reflex anxiety about the country's dependence on world oil markets informs China's foreign policy in many spheres, including its diplomatic relations. It helps, for instance, to motivate China's attempts to promote good relations with its Southeast Asian neighbours (because of the country's reliance on the Malacca Strait for safe transit of its imports); its cultivation of diplomatic ties with states such as Myanmar and Pakistan; and its pursuit of equity-oil investments, including in Africa.[10] In equity-oil investments, concession owners – in this case Chinese state-owned oil companies – retain an agreed proportion of the oil produced for sale as they choose, either on the world market or in the concession holder's domestic market.

Since the early 1990s, China's NOCs have sought to gain control of wellheads in oilfields in Africa, most prominently in Sudan, and elsewhere in the world. Throughout, they have been at pains to assure the Chinese state to which they theoretically answer that their at-source presence will aid national energy security by increasing the diversity of China's supply sources, reducing vulnerability to price fluctuations and creating the possibility that China might play a greater role in dictating downstream pricing in the future. The NOCs employ a 'vertical integration' strategy, in which the company retains control over each point on the line of production, from prospecting to drilling and extraction, through transport to refinery and delivery. The NOCs and their advocates within government have emphasised the possible benefits of this sort of arrangement for energy security by pointing out that it offers the possibility of self-reliance in the event of troubled times.

Many economists, pointing to the fungibility of oil as a product and the global nature of the oil market, view the desire to buy at source as irrational. Some have further warned that bilateral contracts for the long-term supply of oil such as China agreed with Angola in 2005 would not necessarily prove reliable in the event of, for example, hostilities involving China, or even political disturbances in the supplier country.[11] In addition, they argue, such agreements threaten to undermine the good functioning of the market on which China and other countries depend. Others have tried to assuage predominantly Western concerns about the intentions behind China's increasing involvement in African oil extraction by reminding consumers on all sides that every barrel that Chinese NOCs produce is still one more barrel on the world oil market, whether or not it goes straight to China. Furthermore, the oil China acquires at source, its 'equity oil', accounts for only around 15% of its imported crude. Only 10% of China's overseas equity oil was shipped back to China in 2003, leaving 90% to be sold on world markets.[12]

Yet are such reminders of the limited insulation from global oil markets offered by the strategy of securing supplies at source, and the common interests of all oil importers in supporting a reliable global oil market, having any effect on Chinese state support for the NOCs' pursuit of equity-oil investments? China may instinctively favour this approach to acquiring oil for domestic consumption, and be willing to pay a premium to secure supplies either directly or through the negotiation of package deals with host governments, but the investments made by Chinese firms on this basis in some African countries are bringing with them political problems for the state that a simple dependence on the global oil market would not. While the global marketplace acts as a buffer between buyer and original supplier, equity-oil investments involve direct contact with suppliers of all political stripes, with sometimes uncomfortable consequences. The activities of Chinese NOCs in Sudan in particular are a clear example of equity-oil investments that have put the Chinese state under an unwelcome international spotlight.

There are certainly signs of frustration and unease within the Chinese state over the political problems that the activities of the NOCs have been bringing in their wake, most obviously in Sudan. Sudanese oil accounts for around 7% of China's imported oil; given the political problems associated with equity investments in Sudan, a suspicion has developed within some sections of Chinese officialdom that CNPC's engagements in the country are motivated more by the company's inter-est in profits and securing access to reserves than by concerns for China's energy security. In 2008, CASS scholar Zhu Feng voiced publicly what many complained about in private: that state-owned companies, with their powerful interest groups, had 'hijacked China's foreign policy in Sudan'.[13] Seemingly caught off guard by the political entanglements resulting from CNPC's investments in Sudan, state institutions have begun to debate the extent to which the interests of China's NOCs are in fact aligned with those of the Chinese state, and to consider what strategies might best protect China's access to secure supplies of oil.

As experience of energy investment overseas has accumu-lated, a more nuanced understanding of the concept of 'energy security' has begun to emerge in China. It is becoming clear to some at least that ensuring the security of hydrocarbon supply is a more complex task than simply investing at source and then planting flags down the supply chain. For a start, even if the NOCs were willing and able to ship oil to China in a time of crisis – when such supply chains are expected to play a central role in ensuring supply – not all of the crude oil the NOCs are exploiting is well-suited to China's domestic refining facilities. Furthermore, some Chinese experts are now speculating that a vertical-integration strategy may even increase China's vulnerability to hostile targeting of its energy supply.[14]

Some commentators have discerned signs of a reassessment within China of the contribution of equity stakes to national energy security. The International Crisis Group's 2008 report on China's oil and gas strategy echoed a number of other voices when it concluded that 'Chinese leaders are coming to understand that their state companies' investments abroad have contributed far more to those companies' profits than to improving the country's energy security'.[15] The report concluded that there had been a move away from a mercantilist approach towards a more open approach that favoured greater participation in energy markets and the promotion of a more cooperative international environment for dealing with energy-security concerns. In 2007, China issued an Energy White Paper celebrating the benefits to be had from international cooperation on energy issues.[16] The 2008 White Paper on Diplomacy considered energy security in some detail, noting that global competition for energy resources was increasing. The paper set out a commitment to international cooperation, and argued for China's ongoing key role in the global market, as both a major producer and consumer of energy.[17]

Chinese energy scholar Zha Daojiong has suggested that one response to the politics surrounding energy provision has been to increase the focus on domestic coal in the short term, while the authorities consider how best to handle their more troublesome overseas involvements. He notes that the proportion of China's energy consumption derived from coal power rose from 72% in 2000 to 76% in 2007.[18] But though China plays host to the world's third-largest reserves of recoverable coal, with these reserves set to see China through the next couple of decades, the Chinese government is aware that coal does not present a long-term solution. Furthermore, the increased exploitation of coal aggravates other problems, such as environmental damage and unsafe working conditions.[19]

The Chinese state is now faced with the challenge of balancing the goal of ensuring energy security with the need to promote Chinese soft power and protect China's relationships with other countries, while at the same time continuing to support the long-term development and global competitiveness of its NOCs. While Beijing formally recognises the ideal of working in a cooperative international environment to deal with potential supply disruptions to the global oil market, it also fears that if it tries to conform to this ideal too closely without developing a fallback strategy for meeting China's own energy requirements, it may be taking unnecessary risks with the country's security for the sake, some in China feel, of appeasing those overseas who have their own reasons for wanting to limit China's equity resources. There are thus few signs of a decisive shift by China towards a more collaborative approach to the shared challenges of energy security. A recognition of the difficulties surrounding equity oil, and even of internal tensions over the competing agendas of those advocating it, does not mean that the Chinese state is preparing to abandon the pursuit of equity stakes in African oilfields.

The interests of the various parties involved in China's African oil concerns will continue to chafe and sometimes to conflict with each other. As Chapter Two illustrated, the interests of China's state institutions and its businesses are not always well aligned, and tensions can emerge, not only between state and business, but also within state institutions themselves. The debate about how best to ensure a secure national energy supply is complex, and covers many issues, among them questions about the diversification of supply and the levels of protection of supply needed; how and to what degree to exert control over the NOCs; and how much hedging there should be as China works with other states to address the challenges of energy security. This debate can be expected to continue in the context of these tense and sometimes conflicting intra-state relationships. Several commentators, both within and outside China, have echoed the recommendation of the 2006 Central Foreign Affairs Work Conference that a new ministerial-level body, such as an energy ministry, be created in order to coordinate China's interests better, but achieving this will not be easy.[20] The NOCs certainly have little interest in seeing the emergence of a body with real authority over them. For the time being, a coherent energy policy remains some way off.

A further obstacle lies in the fact that, at present, it is difficult to analyse China's vulnerabilities in the area of energy supply because even the most basic data on China's energy activities appears to be lacking. In 2008, the country's National Statistics Bureau rather belatedly announced the creation of a separate section for energy statistics.[21] Even so, problems with collection capacity remain. A comprehensive energy audit would be a useful tool for analysing the extent of China's energy vulnerabilities, and ought to be a priority for the government as it seeks to develop targeted plans for improving energy security and efficiency.

Determining the limits of sovereignty

Once Chinese SOEs have invested in assets in a given country, a degree of interest in that country's stability and development becomes inevitable. Soon the question arises as to whether this interest extends to troubling China's long-standing attachment to the doctrine of non-interference in the domestic affairs of other countries, as first outlined in the 1954 'Five Principles of Peaceful Coexistence'. Challenges to this doctrine can emerge at both inter- and intra-state levels. An inter-state example is Guinea in West Africa, which hosts two-thirds of the world's known bauxite reserves and enjoys sizeable reserves of alumina, diamonds and gold. The situation in neighbouring Guinea–Bissau, now virtually a narco-state as a result of its use by Latin American drug traffickers as a transit point for cocaine on its way to Europe, is beginning to impact negatively on Guinea's own development. Investors in Guinea, including China, thus increasingly need to take note, at the very least, of events in Guinea–Bissau.

At the intra-state level, China holds considerable assets in Sudan's oil-rich Abyei province, on the disputed internal border between the north and the south of the country. It is far from clear that the fragile 2005 North–South Comprehensive Peace Agreement (CPA) between the Khartoum government and the Southern People's Liberation Army/Movement (SPLA/M) will survive the assorted political pressures of the International Criminal Court indictment of President Omar al-Bashir for war crimes, elections, now scheduled for February 2010, and a referendum on southern secession intended for 2011. There are concerns that southern rebels could make a unilateral decla-ration of independence should Khartoum move to jettison the agreement, as some anticipate. What happens to China's inter-ests in Sudan if the CPA falls apart? What measures might the Chinese state take to defend its interests on the ground and how would these fit with its doctrine of non-interference? China's interests are not only vulnerable in Abyei. While most of the infrastructure to export China's oil assets in Sudan is in the north, a substantial portion of the assets themselves are in the south, in the Muglad and Melut basins. China therefore needs to cultivate relations with the leaders in southern Sudan in case of any future break-up of the country – which would impact substantially on China, because of the distribution of its assets and infrastructure across the country – while simul-taneously continuing close cooperation with the government in Khartoum. Furthermore, even if the south was somehow to secede more or less peacefully, and China managed to protect all its interests despite the break-up, China would still need to protect its strategic investments against the threat of conflict among the peoples of the south itself.[22]

So far, China has been spared the worst tests of its much-cherished principle of respect for sovereignty through non-interference. In Sudan, the participation of the SPLA/M in a largely notional 'Government of National Unity' under the terms of the CPA has meant that China has been free to cultivate relations with the south, including with Salva Kiir, the SPLA/M's leader, inviting him to Beijing in 2007 in his capacity as first vice president in the Government of National Unity.[23] The opening of a consulate in Juba in southern Sudan in August 2008 was a prudent step that should allow the Chinese government to develop its ties in the region. The move would appear to reflect an increasing effort on the part of China to prepare for possible secession, working to develop diplomatic as well as commercial links with the south alongside Beijing's close diplomatic relations with the north. But how should China deal with those who are outside the political process altogether? With CNPC prospecting for oil in Darfur, should China not consider engaging with the rebels so as to minimise the danger of disruption to its operations or violence towards its workers? The high incidence of conflict in Africa – which endures in spite of considerable progress over the past decade on the part of many African nations – and the tendency of resource-rich nations to suffer from intra-state conflict mean that Africa is likely to be among the first arenas to present a real challenge to the Chinese state's attachment to the principles of sovereignty and non-interference, as it seeks to secure new and reliable sources of oil on the continent and protect its assets and personnel as it does so.

China's strict Westphalian[24] interpretation of sovereignty has certainly not hindered it from building up its strategic investments overseas, with the idea of China as respectful of sovereignty facilitating transactions with widely divergent forms of government – including 'pariah' states – in Africa and elsewhere. But the approach undeniably has drawbacks once interests are established and need protecting in volatile environments. The reasons behind China's attachment to the position are connected to the 'three Ts' of Tibet, Taiwan and Tiananmen. They also reflect China's traumatic historical experience of foreign intervention and the CCP's use of the notion of national sovereignty in its struggle against the KMT. As a result, even where sizeable investments and a personnel presence on the ground in an unstable region might be thought to give the Chinese state an interest in conflict mediation, the CCP is reluctant to show much enthusiasm for taking a more active part in international conflict-resolution efforts.

Internationally, the principle of national sovereignty was modified in 2005 by the United Nations' recognition of a 'responsibility to protect' in cases where a sovereign government is failing to protect its citizens.[25] Although this has done little to prevent the suffering of, for instance, Sudanese citizens in Darfur, the principle is nevertheless established – and supported by China – and could see greater application in the future. Prior to this, the establishment in 2002 of a permanent and independent International Criminal Court through a statute adopted by 120 countries (not including China) sanctioned international involvement in state affairs, albeit retrospectively, in cases that involved the most egregious crimes 'of concern to the international community'.[26]

As the Chinese state comes under pressure to use the economic leverage its investments in Sudan have brought it to contribute further to conflict resolution in Sudan in this context of evolving international approaches to the notion of sovereignty, Chinese analysts and policymakers have been considering how to harmonise China's doctrinal position on sovereignty issues with mounting international expectations and its growing investments overseas. Quietly, some greater flexibility on the non-interference principle is emerging. It is no longer quasi-sacrilegious in China to question the limits of sovereignty. From the 1990s onwards, there has been a steady stream of Chinese academics at all levels prepared to advance unconventional positions on the issue. International-relations analyst Pang Zhongying, for example, has been critical of China's predilection for abstaining from UN Security Council votes on issues that do not directly impact on China's national interests, calling for China to show greater leadership in setting and adhering to international norms.[27] In January 2008, another influential academic, Wang Jisi, who informally advises the Chinese government on foreign policy, published an interesting article that appeared to ask whether there might be a way of decoupling China's foreign policy from its domestic concerns about sovereignty, so as to allow it freer range to be a responsible actor in international affairs.[28]

With China under particular international pressure in recent years as a result primarily of its commercial engagements in Zimbabwe and Sudan, the momentum towards some modification of the official stance has been increasing. By summer 2008, a revised interpretation of the principle of non-interference incorporating such notions as 'proactive non-interference' and 'constructive mediation' appeared to be under discussion in Beijing, along with early attempts to define what such a policy might mean in practice.[29]

In the African context, Chinese diplomats are at pains to emphasise that, on specific dilemmas about diplomatic 'interference' or military intervention, its position is aligned with that of the AU and, implicitly, that of 'Africa' in general. The fragility of this position lies in the fact that it fails to appreciate the diversity of African opinion on these issues. For example, mixed reactions on the continent to the suspected vote-rigging and intimidation and violence that accompanied Zimbabwe's 2008 elections should have reminded the Chinese authorities that Africa is a large and diverse place, where appeals to a blanket principle of non-intervention may not always be welcomed, and may sometimes be repudiated. Such reactions are not confined to civil society; they may even be shared by governments. In a speech in July 2008, Liberian President Ellen Johnson-Sirleaf spoke hopefully of a 'new Africa unfolding' that cherished democracy, human rights and a free media. Expressing solidarity with the peoples of Darfur, Somalia and Zimbabwe, she denounced the second round of presidential elections that had been decreed in Zimbabwe, remarking that 'in 1985, Liberia held a sham election that was endorsed by Africa and the world. Thirty years of civil war and devastation followed, with thousands dead and millions displaced. It need not have happened.'[30] Leaders such as Botswanan President Ian Khama and Kenyan Prime Minister Raila Odinga have also criticised Mugabe and the Zimbabwean regime.[31]

Official Chinese attitudes to Africa's political problems have at times shown an insensitivity to the multiple strands of African opinion. For example, when violence broke out in Kenya following elections in early 2008, Chinese representatives merely remarked that in developing countries, democracy brought with it such outbreaks of violence: in the words of *People's Daily* reporter Li Xinfeng, 'Western-style democracy isn't suited to African conditions, but rather carries with it the root of disaster'.[32] Taking a very different tone, an editorial in Kenya's *The Nation* in February 2008 called on China to win respect through global leadership on addressing Africa's problems in Darfur and elsewhere.[33] The diversity of African opinion on these issues sets limits on the usefulness to China of its traditional appeals to developing-world collegial ties with 'Africa' as an entity.

In practice, China's investments on the ground in Africa are bringing a level of involvement in host countries' domestic affairs that is well ahead of any adjustments to the theory. Among these involvements, there have been some that have proved more embarrassments than assets to China. Notoriously, when the opposition in Zambia's 2006 elections accused foreign firms, including Chinese ones, of exploitative investment practices, the Chinese ambassador to Lusaka protested vehemently and suggested that Chinese companies might withdraw their investments should opposition candidate Michael Sata win.[34]

But some more positive practical adjustments to China's 'non-interference' posture are beginning to emerge at a political level. For example, by 2007, the Chinese leadership appeared to have decided to step back a little from its hitherto close relations with Zimbabwean President Robert Mugabe. When President Hu toured Africa that year, he visited South Africa, Mozambique, Zambia and Namibia, but not neighbouring Zimbabwe. Although the Chinese embassy in Harare was forced to deny that any snub was intended by this itinerary, a message was being sent both to Mugabe and to the West. Yet it is unclear whether this diplomatic recalibration was a consequence of a new strategic calculation in China about the problems of associating with a destructive and dictatorial regime, the result of a growing fatigue with a country that was defaulting on its payments and where it was becoming more and more difficult to make money, or indeed a political smokescreen for ongoing commercial involvements in Zimbabwe. Whatever the motivations, the diplomacy of 2007 was certainly very different from that of 2005, when Beijing hosted Mugabe on a state visit to China only weeks after his launch of the brutal and politically motivated 'Operation Murambatsvina' to 'cleanse' Zimbabwe's slums.

China's scope for quiet diplomatic adaptation is to some extent limited by the strategic importance it attaches to emphasising its 'developing-world' platform in contexts where intervention is often seen as a quasi-colonial activity of the developed-world powers. Thus, in July 2008, when Russia vetoed a UN resolution imposing sanctions on Zimbabwe, China did the same.[35] Under pressure from both pro- and anti-sanctions lobbies, and with South African president and lead mediator for the South African Development Community (SADC) in the Zimbabwe crisis Thabo Mbeki reportedly privately petitioning against sanctions, the Chinese authorities appear to have concluded that a veto was necessary to safeguard their credentials as the (self-designated) protectors of the developing world.[36] The fact that Africa's position on the issue was far from uniform did not appear to matter: from Beijing's perspective, the risks to its interests that would be posed by sponsoring a tougher international response to Mugabe's behaviour in Zimbabwe were too great, so China played it safe and aligned itself with the majority of Africa's governments.

Nevertheless, with an eye on its diplomatic relations beyond Africa – perhaps particularly in view of the imminence of the Beijing Olympics – the Chinese government followed up its intransigence here with a proactive strategy of damage limitation. It appears to have sent some strong messages to Mugabe after the vote, and to have contributed substantially but discreetly to Mbeki's brokering of the outlines of a September 2008 power-sharing agreement between Mugabe and the opposition in Zimbabwe.[37] However, the Chinese convention of non-interference and the country's relative inexperience in conflict mediation made China somewhat uncomfortable with developing its behind-the-scenes role in negotiations in Zimbabwe, a discomfort that increased as Mbeki's influence waned following his resignation from the South African presidency in September 2008, and as the SADC continued to fail to adequately address the issue.

Nevertheless, as the situation in Zimbabwe deteriorated throughout 2008, the severity of the crisis appeared to prompt further adjustments to China's approach. As Zimbabwe's cholera epidemic spread towards the end of the year, China's line that Zimbabwe should not be subject to punitive action from the UN Security Council because it was not a threat to international security began to weaken.[38] In December 2008, Chinese Foreign Ministry spokesman Liu Jianchao announced his country's plans to provide humanitarian assistance to Zimbabwe. Though he did not call for Mugabe to stand down, he did note China's 'concern with the current constant deterioration of the economic and political situation in Zimbabwe'.[39] By the standards of Chinese diplomacy, this amounted to clear criticism of the regime, criticism that Harare, along with other African governments, will have noticed.

However, adjustments to political messages are not always well aligned with commercial practice: by December 2007, the SASAC-supervised central SOE Sinosteel had bought 67% of Zimasco Consolidated Enterprises, the holding company for Zimbabwe's largest ferrochrome producer.[40] China's commercial engagements with Zimbabwe continued through 2008, despite the country's dire economic situation. The Jiangxi Corporation for International Economic and Technical Cooperation agreed to a joint venture with the Zimbabwe Mining Development Corporation to mine chrome in Midlands province and the Zambezi Valley.[41] Meanwhile, Hebei province's Jingniu Group continued with its plans to spend $400m on the development of a glass factory in Kadoma.[42] The same year the Chinese embassy in Harare hosted a trade fair sponsored by the Ministry of Commerce, in which 30 Chinese companies showcased their products. Notwithstanding Zimbabwe's economic implosion, in late 2008, an embassy official predicted that Sino-Zimbabwean trade for 2008 would surpass $500m, up from $275m in 2006.[43]

Even assuming it wanted to, after years of encouraging investments in Zimbabwe's mineral resources in particular, it would not be easy for the Chinese state to disengage from the engagements that have developed. Yet despite its ongoing commercial engagements and the relatively slow evolution of its political stance on Zimbabwe, China's diplomacy has been changing, indicating both a responsiveness to international pressure and a growing appreciation of China's own interest in securing stability and responsible governance in Zimbabwe.

As the case study at the end of the chapter illustrates, developments in Sudan have also played a crucial role in modifying China's approach, highlighting the challenge China now faces as its sizeable strategic investments in Sudan and the stationing of increasing numbers of its citizens there give it a substantial stake in the country's stability, and showing how China might begin to address these issues. Moving from the rather naive belief that it would be possible to keep its commercial engagements in Sudan walled off from the country's political problems, China has begun to take on the role of messenger between opposing parties in Sudan and even, sometimes, that of an active – albeit rather ambivalent and discreet – persuader.[44]

The prominence of Africa in China's adaptations to a new reality of international engagements and responsibilities could also be seen in the December 2008 decision to send two Chinese destroyers and a resupply vessel to the Gulf of Aden in support of international efforts to combat the growing problem of Somali piracy. This was China's first operational naval mission outside Asian waters since Zheng He's explorations 600 years ago. Commending his country for playing a 'more constructive role in international conflicts and crises', Pang Zhongying concluded that 'China is trying to balance its old principle and the new reality ... Non-intervention is in the process of slow change.'[45] With as much as 20% of Chinese maritime traffic in the Gulf of Aden subject to pirate attack in 2008, the provision of Chinese destroyers to protect shipping was undoubtedly grounded in national self-interest.[46] Furthermore, the Chinese authorities are not in a difficult position on this issue: with three UN resolutions in six months calling for an international response to Somali piracy combined with the blessing of the Somali government for such operations, there is no problem with 'intervention'. But while the Aden mission represents a straightforward opportunity for China to develop operational expertise, it also presents an opportunity for those seeking to encourage the emergence of a more responsive and responsible China that operates in partnership with other major players to deal with matters of international concern.

Even before the Gulf of Aden deployment, in a statement to the US–China Economic Security Review Commission in March 2008, US Deputy Assistant Secretary of State for East Asian and Pacific Affairs Thomas Christensen was able to give the following summary of China's sometimes difficult progress on the issue of non-interference:

China's diplomatic activity reflects an evolution beyond its previously strict insistence on 'non-interference in internal affairs of other countries' to a more pragmatic recognition of the merits and obligations of working with the international community

> on areas of concern. In the past few years ... China has adopted policies that would have been hard to imagine several years ago.[47]

But while China has indeed moved a long way from its original rigid stance of non-interference, there is some way to go before its participation in conflict prevention and resolution and promotion of and adherence to international norms and treaties will convince all Western observers that it is a reliable and responsible partner. While accepting that some gaps between policy rhetoric and practical reality are inevitable for any country, the challenge for China of harmonising what are often contradictory interests is not inconsiderable. Among these interests are: the desire to use the non-intervention principle to attract partners for new investments; the need to be able to take a more proactive stance to protect these interests once developed; to shield itself from Western accusations of being a patron and financier of pariah states, and to ensure that it is seen by the West as a partner in the promotion of stability and good governance; and to coordinate and control its diplomatic and commercial operations in order to meet all these demands. For the moment, China's adaptations in the face of these challenges remain piecemeal, limited and tactical, rather than broad-ranging and strategic.

Some commentators on China's development hold that Beijing's approach will necessarily evolve. The increasing stakes of Chinese companies across a range of activities and interests in Africa will lead to government policies that retain their pragmatism, but which also consider long-term stability alongside short-term political advantage. Nevertheless, for the time being, Chinese institutions are still largely wedded to the position that China's status as a developing-world country means that it should be careful to avoid incurring what are seen as premature and excessive responsibilities imposed on it by the West. Participation in international mediation is fine; taking action on Zimbabwe in the form of sanctions or disinvestment, for instance, is a step too far. China's reluctance to back up agreements with penalties for non-compliance continues, as seen in its resistance to sanctioning the Sudanese government for obstructing deployment of a hybrid UN–AU force to Darfur, or Zimbabwe's ZANU-PF for its vacillation and game-playing over the formation of a government of national unity. When tangible measures are needed, Beijing still gets nervous.

While power and influence in Africa is sought by China, responsibility there still tends to be avoided. A change in mindset is surely needed for this aspirant great power – for, of course, not only does power bring responsibility, but responsibility also brings power. Of course, any adjustments China does make to its approach to intervention will not always be in harmony with the interests of the mostly Western powers urging China's greater participation in activities such as conflict resolution. Those in the West who call on China to demonstrate its credentials as a responsible partner for the West through increased international activity may need to be careful what they wish for. Nevertheless, on balance, a common interest in the stability of politically fragile countries – be it pragmatic or principled – should result in greater cooperation and coordination on averting and limiting conflict.

China's approach to the issue of sovereignty also informs its delivery of foreign assistance. Its effects can chiefly be seen in the refusal to attach any non-economic conditions to aid. China's foreign assistance is disbursed independently of the coordinating facility of the OECD Development Assistance Committee, which promotes an aid-effectiveness agenda and offers donors guidance on policy and best practice on encouraging democracy, good governance and transparency. This has been the cause of some concern, particularly to donors whose programmes are operated under Development Assistance Committee standards and guidelines. Although China is a signatory to the OECD's Paris Declaration on Aid Effectiveness, it is quick to point out that it signed the declaration as a recipient of foreign assistance rather than as a donor. It is free to provide non-conditional assistance, aware of the advantage this gives it in its dealings with a number of recipient governments in Africa, including those that are eager to take dubious advantage of its no-strings-attached support. In July 2008, China's special envoy to Africa and Sudan, Liu Guijin, reiterated China's position on aid to Mugabe's Zimbabwe and al-Bashir's Sudan: 'We don't attach political conditions [to aid]. We have to realise the political and economic environments are not ideal. But we don't have to wait for everything to be satisfactory or human rights to be perfect.'[48] As long as the US and the EU explicitly link aid with the issues of good governance and democracy and China continues to see commercial and political value in taking a neutral approach, tensions with the West over China's foreign-assistance programmes are likely to continue.[49]

Managing peacekeeping and arms control

Differing views of the limitations of sovereignty are a recurring theme in meetings of the United Nations, where African issues currently occupy around a quarter of the Security Council's time. Historically, Chinese resistance to active participation in the UN has been particularly acute in the area of peacekeeping. Maoist ideology and memories of the UN intervention in Korea, which saw Chinese soldiers fighting UN forces, meant that the PRC declined to participate in UN peacekeeping operations in the early days of its membership of the Security Council.[50] China did not support any peacekeeping operations until late 1981, when it voted to extend the mandate of UNFICYP, the peacekeeping force in Cyprus. However, following these reluctant beginnings, China's progress in this area has been substantial. In 1982, China began to contribute financially to UN peacekeeping. By 1988, it was applying for membership of the UN Special Committee on Peacekeeping Operations. The following year, China participated in UN peacekeeping for the first time, sending 20 civilians to work for UNTAG in Namibia.[51] During the 1990s, limited support for UN peacekeeping operations gradually emerged, with China contributing impressively to UN operations in Cambodia through, among other things, the provision of 800 military engineers to the UN Transitional Authority in 1992 and 1993. China has even, when its interests have allowed, been flexible with its requirement that the host government grant consent for any deployment. Noting 'the exceptionality of the situation', in 1992, China supported sending UN troops to Somalia in the absence of such consent.[52] In December 2001, a Peacekeeping Office was formally established in China's Ministry of National Defence.[53] In early 2003, China sent 218 peacekeeping personnel to participate in MONUC, the UN's mission to the DRC.

Though its financial contributions to the UN's peacekeeping budget remain relatively small, China now readily provides civilian police, military observers and troops to UN peacekeeping operations mandated under Chapters Six and Seven of the UN Charter. Africa has been the site of much of this peacekeeping activity. As well as UNTAG in Namibia (1989–90), China has contributed personnel to ONUMOZ in Mozambique (1993–94), UNOMIL in Liberia (1993–97), UNOMSIL and UNAMSIL in Sierra Leone (1998–99 and 1999–2005 respectively) and ONUB in Burundi (2004). By September 2008, China was contributing to six of the seven ongoing UN missions in Africa, the exception being MINURCAT, a relatively small mission monitoring the situation in the Central African Republic and Chad. From

January 2007 to April 2008, China was the leading monthly contributor of personnel to UN missions among the P5.[54] In May 2008, France temporarily took the lead in overall troop contributions, with 113 more personnel deployed than China, but in Africa, China remained the pre-eminent troop contributor of the P5. Eleven per cent of France's total of 2,090 peacekeeping personnel was serving in missions in Africa in May 2008, in contrast to 73.5% of China's 1,977 personnel.[55]

The reasons for China's move towards greater participation in peacekeeping are varied, and disputed. They can be found primarily in intellectual shifts within the policymaking elite in Beijing, shifts that were reinforced by lessons drawn from the Western-led interventions in Iraq in 1991 and Kosovo in 1999. The change that has taken place in a couple of decades is undoubted, and Beijing now proudly cites its contribution to African peacekeeping as a demonstration of its role as a responsible stakeholder on the continent. However, while China has taken to the practice of peacekeeping itself with remarkable ease, its contributions are still being undermined by certain factors. For example, China's insistence on a host-government invitation was the source of considerable diplomatic difficulties over the deployment of a UN mission to Darfur. Indeed, the obligation caused difficulties for China, as it found itself having to take responsibility for securing this invitation. Eventually, with the non-interference principle taking something of a back seat, China's Ambassador to the UN Wang Guangya won widespread credit for his lobbying of the Sudanese government to persuade it to accept the deployment of a UN–AU hybrid force.[56]

China's contributions to peacekeeping are also being undermined by the arms it sells to Africa. Though China is not the largest supplier of arms to Africa, its market share is growing.[57] When arms can be bought and sold on to a third party, and regimes and alliances can change so swiftly, the medium- and long-term consequences of weapons transfers are difficult for any power to calculate. However, China's arms deals embrace pariah states such as Sudan and Zimbabwe, and focus on small arms and light weapons which, while making a comparatively minor contribution to China's arms-export earnings, do dispro-portionate damage in the continent's civil wars. China sold arms to Sudan throughout its two-decade-long civil war. That trade continues in spite of a 2005 UN arms embargo on supplies to all forces waging war in Darfur, an embargo which a number of observers, including a UN Panel of Experts, claim the Sudanese government has repeatedly violated.[58] China provides helicop-ters and fighter aircraft as well as small arms and ammunition. UN records show that Chinese arms transfers to Sudan in 2005 were worth $23m, making China Sudan's largest reported arms supplier in recent times and by far its largest supplier of small arms.[59] In late 2005, amid scrutiny of the Sudanese government's role in scorched-earth policies in Darfur, the vice chairman of China's Central Military Commission, Xu Caihou, welcomed Sudan's deputy chief of the general staff, Muhammad Isma'il, to Beijing to 'increase military exchanges and cooperation'.[60] Promises to increase military cooperation further were made at an April 2007 meeting of the chiefs of the general staff of the two countries.[61] If the claims of Sudan's government officials that the country is now largely self-sufficient in light weaponry are accurate, then this is largely thanks to China, which has also built weapons factories in Sudan and appears prepared to continue its trade of arms for natural resources.[62]

In April 2008, as Robert Mugabe was using Zimbabwe's military to intensify his campaign of intimidation following the first-round victory of the opposition Movement for Democratic Change in presidential elections the previous month, dockers at the port of Durban in South Africa refused to unload the cargo of a Chinese ship, the *An Yue Jiang*. Nicknamed 'the ship of death' by protesters, the vessel was carrying a 77-tonne load of small arms, believed to include an estimated 3m rounds of ammunition, together with several thousand mortars and rocket-propelled grenades, all destined for Mugabe's forces.[63] Sales such as these are not usually particularly lucrative in themselves, but in the case of Zimbabwe, it seems likely that arms are used by China as unofficial leverage to enable greater access to the country's plentiful mineral reserves.[64] Beijing's official line on the *An Yue Jiang* was that as Zimbabwe was not under a UN arms embargo, Chinese companies were doing nothing wrong in conducting business with the Zimbabwean government, a response that may well have lost it some friends among ordinary African citizens.[65] The incident seemed to create a new sense of urgency among local observers over the issue of arms sales to Zimbabwe; in June 2008 civil-society organisations in five SADC countries began petitioning their leaders for a moratorium on arms shipments to Zimbabwe.

Nevertheless, with China becoming more involved with the international community from the mid 1990s onwards, the country has made considerable progress on arms control since the days when it argued that all countries had equal rights to all weapons. In 2007, security analyst Bates Gill commented that 'China's new approach to non-proliferation and arms control marks some of the most striking aspects of China's proactive security diplomacy over the past decade'.[66] Since the Beijing Declaration following the first FOCAC ministerial summit in 2000, the issue of the illegal arms trade in Africa has been on the Sino-African agenda. In 2002, China imposed improved controls on its arms exports, publishing a Military Products Export Control List as a supplement to its revised Regulations on the Export Control of Military Items, and expanding missile export-control regulations. In the same year, China became the

46th signatory to the Protocol Against the Illicit Manufacturing of and Trafficking in Firearms. In 2005, a White Paper on arms control was published, and the government began testing a national system for tracking the production, possession and trade of small arms and light weapons and monitoring end users.[67] However, there are still gaps to be filled within this emerging regulatory framework. Furthermore, the framework is limited by China's primary focus on illicit weapons, with controls on the export of legal weapons remaining lax.

While Chinese peacekeepers may be contributing greatly to security in conflict zones in Africa, ill-judged Chinese arms sales are simultaneously fuelling instability that can generate the need for such missions. China's failure to view some of its arms deals in Africa in a wider perspective undermines its attempts to present its increased engagements in Africa as unthreatening, and risks implicating Beijing in human-rights abuses and repression. The challenge is both ethical and practical. As on other issues, China needs to prioritise its interests here more clearly, and tackle problems of policy coordination across departments and between the civilian and military arms of government, problems that are reportedly exacerbated by princeling involvement in the arms industry. This is a particularly important challenge in view of the probability that China will over the next few years be seeking to intensify its security relationships with African countries. Beijing is anxious to ensure the security of the increasing numbers of Chinese people and growing assets in Africa, as well as being privately concerned about the developing naval presence of India in the Indian Ocean and the motives behind the US decision to establish an Africa Command (AFRICOM). Hitherto, it has prioritised the development of strategic resource interests in Africa, with political and security interests taking an important but secondary role. This may be beginning to change as

China's developing resource interests themselves raise the profile of security issues. The January 2009 Defence White Paper made the case for expanding the reach of China's military to better protect Chinese economic investments abroad.[68] In the event that such an expansion goes forward, Beijing will need to communicate effectively with other powers involved with Africa and show transparency about its intentions there in order for its actions not to be viewed askance by the world beyond China and Africa.

Increasing popular engagement

One factor that will help to determine the sustainability of Sino-African relations will be Beijing's ability to move beyond its focus on fellow governments and political elites, with whom it evidently feels comfortable, towards broader engagement with African societies. Even in those African countries where the 'big man' syndrome persists and where the disconnect between leaders and their citizens is most evident, some changing of the guard is inevitable, and China cannot rely on this always taking the form of a smooth handover from a big man to his likeminded protégé. In Africa's increasing number of democratic countries, China will need to work to avoid becoming the target of choice for populist opposition movements seeking to blame outsiders for national development problems.

Development assistance can be one way of securing popular support; indeed, this may be one of the reasons behind the Chinese authorities' repeated pledges to increase foreign assistance. In 2006, Premier Wen Jiabao declared that 'in providing assistance to Africa, we will lay even greater emphasis on public programs, particularly programs in agriculture, poverty reduction, healthcare, education, sports, water supply, housing and environment protection that are essential to the life of African people'.[69] However, winning popular support is only one

among many diplomatic reasons for China to offer development assistance in Africa. As well as improving state-to-state
relations and promoting a positive political environment for
the commercial activities of Chinese companies, aid can also be
used as a means of countering third-party accusations of exploitation. Its development projects are often invoked by China
to defend its relationships with politically 'sensitive' African
countries. By 2008, it had become rare to hear China's special
envoy to Darfur, Liu Guijin, discuss the situation in the region
without also hearing in detail about the various Chinese-led
engineering projects under way there, including projects for
improving access to water.[70]

China needs to find ways of building popular support for
its investments in Africa that go beyond aid, to direct engagement with local communities. The grand football stadiums that
Chinese construction companies have long helped to build all
over the continent may help a little, but more direct contact is
also important. Local communities themselves need to be targets
of Chinese efforts to develop 'win–win' engagements, which are
currently aimed more at state officials than at the communities
they represent. By engaging at a non-state as well as a state level,
China can build a buffer of popular support for its in-country
interests. Such a buffer could offer valuable protection against
the possibility of a popular backlash in the event that the promised benefits of foreign investment fail to materialise. This is a
risk as the global economic crisis threatens to scale back some of
China's African concerns, in particular those of smaller companies operating with little state support. With African jobs being
lost as firms cut their losses and leave, Chinese companies run the
risk of being seen as fair-weather friends, undermining Chinese
claims to a serious commitment to Africa's development.

One CASS academic warned in 2008 that while engagement
with civil society constituted 'the grass-root foundations for a

sustainable partnership with Africa', it was also 'the weakest area in [China's] bilateral relations'.[71] Some typical shortcomings in this area are illustrated by the comments of one CADF official talking in late 2008 about how he and the fund were handling their investment interests in Kenya, a country where civil society is becoming increasingly attuned to the problems that can accompany unregulated Chinese investment. Faced with Kenyan governmental concerns about the reactions from some civil-society groups to certain projects under consideration, the CADF's instinctive response was to focus on problem-solving at a state level. The projects would be moved forward once the personal relationships with the CADF's Kenyan interlocutors had been further cultivated. The aim was to reassure these officials about the proposed projects in the hope that they would be persuaded to override popular concerns, or at least agree to the investments and undertake to handle any complaints and difficulties themselves.[72] The alternative course, of prospective Chinese investors working with Kenyan officials to consider ways that projects might win popular support, for example through the development of some sort of outreach programme, does not appear to have been considered. This is typical of both Chinese investors in Africa and their state sponsors – while the need for greater direct engagement has been recognised at the higher levels of officialdom, change on the ground is still at a very early stage.

The Chinese government's 2006 White Paper on Africa called for broader engagement with both public- and private-sector institutions.[73] On his 2009 African tour, Hu Jintao repeatedly emphasised the need for increased contact and interaction on the ground between Chinese companies, their staff and host communities. The potential for such engagement offered by CSR initiatives has become the focus of some interest in Beijing. Meanwhile, Beijing, conscious of the difficulties that trade-union action can cause to Chinese business interests, is also encouraging the development of contact with the leaders of Africa's trade unions. Since 2004, annual meetings between African trade-union leaders and the state-controlled All China Federation of Trade Unions have been arranged by the Chinese Ministry of Commerce. Little more than public-relations exercises, these events represent a smooth, if superficial, diplomatic outreach to Africa's trade unionists. The 2008 event in China was attended by 26 leaders of the trade unions of 11 African countries.[74]

As the Chinese authorities gingerly begin to seek broader community involvement in Africa, they are having difficulty overcoming their wariness of engaging with opposing or dissident elements. China's engagements with political oppositions remain uncertain, with the CCP's International Department particularly concerned about how to manage such contacts alongside relations with ruling parties. For example, in Zimbabwe, there appears to have been only limited contact between Chinese officials and the Movement for Democratic Change during the turmoil of 2007 and 2008.[75] A near-exclusive focus on the ruling party may be attractive in the short term, especially when relations between contending parties are particularly bad, but a lack of flexibility in engagements can cause problems as and when power changes hands.

Another area in which Beijing would do well to increase its engagements is that of NGOs. Here, the lessons have barely begun to be learned. Beijing is still extremely suspicious that foreign political agendas might be driving even African-origin NGOs, and this suspicion continues to hamper broader Chinese engagement with Africa. However, there have been a few cautious efforts on the part of Chinese academics to learn more about the role of NGOs in Africa, and it appears that the possibility of giving a limited role to NGOs at the next FOCAC meeting in Egypt in late 2009 is at least under consideration.[76] Meanwhile, Chinese officials involved with Sudan are gaining some experience of dealing with international NGOs, even if this involves little experience of partnering with them. Liu Guijin, for example, met representatives of the Save Darfur coalition on his visit to the US in 2007.[77]

Attention to developing community relations is also bringing China closer to human-rights issues. Concerns about sustainable development surrounding China's contributions to hydroelectric power in Africa have already been noted. Such projects also have implications for human rights. The Merowe Dam in Sudan, opened by President al-Bashir in March 2009 and funded by China ExIm Bank and a number of Arab development funds after financiers from OECD countries refused funding, is a prime example.[78] Projected to more than double Sudan's power output, the dam and its reservoir cover a fertile area that had been the home of more than 50,000 people of the Manasir, Hamadab and Amri tribes, who are now being forced to move to more arid areas.[79] Since the start of the project in 2003, protesters have been subject to harassment and detention. During demonstrations in April 2006, dam security forces opened fire, killing three people and injuring dozens.[80] Managing the environmental and human consequences of such engagements is no easy task for China; the country is once again exporting the experience it knows. For example, its ambitious Three Gorges Dam on the upper Yangtze will add valuable power capacity and could also help to save many lives from floods, but there are ongoing serious concerns about the environmental sustainability of the project, while the impact on those displaced has often been more severe than official publicity suggests.

Chinese professionals in Africa are now learning local languages, deploying the vocabulary of CSR to generate positive local responses, and even engaging more with local and international media. But viewed in the wider context of Chinese engagements in Africa, such efforts remain somewhat isolated and piecemeal. In general, the Chinese authorities are still a long way from dealing effectively with opposition movements and trade unions, working through NGOs, or more broadly engaging with civil society in a way that would build more solid and sustainable relations with local communities.

Operating multilaterally as well as bilaterally

For some time, there has been a growing sense, both in Africa and in the watching West, that African nations would do well to respond to China's 'Africa strategy' by forging clearer 'China strategies' for exploiting the opportunities that China's interest in their continent brings. There is widespread recognition that for such strategies to be truly effective, they need to be coordinated at a regional level. This concern for Africa to develop a clearer and more cohesive strategy for managing Chinese interests has resulted in increasing attention being paid to the quality of China's own multilateral engagements in Africa outside the triennial showcase of FOCAC. Both African and Western governments have privately and publicly engaged China on the issue of working more closely with the AU and its New Partnership for Africa's Development (NEPAD), as well as with Africa's various sub-regional organisations.

China's conversion to multilateral engagements came relatively late, due to the leadership's initial tendency to view multilateral regional institutions or agreements as US-sponsored mechanisms for China's containment. Even when the country did begin to participate more in international organisations, in the 1980s, its involvements appeared more presentational than driven by any genuine strategic enthusiasm. Nevertheless, China began its engagement in Asia-Pacific regional coordinating initiatives around this period, joining, for example, the Pacific Economic Cooperation Council in 1986 and the Asia-Pacific Economic Cooperation forum (APEC) in 1991. As China's thinking on security developed in the mid 1990s further in the direction of greater engagement with the international community, its approach to multilateral engagement – alongside ongoing bilateral relationships – became more positive and proactive.[81] In 1994, three years after having established or resumed diplomatic relations with all members of the Association of Southeast Asian Nations (ASEAN), Chinese officials attended the establishment of the ASEAN Regional Forum, then the only region-wide security institution in the Asia-Pacific. In 2001, China hosted an APEC summit in Shanghai. As its thinking on security continued to develop, the prestige China associated with membership of multilateral organisations increased, and its willingness to join such organisations grew further. Susan Shirk, under secretary for Asia in the Clinton administration, has even called China a 'born-again regional multilateralist'.[82]

Historical links with the AU (which replaced the Organisation of African Unity in 2002) have meant that China has traditionally been more comfortable with this particular multilateral body than it has with many others in the international arena. Further effort is being made to develop more substantive regional relationships in response to African and Western lobbying. China has, for example, made repeated, if sometimes symbolic, financial donations to AU capacity building, including to its Peace Fund and NEPAD.[83] At FOCAC 2006, President Hu announced the financing of a new AU conference centre. Here, the sums involved were more substantial; construction of the $61m project is scheduled for completion by 2011. In November 2008, the first China–AU Strategic Dialogue was launched, intended to be an annual event to be held alternately in Addis Ababa and Beijing. Among the achievements of the dialogue was the decision that the AU Commission would in future participate in FOCAC meetings as an official delegate, rather than an observer.[84]

China's engagements with Africa's multilateral financial institutions have also been gathering pace. In recent years, China has increased its involvement with the African Development Bank, having first become a non-regional member in 1985. The bank acknowledged China's role in Africa by holding its 2007 annual meeting in Shanghai, only the second time in its history it had convened its annual meeting outside Africa. China is also becoming more open to multilateral involvement with other foreign actors interested in Africa. In 2007, China's ExIm Bank signed a memorandum of understanding with the World Bank to promote multilateral cooperation, particularly on Africa.[85] ExIm also appears to be becoming more flexible about funding projects undertaken by foreign companies. For instance, the bank is the major financier of the Mphanda Nkuwa Dam in Mozambique, which is to be built, not by a Chinese company, but by a Brazilian–Mozambican consortium. In addition, despite initial reluctance, China is slowly becoming more open to discussing its African relations with counterparts in both West and East. In December 2008, the leaders of Japan, South Korea and China agreed at their first trilateral dialogue to 'reinforce dialogue and consultations on African affairs'.[86]

However, despite such progress, China's engagement with Africa at a multilateral level remains far from comfortable. There is a tendency on the part of China to pay lip service to the promotion of African unity, while its companies continue to take advantage of the more favourable negotiating conditions associated with bilateral deals with individual countries. When it is convenient for China – as in the announcement of balance-of-trade figures that show an apparent broad parity between itself and African countries, or in the political theatre of FOCAC meetings – a pan-African ideal is promoted. But China's declaration of a commitment to multilateralism has less to do with a recognition of the need to engage with a strong and united Africa than with a pragmatic interest in promoting multipolarity in the face of continuing Western dominance of the international community. Beijing now sees multilateralism, once viewed as a mechanism for the US to contain China, as a tool for bringing about a more balanced, multipolar world, free of US hegemony. Of course, how much Chinese commitment to multilateralism there will be in a world in which China enjoys greater relative power remains to be seen.

NEPAD is a potentially important multilateral body for Africa. The organisation lists ensuring democracy and good governance among its priorities, stating that one of its 'immediate desired outcomes' is that 'Africa adopts and implements the principles of democracy ... and the protection of human rights becomes further entrenched in every African country'. The acceleration of regional and continental integration are also among the organisation's guiding principles.[87] The African Peer Review Mechanism, one of NEPAD's centrepiece initiatives, invites countries to review one another's performance on various criteria, including democracy and political and corporate governance. NEPAD has identified priority projects in areas such as infrastructure, agriculture and health in which China has proclaimed itself eager to help. The organisation's Short Term Action Plan for Infrastructure sets out the continent's most urgent requirements in these sectors. Yet there is still considerable scope for closer coordination between Chinese interests and recipient-country priority requirements, as well as for more Chinese engagement in multilateral projects. The director of NEPAD's Business Foundation has suggested that China consider the 'high-potential development corridors' identified by NEPAD when deciding the location of future ECZs.[88] As well as building transport links between mines and newly developed ports, China could gain strategic advantage by contributing more towards repairing the deficit in intra-African infrastructure. Combined with prohibitive trade barriers, this weak infrastructure acts as a key inhibitor of African development by limiting access to neighbouring markets, with the result that it is often cheaper for an African country to trade with China than with its next-door neighbour.

If Chinese declarations of support for Africa's multilateral institutions are to be matched by reality, China's FOCAC secretariat will need to develop better ways of engaging with NEPAD to ensure that China's commercial activities in Africa, which it promotes as benefitting Africa as well as China, are designed in harmony with the declared priorities of NEPAD and the AU. Speaking in early 2008, one special adviser to NEPAD criticised China's 'inadequate coordination and engagement with the AU/NEPAD framework and principles', observing that this prevented Chinese engagement from helping to maximise regional coordination and integration.[89] To be fair to China, progress towards regional coordination has not been aided by poor coordination between the NEPAD secretariat and the AU Commission, a problem that it is hoped will be overcome by the planned integration of the two bodies.[90] Nevertheless, it is likely that tensions will remain in China's dealings with NEPAD. Unfortunately for Africa, but perhaps fortunately for China, given its ambivalence towards engaging substantively with the organisation, NEPAD has proved something of a sickly child since its conception in 2001. The wariness shown by some African states towards NEPAD as a potential source of criticism and scrutiny has had the effect of rather emasculating the organisation, giving China something of a reprieve from having to work proactively with it on a number of the issues identified.

Though it nominates special representatives to Africa's myriad sub-regional organisations, China's engagement with these organisations has also been somewhat reluctant. Since too many of these organisations are fragile and ineffective, it is perhaps unsurprising that China is tempted to see participation at this level as little more than a tool for smoothing the passage of its commercial and political projects in Africa, rather than as a serious exercise in capacity building. The complex interweaving of the various organisations is not always conducive to doing good business. World Bank economist Harry Broadman has recorded that every African country is a member of at least four different agreements, with eight different customs unions and eight other types of regional integration projects active on the continent.[91] Nevertheless, though Beijing is far from comfortable with Africa's multilateral sub-regional bodies, efforts are being made to develop relations with them. The Economic Community of West African States (ECOWAS) is, arguably, the most developed of Africa's sub-regional organisations. In September 2008, the first annual four-day ECOWAS–China Economic and Trade Forum took place in Beijing, attended by around 500 business leaders from China and ECOWAS member nations.[92] In December, China donated $100,000 to the ECOWAS Peace Fund. In early 2009, China donated the same amount to the executive secretariat of the International Conference on the Great Lakes Region to promote relations with that body, which brings together 11 countries from eastern and central Africa.[93]

Although China is making moves to be seen as a supporter of greater pan-African cooperation, there remains the risk that a persistent air of bilateralism will linger in its African engagements, generating frustrations among its partners on the continent. The question is open as to whether such frustrations could push African nations, which are often every bit as suspicious of each other as they are of outsiders, to cooperate more closely and effectively with one another. If this does prove to be the case, China will have unwittingly done African development a great service.

Assessing China's responses

In a short space of time, China has faced numerous political challenges in Africa. A number of these will be familiar to developed Western nations accustomed to this kind of international engagement. But to a state and businesses only recently 'gone global' and often simply exporting the standards and principles relevant to their own development, some challenges have come as a surprise. Furthermore, in some ways, the challenges are only just beginning. China currently has a window of opportunity in which to learn from its mistakes and consider how to adjust its African associations so as to forge relations that are more complex and mutually beneficial. Other suitors, old and new, are jostling for Africa's attention, and as China's African partners become increasingly habituated to its presence on the continent, any novelty appeal it retains as a generous and unconditional investor is likely to diminish. But if China can continue to recognise and adapt to the challenges it faces in maturity as impressively as it has orchestrated its African campaign in courtship, the window of opportunity should remain open a little longer. If China fails to adapt, it is likely to rapidly accumulate a similar burden in its African engagements to that borne by many Western countries, but without having had sufficient time to make up the gap in technological expertise so as to be able to compete in Africa at an equal disadvantage. Such a failure could also limit Africa's own opportunities for development, as well as damaging the reputation of China's businesses and government on the continent and beyond.

As China's commercial enterprises increasingly try to develop their familiarity with and understanding of Africa, the Chinese government is doing likewise. Yet the financial resources it has poured into supporting the activities of Chinese companies in Africa continue to be poorly complemented by investment in independent expertise on the region and the issues that the government can expect to face there. Research centres such as the Institute for West Asian and African Studies at CASS in Beijing may enjoy a reasonable profile internationally but, controlled by the CCP and confused between their roles as analysts and defenders of government policy, their ability to conduct genuine independent and scientific research remains limited. African-studies institutes have been established in some universities around the country, notably at Zhejiang University, but these will need to be well managed and removed from state and Party influence if real expertise is to be developed.

As challenges continue to emerge for all players in Africa, it will be important for non-Chinese parties to be honest about where the problems lie, and about which are and are not connected to Chinese engagement. If, for example, other powers are concerned about their diminishing influence in Africa, they should begin by re-examining their own policies of engagement, and resist the temptation to ignore their individual policy failures in favour of fretting about a supposed Chinese menace. In its consideration of Sino-African relations, the West will need to focus on the issues that matter. It does not need and should not seek to limit fair commercial competition on the continent. Chinese commercial activities evidently do pose some challenges to both Africa and the West, but these should prove manageable if China can begin to make, if not a rapid rise to the standards that Western NGOs desire, at least some progress to the point where Chinese investments no longer have a reputation for falling short on certain key criteria.

The issues that have a real capacity to threaten sustainable, positive Sino-African relations and, by extension, to disturb relations with the West are political, rather than commercial, in nature. This is underlined by the fact that when international commentators agree that China's interest in Africa presents opportunities for Africa, they mean opportunities for economic advancement, not political opportunities. The West will need to develop its dialogue with both China and Africa to push for greater acceptance of the advantages of good governance, human-rights protection and democracy in the context of Sino-African relations. For China, the challenge of dealing with a developing and differentiated Africa will be a major test of its notions of what it will mean to be a global power. The political framework China is constructing around its economic relationships is still being shaped. African and other stakeholders will need to work hard to ensure that China's progress in tackling the challenges it is facing is substantive, and that what currently amount to cautious tactical changes can develop in time into genuine strategic choices. Can China modify its approaches to Africa to ensure that it can meet its resource requirements there without, for example, giving financial support to pariah leaders? Only inveterate pessimists about the future of Africa would conclude that China would be able to sustain stable relations with Africa without adapting in this way. To maintain its momentum in Africa and protect its position there, China will need to make policy changes. If it succeeds in so doing, these adaptations will change for the better not only Africa's situation, but also the modus operandi of Chinese foreign policy.

Dealing with political dilemmas
arising from commercial engagements

Case Study: Sudan

In the 1990s, arms exports dominated China's bilateral relations with
Sudan. Signs of the potential political difficulties associated with
dealing with Sudan were in evidence as early as 1993 when, two
years after Osama bin Laden moved his base to the country, the US
designated it a 'state sponsor of terrorism'. UN Security Council sanctions followed in 1996, and US sanctions forced the withdrawal of
US companies from Sudan in 1997.[94] This helped to create the conditions in which China's economic engagements with Sudan would
begin to grow, adding a new dimension to Sino-Sudanese relations
in the process. In 1997, Chinese state oil company CNPC became
the largest stakeholder in the newly incorporated Greater Nile
Petroleum Operating Company, the joint-venture petroleum exploration and production company that now extracts and processes
most of Sudan's oil. In the ten years following this agreement, China
invested at least $15bn in Sudan in package deals, whereby it
provided infrastructure projects and arms sales in return for access
to oil.[95] Petroleum sales now account for around 70% of the government's revenue; as much as two-thirds of Sudan's oil is purchased by
China. China is Sudan's top source of imports and top recipient of
its exports.[96] In 2006, 32% of China's overseas equity-oil production
was Sudanese.[97] Chinese companies are also engaged in other types
of business in Sudan, including telecommunications, agribusiness,
textiles and shipbuilding. While companies from countries other
than China continue to do business in the country, in 2008, 13 of
the largest 15 foreign companies operating there were Chinese.[98]
China enjoys majority drilling rights in eight of the nine oil blocks in

Sudan (out of a total of 19) understood to hold significant reserves.[99] Since 1999, when the Greater Nile Petroleum Operating Company completed a pipeline connecting the oilfield of Heglig in central Sudan to the Port of Sudan in the north, Sudan's oil production has risen from near zero to more than 500,000 barrels per day. This has provided the Sudanese government with a reliable and growing source of revenue that has the potential to be a major resource in support of development, but a substantial proportion of which has been used instead to fund the purchase of arms for use against Sudan's assorted rebel groups.[100]

The long-running civil war between the north and south of the country has been a perennial source of security problems for Sudan's foreign oil investors. Between 2003 and the signing of the CPA in 2005, it seemed as if progress was finally beginning to be made on bringing the fighting to an end. However, as the peace negotiations between Khartoum and southern rebels progressed, the situation in the west of the country deteriorated, with rebel groups beginning to attack government targets. Khartoum responded by mobilising 'self-defence militias'. Though the government denies any links with the janjaweed, the mounted gunmen held to be responsible for much of the killing and rape in Darfur since 2003 and who have frequently operated alongside the government's militias, accusations from the international community that Khartoum was complicit in the janja-weed's actions grew louder as the death toll in Darfur increased. For some time, the Chinese diplomatic response to the extreme suffering in Darfur was characterised by an intransigent insistence that this was an internal issue for the government of Sudan. China's respect for national sovereignty meant that it could not offer substantive comment or response. However, in recent years, spurred by Western scrutiny, China has been showing some signs of flexibility on the issue. At FOCAC 2006, President Hu appealed to the Sudanese government to agree to the deployment of UN peacekeeping troops to Darfur under UN Security Council Resolution (UNSCR) 1706, which expanded the mandate of the UN Mission in Sudan to include Darfur (a resolution on which China had abstained). In February 2007, Chinese Ambassador to the UN Wang Guangya was at pains to highlight the pressure China had been putting on Sudan: 'Usually China doesn't send messages, but this time [it] did'.[101] In March 2007, the NDRC released its list of priority countries for investment, which now conspicuously excluded Sudan (although this did not stop the CNPC from acquiring further assets there).[102] In April 2007, China's assistant foreign minister with responsibility for Africa, Zhai Jun, met President al-Bashir in Khartoum and again lobbied for Sudan to accept the proposed UN force. In May 2007, China appointed Liu Guijin, a veteran diplomat with considerable experience in Africa, as its special envoy to Darfur, after Andrew Natsios had been nomi-nated as the US special representative the previous September. With the peacekeepers mandated by UNSCR 1706 having failed to deploy, partly as a result of a lack of international support, in July 2007, during its term as chair of the Security Council, China supported a new resolution, UNSCR 1769, which authorised the deployment of UN peacekeeping troops to Darfur in support of AU troops under a Chapter Seven mandate, in a new mission to be known as UNAMID.

In February 2008, Natsios, having retired from his special-envoy role, remarked of China's contributions on Darfur: 'China in my view has been very cooperative. The level of coordination and coopera-tion has been improving each month.'[103] One Chinese foreign-policy expert interviewed reflected that 'China has been forced to play a role in Sudan's domestic agenda'.[104] In a speech in February 2008, Liu Guijin tacitly acknowledged the role of international pressure in China's adjusted approach when he remarked that 'since 2007, when the Darfur issue began to heat up, Chinese President Hu Jintao has used ... opportunities to talk to President al-Bashir and other Sudanese leaders and urge Sudan to actively collaborate with the rest of the international community'.[105] Liu's citing of 2007 as the date when the Darfur issue began to 'heat up' surely refers to the point at which China recognised the need to respond to ongoing international attention, rather than to events on the ground in Darfur.

In July 2008, the war-crimes charges brought against Omar al-Bashir by ICC prosecutor Luis Moreno Ocampo put Sudan into the spotlight once more. China's response was careful. Arguing that the indictment was not in the interests of the peace process, Liu Guijin commented: 'This is like having a house on fire. The pressing need is to put out the fire and not look for the identity of the arsonist. We are focusing on extinguishing the fire first, but that doesn't mean we are turning a blind eye to the arsonist.'[106] China ignored Sudanese lobbying for help in sabotaging the indictment, choosing instead to simply join African countries such as South Africa in expressing regret and concern when an arrest warrant for al-Bashir was issued in March 2009.[107]

Though there have been adjustments in China's international diplomacy on Sudan, the country's bilateral military and economic relations with Sudan continue. During his two-day visit to Khartoum in February 2007, Hu Jintao put forward a 'four-point principle' for the pursuit of a comprehensive political solution in Darfur and privately pressed al-Bashir on the problem, but he also approved seven economic and technological partnership agreements, including one for the provision of an interest-free loan for infrastructure projects, among which was the construction of another presidential palace.[108] In June 2007, in the run-up to UNSCR 1769, the CNPC acquired a 40% stake in Sudan's Block 13.[109] A year later, in June 2008, President Hu took a more overtly forceful diplomatic line with Sudan, urging visiting Vice President Ali Osman Taha to

'achieve substantial progress' in Darfur and calling for a 'comprehensive ceasefire'.[110] Yet eight new economic deals were also signed
in the course of Taha's visit, during which he implicitly contrasted
China's approach to the Darfur issue with that of powers that were
'infringing Sudan's sovereignty', and praised Sudan–China ties as a
'paradigm' of bilateral relations.[111] Chinese companies are now prospecting for oil in Darfur.[112] This exploration will increase China and
Sudan's security cooperation, as the Sudanese army provides security to prospecting operations. As Chinese weapons sales to Sudan
continue, recent deliveries have included K-8 fighter trainers fitted
with 23mm machine-gun pods, and A-5 attack aircraft.[113] Modern
T-92 wheeled infantry fighting vehicles and T96 main battle tanks
have also been exported, reportedly the first sales of such equipment by China to any African nation.[114]

Thus the concern remains that any reassessment by Beijing of its
policy towards Khartoum is limited and tactical. China recognises the
need for stability in Sudan, but its will to push actively for conflict
resolution is weak. On a number of occasions, China has sought to
water down the wording of UN resolutions, often to a point where
the substance is radically diluted, only to still abstain. This strategy
was seen in the preparation and passage in 2004 of UNSCR 1556,
which established the near-unenforceable targeted embargo on
arms destined for Darfur. The same strategy was in evidence with
UNSCR 1591 in 2005, which reaffirmed the embargo and called for
travel sanctions and asset freezes to be placed on those impeding
the peace process in Darfur. Although China did support UNSCR
1769, its subsequent handling of problems that have prevented the
full deployment of the UN–AU hybrid force has raised suspicions
that this support may have been motivated more by political expedi-
ency than by a genuine desire to see the mission at work.[115] When
this does not threaten its economic interests, China contributes well.

In April 2007, it committed 315 military engineers to Darfur to help with development work, becoming the first non-African country to deploy peacekeepers there.[116]

Although Chinese diplomacy is shifting, it is doing so under pressure and warily. Further challenges await. If the situation in Sudan worsens, China's struggle to integrate its interest in limiting damage to its reputation in the West with its interest in protecting its economic and energy concerns in Sudan will become more difficult. China will also need to consider what measures it is prepared to take to protect its oil facilities in southern Sudan in the event that the CPA breaks down. Even if the agreement holds until the referendum on southern secession in 2011, China will still need to plan strategies for protecting its investments on the north–south border in case of a vote for secession, and the probable violence that would result. How would China respond to repeated kidnappings and murder of its workers, or handle protracted negotiations for hostage release? The list of possible scenarios and the problems they could entail is long. It is likely that China will find contingency planning for these scenarios and the pursuit of preventive diplomacy to limit their probability somewhat challenging.

CHAPTER FIVE

Dealing with the Implications

While the appeal of Africa endures among Chinese policy-makers, some of the early naivety has gone: few Chinese now involved in Africa view the continent simply as a land of unbridled opportunity. As China's appreciation of the complexities of its diverse engagements in Africa's developing and sometimes fragile states grows, the consequences of these engagements increasingly need to be faced. China's ability to recognise and tackle the more negative effects of its engagements will impact greatly on the sustainability of developing Sino-African relations. The danger here is that China's government might fail to look beyond its own rhetoric about equal engagements with Africa to acknowledge the practical reality that many of these relationships are far from equal, and that China incurs certain responsibilities as a consequence of this, notably the responsibility not to be overly exploitative of its relative advantage. The implication of China's line that its relations with African countries are equal is that it is the responsibility of China's African partners to develop policies that make their relationships with China beneficial and sustainable, and that China's role is simply reactive. But China's relative power means that,

:e, it has the greater say in determining the terms on
vestments and other engagements are made, which
___ ____ e it difficult for individual African nations to build
more stringent frameworks for Chinese investment activity.
Thus, the best way for China to protect its investments and
its image abroad is for it to prove itself an active supporter of
robust African strategies for ensuring that Chinese investments
bring African benefits.

African civil society is unlikely to confine its scrutiny of
Sino-African engagements to the behaviour of African leaders
in their dealings with China; China's own activities will also
receive attention. China's international image and its relations
with Africa's citizenry will not escape untainted in the event
that African leaders cheat and steal their way through the
proceeds of Chinese exploitation of their countries' resources.
Indeed, failure to modify its modes of engagement could lay
China open to becoming a scapegoat for the failures of African
regimes that do not make the progress on development that
Chinese investments seemed initially to promise. Furthermore,
China's deployment of non-conditional assistance in support
of Chinese commercial activities in Africa threatens to make
it a favoured sponsor of pariah regimes and corrupt leaderships.

Before considering in detail the implications of the challenges that China is facing in Africa for China, Africa and other
interested parties, and China's ability to adapt to them, it is
worth reflecting once more on the context in which they are
arising. By no means are all these challenges unique to China.
Other developing countries seeking to increase their ties with
Africa face many of the same commercial and political issues.
For example, the disparity between domestic standards of
labour and environmental protection in the developing world
and those of established industrialised nations means that even

where developing countries export their best practice to Africa, concerns still arise in the West about the possible impact on Africa's development.[1] Countries such as China and India are going through their industrial revolutions against the backdrop of the ethical and legal frameworks, media scrutiny and global concerns of the twenty-first century. Such disparities are, of course, hardly unprecedented: US historian Stephen Mihm has recalled how, during the nineteenth century, Europeans fretted about another fast-growing nation with 'a reputation for sacrificing standards to its pursuits of profits' – the United States.[2]

Furthermore, some of the challenges that China is facing are not unique to developing nations. Whatever their nationality, many foreign businesses operating in Africa grapple daily with issues of security and risk assessment, and the various problems associated with working under unstable, undemocratic or corrupt regimes. It would be hypocritical to ignore the ongoing operations of Western oil companies in the dubious political and human-rights environments of Obiang Nguema's Equatorial Guinea or Idriss Déby's Chad. It is, of course, not just Chinese companies that have been criticised for a lack of concern for the environment or for the damaging effects their African exploits have had on local communities. In the 1990s, Shell attracted strong criticism for its activities in Nigeria, accused by NGOs not only of causing severe environmental damage in the Niger Delta but also of being complicit in human-rights abuses, after writer and activist Ken Saro-Wiwa, who had been campaigning against the exploitation by oil companies of the lands of his Ogoni ethnic group, was executed by the military regime of Sani Abacha in 1995.

In some cases, it is the sheer scale of China's activities and apparent ambitions in Africa, rather than the precise mechanisms for engagement it chooses, that attracts attention. For instance, China is not the only country to make use of the packaged 'resources-for-infrastructure' deals that spark the envy of commercial competitors and the concern of other states about low levels of transparency and opportunities for corrupt practice. But China's deals of this kind – for example, its multi-billion-dollar loans to the governments of Angola and the DRC – tend to be of a different order of magnitude from those of other investors. Nevertheless, Chinese companies can sometimes play it safer than Western businesses. For example, ICBC's 2007 purchase of a 20% stake in South Africa's Standard Bank gained it only two non-executive seats on the bank's board of directors and no veto power over board decisions. In contrast, in 2005, to some popular disquiet in South Africa, Barclays Bank provided South Africa's largest foreign direct investment since 1994 with the purchase of a majority stake in ABSA, South Africa's biggest retail bank, proclaiming as it did so its intention to become the 'pre-eminent African bank'.[3] UK-based Vodafone has been expanding its presence across the continent, securing a controlling stake in South Africa's largest mobile-phone company, Vodacom, in 2008. Vodafone's successful $900m bid for a 70% stake in Ghana Telecommunications in the same year met considerable opposition both in Ghana's parliament and among the public of that country, partly in response to concerns about the transparency of the bidding process.[4]

Similarly, it is not only Chinese companies that can get caught out by their involvements with politically sensitive countries. In June 2008, in the midst of a post-election political crisis in Zimbabwe, Anglo American became the focus of unwelcome attention when it announced its intention to invest $400m in the development of the country's Unki platinum mine. In response to criticism, the company played the history card – in much the same way that some Chinese actors have done – by citing its 60-year involvement in Zimbabwe as evidence of a long-standing investment interest in and commitment to the country.[5] In late 2008, 42 people, many of whom were members of the French business and political elite, went on trial accused of selling arms to Angola in the face of a 1990s UN arms embargo. Among the defendants were a former interior minister and the son of former President François Mitterrand. The investigation, with its allegations of bribe-taking at the highest levels, has also embarrassed members of the Angolan government, which has repeatedly tried to halt it. The scandal has damaged Franco-Angolan relations for much of the past decade. For example, in 2004, the Angolan government refused to renew French oil company Total's licence on shallow-water Block 3/80, and forced it to relinquish parts of the 'ultra-deepwater' Block 17 and other Angolan assets the following year.[6]

However, some of the political difficulties that arise as a result of business activities in Africa are more acute for the Chinese government than for other governments. This is partly a result of the Chinese state's involvement in business. Even if a particular Chinese SOE does not uniformly obey state commands on investments abroad (as it is often assumed such companies automatically do), if that company is identified as a particularly poor employer in a given overseas community, this will still rebound on the reputation of the Chinese state. The belief that the Chinese state routinely supervises the ongoing investments of large Chinese companies overseas, including private ones, is partly a consequence of the way in which many Chinese firms enter foreign markets, with initial entry being heavily state-supported.

Still, it remains the case that several of the political challenges faced by the Chinese state in Africa are universal. Furthermore, the West can hardly be said to have developed a perfect formula for balancing the imperatives of generating profit and sponsoring sustainable and responsible development in Africa, which

China needs simply to adopt for all to be well. The design and consistent delivery of responsible development policies for Africa has also proved to be challenging for Western powers, with no blueprint available so free of flaws that the Chinese government cannot but choose to follow it. The terms and conditions of the provision of aid, for example, remain highly contentious even in the West itself. China is far from alone in favouring bilateral and tied aid. The US ties nearly three-quarters of its bilateral aid, despite the recognised inefficiencies this brings.[7] The progress that has been made by many OECD parties on untying their aid is relatively recent.[8] Likewise, it is not only Chinese companies that can fail to deliver tangible benefits to local communities from their resource-extraction operations. For example, the long-standing presence in Nigeria of international oil companies such as Shell has coexisted with enduring poverty in the country, with some 70% of the population continuing to live below the poverty line.[9]

Finally, some of the challenges China is facing in Africa are not only relevant to its international relationships, but also have domestic relevance, with implications for China's own development. While the state's primary mechanism for managing China's resource requirements will remain the engagement of local elites, both abroad and at home, the question of how to rapidly extract primary resources from an area while maintaining at least reasonable relations with the local population is of importance to the Chinese authorities not just in Africa, but also at home, in regions such as resource-rich Xinjiang in the west. There is considerable resentment in Xinjiang, which has a substantial population of Turkic-speaking Uighurs, over preferential employment for Han Chinese, and the transfer of the great majority of taxes collected from the region's petrochemical industry to the centre, rather than to local government. Thus far, in Xinjiang, Beijing's answers to the challenge of how to minimise such resentments and engage with the local population have not been particularly sophisticated: a billboard advertisement in one Xinjiang town suggests that locals 'Offer energy resources as tribute [to Beijing] to create harmony.'[10] Yet this may be beginning to change, as developments in Chinese practice overseas, precipitated by pressure from African and Western civil society, start to reveal the benefits of a more nuanced and inclusive approach to resource exploitation. While the CCP has considerably more power over its own citizens than it does over Africans, and thus has greater leeway to rely on cruder methods for limiting dissenting responses to its policies, Africa may yet be the source of some important lessons in the value of popular engagement and support in creating sustainable engagements. Just as some developments inside China have been pointing the way for Chinese companies and the Chinese government to improve practice overseas, so developments in overseas practice may help to show the way at home.

Such contextual points are important for ensuring that any debate on China in Africa remains grounded in reality and avoids hyperbole or paranoia. Exaggeration and simplification are too often present in Western media treatments of the subject. For example, one 2008 article in the UK's *Daily Mail* ran under the headline 'How China's taking over Africa ... and why we in the West should be very worried', and credited China with a 'vice-like grip' on the continent.[11] In reality, the many challenges facing China in Africa ensure that China's grip is far from vice-like. Furthermore, as we have seen, Western businesses and states have made many of the same mistakes in Africa and face many of the same challenges there, and other actors interested in increasing their African engagements will also be confronted by similar issues. The question is to what extent China's attempts to answer these challenges have characteristics – in the area of 'values' in particular – that distinguish them from those of the West and, if so, what implications this might have for China's international relationships.

China's impact on international terms of engagement with Africa

The inroads China has made into Africa have brought lessons for other countries and institutions involved in the continent. The consequences of China's African engagements can therefore be assessed not only in terms of direct Sino-African relations but also in terms of how China has altered the environment in which other powers engage with Africa. Even the strongest critics of China's involvements in Africa would find it hard to deny that Chinese activities have offered some positive lessons for Africa's development.

One such lesson is that trade is a more sustainable way to advance Africa's development than aid. China has used its status as a developing country and the fact that aid has played and is playing little part in its own development to defend its focus on trade over foreign assistance in Africa. The country's engagement in infrastructure projects on the continent, often undertaken in connection with its resource-focused trading interests, has helped to remind Western development agencies of the importance of this area, which fell out of favour with the promotion of structural-adjustment programmes and privatisation policies in the 1980s. While the scaling back of spending on infrastructure projects by both African governments and Western donors during the 1980s and 1990s did reduce the resources lost to 'white-elephant' projects, it also hampered the development of Africa's internal and international trade. Coming into a setting in which only around one in four Africans living south of the Sahara enjoys access to electricity, and where poor road, rail and harbour facilities create remarkably high transit costs, the Chinese state sees an opportunity for 'win–win' engagement in the form of infrastructure projects that make money for Chinese companies while helping to better connect African goods and workers with their markets.[12] A World Bank report estimates that in 2006, China's 'Year of Africa', China spent $7bn on roads, railways and power projects in Africa, followed by another $4.5bn in 2007.[13]

With donor interest in Africa's severe infrastructure deficit reviving, in 2006 the European Commission established the EU–Africa Partnership on Infrastructure, with €5.6bn allocated from the European Development Fund for cross-border and regional development in Africa.[14] In 2007, an Infrastructure Trust Fund for Africa was established as part of the partnership, backed by €90m, plus a further €260m in loans.[15] Through its Millennium Challenge Corporation, the US has also returned to funding infrastructure projects, in Africa and elsewhere.[16] The impetus provided by Chinese engagement in African infrastructure projects has played a role in these developments. One Southern African diplomat described the change in the following terms: 'Before China became interested in Africa, we used to try to talk to Western governments about infrastructure or agriculture and their eyes would simply glaze over. Now our phones ring with offers of support.'[17]

More broadly, China's trade-focused approach and its preference for using government agencies over the private sector to stimulate development have even given rise to talk of a 'Beijing consensus' as a possible new model for African development.[18] But while China certainly sees both political and commercial advantage in differentiating its approaches to its African partnerships from those of the West, it is unlikely that it is deliberately exporting an alternative model of development to compete with the traditional thinking of international financial institutions. Nevertheless, both China's domestic development and its interactions with Africa have seriously challenged what economist Joseph Stiglitz has labelled 'market fundamentalism', reminding African and Western governments alike that recipes for progress can vary.[19]

In addition, China's flexible and rapid disbursements of assistance to Africa have highlighted the fact that the assistance policies of the international financial institutions and many Western development agencies still fail to appreciate the need for the quick provision of a limited quantity of aid tailored to immediate local requirements. Contrary to the assumptions of some in the West, it is not only pariah leaders seeking self-aggrandisement who are attracted to China's 'no conditions' aid. While it is right that larger assistance funds should focus on longer-term projects with well-targeted conditionality clauses, there are still not enough funds quickly available on more flexible, less bureaucratic terms for the sorts of rapid-delivery projects that can play a crucial role in post-conflict transitions. Sometimes, as President Johnson-Sirleaf of Liberia remarked to World Bank President Robert Zoellick in 2008, 'A dollar today is worth more to us than 50 dollars in three years' time.'[20]

China's pragmatically motivated appeals to notions of a shared 'Global South' identity against the more developed 'North' have also helped to focus Western actors on their own African commitments. So far, however, the shadow of China appears not to loom quite large enough to ensure the full enactment of the impressive aid promises made to Africa at G8 summits from the 2005 meeting in Gleneagles onwards.[21] The 2008 report of the Africa Progress Panel suggested that 'without major changes', most countries would fall 'well below' their targets.[22] In April 2008, the OECD's Development Assistance Committee concluded that donors would need to oversee 'unprecedented increases' to meet the targets for 2010.[23] Past unfulfilled pledges of financial support have undermined relations between the West and Africa. Chinese leaders are acutely aware of the diplomatic advantage these shortcomings give them, as they cultivate the image of a China that forms more 'reliable' partnerships with African nations.

Chinese engagements are, meanwhile, offering lessons to others on respect and rhetoric in African diplomacy, and are even illuminating the opportunities that Africa presents. The emphasis on 'equal partnership' and the scrupulous avoidance of the language of aid and dependency in China's official pronouncements are beginning to influence other actors, anxious to declare their own good intentions. When French President Sarkozy visited South Africa in March 2008, he called repeatedly for 'partnership' and showed a humility traditionally lacking in Western diplomacy on Africa, as he echoed Chinese talk of lessons learnt from Africa.[24] Impressive year-on-year continent-wide rates of growth spurred by developing trade with China are recasting Africa as a land of commercial opportunity. The theme of Japan's May 2008 Tokyo International Conference on African Development (TICAD) – 'Towards a Vibrant Africa: A Continent of Hope and Opportunity' – reflects how the Chinese approach to Africa is affecting the attitudes of the richer nations.[25] China has also set an impressive benchmark on maintaining regular, high-level diplomatic contact with Africa's leaders; lessons need to be learned here by Western powers.

Non-African powers react to Sino-African relations

Relationships between Africa, China, established Western donors and other emerging powers are increasingly interconnected. All those involved in Africa conduct their business on the continent with a careful eye on the progress being made by others, a dynamic that some African governments are beginning to seek to exploit. The wary presence of other powers adds another dimension to a situation in which China has set itself the already challenging goal of achieving 'win–win' engagements. Not all of those in the West who repudiate the idea of a clash of interests between the West and China in Africa do so simply by arguing that there is sufficient space in Africa for all interested parties. In a speech in 2007, then-UK Prime Minister Tony Blair argued that 'we can work with China to serve the development of Africa in a way which benefits us all'.[26] For China, the demanding reality may be that, if Western states are not to feel overly threatened by closer relations between China and African countries, these relations will need to show at least the potential to be not just 'win–win', but 'win–win–win'. This means that China, the West and Africa will need to find ways of ensuring that commercial competition develops in such a way that the core interests of all states involved are protected, thereby allowing each bloc some reassurance about the bilateral dynamics between the other two.

Competition from China has had the effect of increasing the West's attention to its own interests in Africa's resources and how it pursues them – interests which had to some extent previously been taken for granted. Like those of China, US imports from Africa are heavily resource-focused. In 2007, oil accounted for 80% of all US imports from sub-Saharan Africa.[27] In the same year, Nigeria was once more the US's largest supplier of oil in Africa and its fourth-largest oil supplier worldwide.[28] American interest in Africa's natural resources and the continent's potential role in ensuring US energy security is, furthermore, increasing as US anxiety about dependence on Middle Eastern energy grows. As a result, American initiatives to promote African development are not always as isolated from the issue of domestic resource requirements as some US critics of China's resource-focused African engagements might like to imagine. The 2000 African Growth and

Opportunity Act (AGOA) is a good illustration of the mixed results of some US African development initiatives. The Act (which has undergone several revisions since 2000) offers a number of sub-Saharan African countries the freest access to the US market that is available to countries without a free-trade agreement with Washington. Its aim is to promote economic reform and encourage the development of free-market economies in the region.[29] At first glance, AGOA's record on opening up US markets to African products appears impressive. In 2007, 98% of imports from AGOA-qualified countries entered the US duty free.[30] However, imports are heavily focused on the resource sector and highly concentrated geographically.[31] In 2007, non-oil AGOA trade was worth only $3.4bn out of a total of $51.1bn in AGOA imports.[32] One of the disadvantages for Africa of AGOA's focus on the market for Africa's resources is the resource sector's tendency to provide fewer employment opportunities than others, such as the textile and manufacturing sectors.

However, the US differs markedly from China, both in the scale of its African engagements and, broadly, in the way in which it undertakes them. As well as being Africa's largest trading partner, the US is also one of the continent's main sources of foreign direct investment. In 2006, US foreign direct investment in Africa amounted to $13.8bn; in contrast, China offered $1.6bn.[33] While there undoubtedly are loopholes in the theory and shortcomings in the execution of US directives on development and trade, the US government explicitly emphasises the promotion of values such as good governance, accountability and respect for human rights as it seeks to fulfil its resource requirements, aiming where possible to trade with and partner like-minded governments. The particularly asymmetric quality of US relations with African countries, and an historical lack of serious competition for African resources from powers with a

similar desire to assert their moral leadership, have meant that
the US has felt able to promote these issues more explicitly in
Africa than it has in other regions, most obviously the Middle
East. Where China remains reluctant to engage substantively
in Africa beyond its contacts with local elites, inexperienced
as it is in dealing with organisations such as trade unions and
uncomfortable working with NGOs and civil society, the US is
more likely to engage. For example, in Ghana in 2007, the sixth
meeting of the US–Sub-Saharan Africa Trade and Economic
Cooperation Forum established by AGOA brought together
for the first time representatives of government, civil society
and business in joint discussions to develop relations.

The challenge for China of developing a more sustainable
base for its relations with Africa is highlighted not only by
the more inclusive approach to African engagements adopted
by the US, but also by the broader framework of engagements within which US resource interests in Africa are being
pursued. The US is more directly concerned than China with
issues such as terrorism in ungoverned spaces, democracy and
good governance, development and disease. One illustration
of this broader interest can be seen in the impressive record –
a controversial abstinence agenda in the area of sexual health
notwithstanding – of the George W. Bush administration on
developing channels of African engagement unconnected to
US resource requirements. Official US development assistance
to Africa doubled during the Bush administration's first term.[34]
Spending on the Presidential Emergency Plan for AIDS Relief
(PEPFAR) launched by Bush in 2003 reached $6bn in 2008, and
the US also leads the way in the fight against tuberculosis and
malaria in Africa.[35]

However, other initiatives aimed at broadening US engagement with Africa, designed to demonstrate a commitment to
the continent's security and development, have thus far met

with rather less approval from African governments and citizens. In September 2008, AFRICOM became the US's sixth unified overseas military command, with a brief to focus on war-prevention, rather than war-fighting, and to boost regional security and crisis-response capacity.[36] The force's inception was greeted with considerable unease both in Africa and China, with suspicion rife that its true purpose was to protect US resource interests on the continent, if necessary at China's expense.[37]

Some US initiatives in Africa predate the emergence of concerns in the US about China's increasing interests on the continent, while others have developed in parallel with them. As US analysts have scrutinised Sino-African relations, the challenges presented by China have brought the relative strengths and weaknesses of the US's own African diplomacy into sharper focus. With China's non-conditional assistance and the terms of its extensive provision of loans to African governments continuing to cause disquiet in the US (and elsewhere in the developed world), there has been little regression of US confidence in the moral and practical rectitude of its own positions on these issues. Enthusiasm for the US's more inclusive approach to its African relationships and for the promotion of a broad spectrum of African engagements has increased in response to China's African activities. In addition, the US government watches China closely in Africa. For example, in June 2008, the Senate Committee on Foreign Relations held a hearing on China's African relations and their implications for US policy.[38] China's relations with Sudan have come under particular scrutiny. China itself has not been indifferent to this attention: when interviewed, several Chinese officials indicated that the importance of protecting Sino-US relations had trumped that of developing Sino-Sudanese relations to lead Chinese policymakers to begin making some adjustments to their diplomacy here.[39]

Challenges remain for the US in developing its African relations. These gain urgency as other suitors, led by China, compete for Africa's attention. One obvious challenge for all developed countries is the need to support the development of a more equitable trading regime that would ensure that the poorest in Africa do not suffer effective discrimination through substantial subsidies to the West's powerful domestic agricultural lobbies. Ongoing unresolved issues such as this, which are widely felt to represent patent injustices, enable China to play the role of moral envoy from the developing to the developed world. This kind of identity-politicking on the part of China has a divisive effect, undermining the pursuit of broader cooperation among all parties, whether developed or developing, 'North' or 'South'.

Like the US, EU countries have also been pursuing their resource interests in Africa, though traditionally in combination with a more aid-focused development agenda. Over the past decade, measures have been taken by EU countries to stimulate the development of African trade alongside increasing the provision of aid. Following in the footsteps of the US AGOA initiative, the EU has since 2001 operated an 'Everything but Arms' (EBA) programme, which enhances the duty-free access offered by the EU's 2000 Cotonou Agreement with African, Caribbean and Pacific nations, enabling the least-developed countries, including those in sub-Saharan Africa, to export goods to the EU free of duties and unconstrained by quotas.[40] The AGOA and EBA programmes – which have been copied by China in its introduction of its own tax-exemption measures – have their flaws, many of which are substantial. Nevertheless, the existence of such programmes does at least create the possibility that, with careful scrutiny of these flaws and consequent improvements, the goal of opening up overseas markets to

African goods might be brought closer, thereby providing a major stimulus for African development.

China's African activities have helped to generate discussion within the EU about the union's own resource strategies and how these might best be coordinated with the interests of others. In 2008, the EU Commission proposed the development of 'raw-materials diplomacy' with Africa, China and Russia.[41] The same year, the European Parliament debated a resolution on 'Chinese Policy and its Effects on Africa'. The resolution, passed by 618 votes to 16, discussed the challenges presented by Chinese engagements on the continent. It 'regretted' China's 'cooperation with repressive regimes in Africa' and called, among other things, for greater transparency in China's activities, as well as for China ExIm to give greater consideration to environmental concerns when deciding which projects to fund.[42] At the same time, as in the US, some European initiatives in Africa have been developed largely independently of any serious effort to respond to Chinese engagements there. For instance, the 2005 report of the Commission for Africa established by Tony Blair mentioned China only once in passing, seemingly failing to view it as either a potential partner or a challenger.[43]

EU relations with African countries have been complicated over the past decade by the deteriorating political and economic situation in Zimbabwe, as Europe has struggled to determine the appropriate response to the country's problems. The EU–Africa summit established in 2000 failed to reconvene in 2003 following disputes over the attendance of Zimbabwean President Robert Mugabe. The fact that a second summit was eventually convened in December 2007, with the EU conceding to Mugabe's attendance at the meeting, appeared to be a sign of the pressure Europe was feeling from China's engagements with Africa. The Lisbon Declaration that emerged from the meeting announced a resolve to build a 'new strategic political partnership for the future', apparently echoing Hu Jintao's announcement of China's 'new strategic partnership' at FOCAC the previous year.[44]

It is not only the West that has found itself viewing its African diplomacy in part through the prism of China's African advances. New Delhi too watches China's progress in Africa with some concern, though for India, the dismay may be more over the fierce competition presented by the rapid advances of a rival power with similar resource and political motivations for its activities than about the impact on Africa of Chinese engagements.

India's interest in cultivating closer relations with African countries is primarily motivated by resource interests, though it also needs to garner support for a permanent seat on a restructured UN Security Council. India currently imports around three-quarters of its oil, with about a quarter of these imports coming from Africa. Both figures are rising. By 2025, India is projected to overtake Japan to become the world's third-largest net importer of oil after the US and China.[45] Although its activities on the continent remain small-scale compared with those of China, India is thus making a considerable effort to expand its engagements with Africa.

Theoretically, Indian diplomatic and commercial interests in Africa have some clear advantages over Chinese ones, but these have generally been under-exploited. They include a long-established diaspora on the continent that is on the whole more integrated into local communities than its generally more recently arrived Chinese equivalents; a shared language (English) in many regions; and a tradition of paternalistic philanthropy that should support CSR and community integration. However, as one Indian official has commented, 'There is no race between us [China and India];

the Chinese have left us far, far behind.'[46] To express this gap in trade terms, India's trade with Africa reached $36bn in 2008 – having risen from $967m in 1991, when India's own economic overhaul began – while Sino-African trade reached $106.8bn in the same year.[47]

Some initiatives are under way to try to close the gap. These include the 'Focus Africa' project launched in 2002 by India's Export–Import Bank and the same bank's work with the Confederation of Indian Industry, begun in 2005, to promote economic relations through 'conclaves' on Indian–African partnership.[48] Influenced by China's example, India has also launched its own, relatively modest, Africa forum, the first summit meeting of which was held in April 2008, attended by leaders from 14 African countries nominated by the African Union, as well as by the chairman of the AU Commission. At the meeting, the Indian government announced the provision of $500m in support of aid projects in Africa over the following five years, along with an additional $5.4bn in credit lines.[49] The Indian Ministry of External Affairs is also increasing its presence in Africa. While it may be chasing China on economic diplomacy in Africa, India has been comparatively more successful in its cultivation of security partnerships in Africa in support of its interests in the Indian Ocean. Since 2007, India has had an operational listening post in Madagascar, its first on foreign soil. The Indian and South African navies have conducted a number of joint exercises off the coast of South Africa. Security relations with Tanzania, Kenya and Mozambique have also been expanded, with the Indian Navy helping to provide security for the AU summit in Maputo, Mozambique, in 2003, while naval cooperation with Madagascar, Mauritius and the Seychelles has also increased in recent years.

India appears to be employing some restraint in the development of its commercial interests in Africa, aware that the comparative amateurishness of India's engagements with Africa to date might yet become an advantage should China fail to adapt its resource-focused diplomacy sufficiently to win broad popular support for its activities. In the event of a backlash against the Chinese approach, in which China's government is seen as cynically attempting to 'lock down' African resources for Chinese use, India's less state-centric, rather more haphazard approach to engaging with the continent may well work in its favour. Mindful of the strong criticism Chinese engagements in Africa have received for their initial focus on the extractive industries, India has also sought to highlight its broad commercial agenda on the continent. One important project in this regard is India's $1bn investment in a joint venture with the AU to build a pan-African 'e-network' linking India's leading universities and hospitals with their counterparts in Africa.[50] Lacking the deep pockets of the Chinese state that have often enabled Chinese SOEs to outbid competitors, India is cultivating an alternative emphasis on technology transfer, training and know-how. It would appear that the Indian government is interested in at least working towards the realisation of Gandhi's ambitious prediction that 'the commerce between India and Africa will be of ideas and services, not of manufactured goods against raw materials after the fashion of Western exploiters'.[51]

Japan's forum for dialogue with Africa, TICAD, is longer-established than China's FOCAC, and in the early years following its first meeting in 1993, the conference played an important role in keeping African development on the international agenda at a time when the developed world was suffering from 'aid fatigue' in the aftermath of the Cold War. Indeed, Japan's work here may even have helped draw the attention of China's leaders back towards Africa. Today, the conference's role is more modest, with efforts to continue to position the event as 'the major global framework for Asia and Africa to collaborate in promoting Africa's development' increasingly tortuous and unconvincing in the light of China's arrival on the scene.[52] The role of TICAD aside, Japan's commitment to using multilateral channels as the main conduit of its overseas aid has had positive results in terms of aid delivery. While budget constraints forced Japan's overall aid contributions into decline following a peak in the early 1990s, when the country was the world's top donor, the sums flowing from Japan to Africa have been increasing again in recent years. Though the commitment will be severely tested by the global financial crisis and Japan's own struggling economy, at the 2008 TICAD meeting, Prime Minister Yasuo Fukuda announced that by 2012, Japan would double its aid to Africa, to $1.8bn on top of debt-relief measures.[53]

Japan, like other powers, is conscious of the rapid early advances China has made in Africa, and seeks to learn lessons from China, as well as compete with it. One effect of China's activities has been to prompt Japanese companies that had previously focused on the opportunities offered by government-led foreign-aid programmes in Africa to consider the potential of Africa's resources and markets in their own right. Japanese investment in Africa may be some way behind both China's and India's, but interest in Africa is slowly increasing. This interest is not only fuelled by Japanese concerns about Chinese aspirations in Africa, but also by the ongoing desire to find ways to bolster Japan's contributions to the US–Japan alliance in the context of the post-war constraints on Japanese military activity. At a meeting in 2008, US President Bush and Prime Minister Fukuda agreed collaborative initiatives on African health care and food security.[54]

Other countries, both developed and developing, resource-hungry and relatively resource-rich, have also been paying increased attention to Africa, in line with the trend, exemplified by China, of actively seeking to increase commercial relations, in particular in the hunt for diversified supplies of natural resources. This has in many cases been taking place alongside enlarged aid commitments resulting from the adoption by 189 countries of the Millennium Development Goals set at the UN's 2000 Millennium Summit. In 2006, South Korea inaugurated the Korea–Africa Economic Cooperation Conference (KOAFEC), the country's first ministerial-level Africa forum, a few days after China's much higher-profile event. South Korea is the world's fifth-largest net importer of oil, but its interests in Africa are also market-based, with a number of Korean businesses, including arms manufacturers, seeking to expand into the continent.[55] As with China, the ambitions of some of South Korea's companies in Africa are substantial. In late 2008, as part of an effort to reduce South Korea's reliance on imports from the US and South America, South Korean conglomerate Daewoo expressed an interest in taking over around a million hectares of land in Madagascar for the cultivation of corn and palm oil in a proposed deal with the Madagascan government that Daewoo initially suggested could have seen it renting the land for free in return for the provision of local employment opportunities.[56] In an example of the potential for a popular backlash in Africa against foreign investment deals that are perceived to be exploitative, by March 2009, the arrangement had been cancelled by Madagascar's new government, with resentment over the proposed deal thought to have contributed to the dramatic fall of President Marc Ravalomanana following months of demonstrations.[57]

In August 2008, Turkey inaugurated its own 'cooperation summit' with Africa. By the time of the conference, 355 Turkish firms were operating in Africa with investments worth more than $400m.[58] The African engagements of medium powers such as Turkey are, however, generally beginning from an extremely low base, and are more than anything belated corrections of previous under-engagement. Among the relatively resource-rich countries that have also been taking note of the opportunities on offer in Africa are Malaysia, Vietnam, Canada and Russia.

While many companies have found themselves in increasing competition with Chinese businesses in Africa, others have found ways to gain opportunities from China's increasing interest in the continent. In 2007, the Brazilian state-owned agricultural-research corporation Embrapa announced a strategy to slipstream Chinese infrastructure investments in certain African countries in the hope that its parallel investments might enable it to gain a portion of the market for training, consulting and technical assistance, and facilitate market entry for Brazilian goods, in particular food and agricultural machinery and equipment.[59] In Mozambique, the Brazilian building firm Camargo Correia is helping to construct the Mphanda Nkuwa Dam backed by Chinese finance.

China's African advances have, therefore, brought both challenges and opportunities for other non-African powers involved in the continent. China's African diplomacy has prompted others to more carefully consider their own bilateral ties with Africa, and to examine how their engagements might be developed in such a way that commercial competition takes place within a cooperative diplomatic environment that supports the sustainable development of Africa and functioning global markets for its resources. While it may be unrealistic to expect a smooth 'win–win–win' outcome for China, Africa and the West at a purely commercial level, the challenge remains to ensure that it is not unrealistic at a diplomatic level. This broader challenge will be returned to in the concluding pages of this book.

African responses to China

African responses to Chinese interests have inevitably been complex and diverse, varying according to political and social context, and factors such as the export basket of a given country or region. For some time, acknowledgement of this broad range of responses was absent from much of the discussion of China's role in Africa as a result of the elite-to-elite dynamic of China's initial engagements. However, a more diverse range of African voices is now beginning to make itself heard. Feedback from different layers of African societies, involving governments and citizens alike, has the potential to play an important role in influencing the direction of Chinese engagements. The process of gathering popular feedback is aided in Africa's democracies by the existence of mechanisms for holding governments to account for their roles in determining the nature of foreign engagements. However, as international scrutiny makes the Chinese state more sensitive to carefully targeted pressure on specific aspects of its commercial activities, and as Chinese companies gradually begin to show signs of recognising the importance of engaging with local African communities, grassroots attention to the impact of China's interests on Africa can make a difference even in non-democratic countries whose governments are failing in their responsibility to represent and protect their citizens. The process of subjecting China's activities in Africa to broader African debate can itself be expected over time to impact positively on the development of China's methods to a degree that the voicing of Western concerns alone cannot hope to do.

An awareness of the need for a more detailed analysis of the impact of China's activities on Africa is slowly growing in African civil society, along with an appreciation of the need to hold those involved to account. Organisations such as the African Forum and Network on Debt and Development are sponsoring research into China's contribution to the advancement of good economic governance and development in Africa, while Fahamu, which declares its mission to be to 'support the strengthening of human-rights and social-justice movements', has developed a 'China–Africa Watch' element of its *Pambazuka News* publication.[60] It was not only Westerners who took the opportunity of China's 2008 Olympic torch relay to protest against certain Chinese policies. In Tanzania, the Tanzania Consumer Advocacy Society used the occasion of the torch's passage through Dar es Salaam to highlight China's role in producing counterfeit goods.[61] Also in 2008, campaigners for transparency in Niger called for a parliamentary investigation into the precise content of a contract between Niger and China for oil exploration in the Diffa region in the southeast of the country, and for greater transparency on environmental and labour-protection issues.[62] Their calls were taken up by Niger newspaper *L'Action,* and prompted questions in parliament about the transparency of the deal and the bidding processes that led to it.[63] In Namibia in July 2008, the chief labour-relations officer of the Erongo region appeared on national television accusing the Jiangsu International Construction Company of exploiting workers at a site near the port of Walvis Bay. Claiming that her attempts to discuss pay and safety standards directly with the company had been to no avail, the officer emphasised that her media appearance was intended to generate public pressure for such issues to be tackled.[64] Examples such as these are still the exception rather than the rule, and where action is taken by NGOs and campaigners, it often does not immediately achieve its aims, and can result in the persecution of those involved. Nevertheless, such action makes an important contribution as African civil society begins to examine the implications for different sub-sections of Africa's population of the realities behind the rhetoric of 'win–win' China–Africa engagements.

Among Africa's governments, there is broad agreement over the opportunities that China's interests present. Even countries that do not object to the West's imposition of conditions on assistance have, quite naturally, shown themselves to be interested in developing new customer bases and in diversifying their international relationships beyond Africa's traditional westward orientation. However, there is also an increasing recognition within these governments that African nations could do more to coordinate among themselves, both bilaterally and multilaterally, in order to ensure that the opportunities offered by China's new interests are harnessed and their promised benefits to Africa fully delivered. Rwandan President Paul Kagame has emphasised Africa's responsibility for managing any foreign interests in the continent with the sharp warning that if 'they find you sleeping and they want to help themselves to something, they will take it ... they will not wake you up'.[65]

Individual African governments are gradually becoming more assertive in their dealings with China, recognising their interest in helping to define how China's engagements in the continent should further evolve and change. In Senegal, a Chinese company cannot be awarded an infrastructure-related contract without being partnered with a Senegalese company. The purpose of this rule is to ensure that Senegalese firms not only benefit from individual Chinese investments, but that they also gain the long-term benefits of access to Chinese technology and training. Central and local authorities from Sierra Leone to the DRC have attempted to impose usually temporary bans on the export of selected unprocessed materials in an effort to secure a better share of the benefits of resource extraction.[66] In Zambia, while acute problems with labour rights remain, with the number of child labourers estimated to have increased in recent years, new initiatives have been undertaken to try to ensure that foreign investments contribute

to development.[67] In December 2006, the Zambian government outlined its 'Vision 2030' aimed at making Zambia a
'prosperous middle-income nation' by 2030. The government
has taken a number of measures to increase domestic capacity to manage the effects of foreign investment, for example
through improving the capacity of the Ministry of Labour and
Social Security, increasing the minimum wage and conducting
reviews of labour legislation, including the Factories Act, the
Minimum Wages and Conditions of Employment Act and the
Employment of Children and Young Persons Act.[68] A 'Citizen
Economic Empowerment Fund' has also been launched, aimed
at ensuring the participation of targeted categories of Zambian
citizens in national industries and development. In Uganda,
the Federation of Ugandan Employers has, with support from
the Federation of Norwegian Enterprises, translated Ugandan
labour laws into Chinese in an effort to support Chinese compliance with local standards.[69]

In attempting to hold Chinese business and the Chinese state
more effectively to account, Africa would do well to scrutinise
and even mirror China's own handling of foreign investors.
African governments could, for instance, make use of the CSR
guidelines that China drew up in late 2008 for foreign investors
in China as a template for guidelines for Chinese activities in
their own countries, adapting and applying them to the African
context as appropriate.[70] For example, the local government of
the Pudong district of Shanghai offers financial incentives to
foreign companies implementing comprehensive CSR strategies. Could African local and national governments consider
something similar?

As African governments work to improve the terms of their
trade with China and harness the potential of Chinese interests
for their own development, their demands are likely to be more
effective if they can be made regionally rather than bilaterally.

Improved regional cooperation would increase the capacity of African governments to impact on China's engagements in a more sustained, less piecemeal way. Standardised agreements or at least coordinated attention could help to guard against monopolistic behaviour and uncompetitive practices, better target aid and determine its effectiveness, and push for greater transparency on transactions and respect for Africa's domestic development agenda as outlined by NEPAD, for example. Strengthened regional coordination would also help to increase Africa's influence on the China-dominated FOCAC agenda and thus better tailor Chinese activities to African requirements. An African counterpart of China's FOCAC secretariat could, for instance, be charged with feeding suggestions and requests into the FOCAC process, as well as monitoring the fulfilment of pledges made. If Africa can act together through its multilateral institutions in these and other ways, it will be the more powerful for it. Africa's immense reserves of natural resources are a major source of potential power and influence: bolstered collective diplomacy and leadership could yet realise this potential.

African governments might also remind themselves that they can afford to be confident in their collective dealings with China. China needs a positive dynamic in its engagements in Africa, both in order for these engagements to be sustainable in the long term and for the benefit of its relations with the West. China certainly has a role to play in Africa's development, but Africa should also play a role in China's.

As Sino-African relations develop, it will be important for outsiders to keep in proportion the basic appeal of China in Africa. It is not so much any particular 'China model' of development that is attractive to Africa's governments and citizens, but rather the wider market for African resources and the broader interest in Africa internationally that China's interest in the continent has helped to stimulate. African countries are increasingly identifying welcome new opportunities from among the alternatives presented by the markets of emerging powers. Angolan officials have been clear that closer relations with China are part of a broader plan to increase Angola's independence from the West. In 2008, the country's deputy prime minister, Aguinaldo Jaime, observed that 'China has an important role to play because it is providing huge financing for our economy. But our policy is really to diversify.'[71] This is not to say that the highly elite-focused character of China's engagements and the opportunities for enrichment they offer may not also have a particular appeal for corrupt leaderships. But commercial engagement with China by state elites is not always motivated by a narrow interest in self-aggrandisement. The negotiation and implementation of agreements with China can be quicker, the delivery of projects cheaper, and a diverse customer base more assured. As the differential impacts of the financial crisis begin to emerge, African nations are reminded that dependence on just one set of markets or relationships is simply not in their interest.

As African countries become more confident in their dealings with external investors, there is some danger that they may try to exploit the developing diversity of their commercial and political engagements by encouraging rivalry among Africa's various suitors. While this might in the short term appear to bring rewards for Africa, if it results in unrestrained rivalry between, for example, the West and China, the interests and development of Africa will suffer along with those of China and the West. Western and Chinese actors should, therefore, recognise their vulnerabilities here, and counteract the risk of unnecessary and destructive competition with dialogue and, where possible, cooperation on their African interests.

Greater East–West coordination on Africa would generally be welcome. For one thing, if Western and Chinese actors liaised more closely with one another, African bureaucracies would be spared at least some of the multiple disconnected donor visits and demands they currently receive.[72] However, if African nations are to be truly supportive of such improved coordination and reject any temptation to encourage rivalries for short-term commercial advantage, African concerns about the possible limits of this cooperation will need to be acknowledged and addressed. After all, how much does a salesman really want his customers to collaborate? In the event of closer cooperation, healthy commercial competition in Africa must still be allowed to thrive, and be appreciated as a sign of strength in East–West relations, rather than viewed as a possible flashpoint for problems.

With or without improved coordination between China and the West, other new challenges will doubtless emerge as a result of Africa's diversification of its commercial and political partnerships, and any increased assurance in its dealings with Chinese and other foreign interests. As African elites seek to capitalise on foreign interest in their continent and ensure they are seen as important players in the diplomatic game, rather than mere occupants of the ground on which the game is played, these elites should in time acquire increased financial reserves and improved political capacities. This will herald a still more complex world, with such states liable to develop their capacity for more autonomous political or even military action. The international community may yet be faced with the rise in Africa of more resource-emboldened wayward leaders akin to Sudan's al-Bashir. Despite such risks, a more equitable world such as this should nevertheless be the one that the West seeks as it explores ways to help Sino-African relations bring mutual and stable development as well as commercial profit. However, such prospects are also why the West will wish to continue to encourage and try to protect the growth of democracy in Africa and elsewhere. The self-correcting, stabilising mechanisms of a functioning democracy should help to ensure that the increased leverage that awaits the leaders of prospering African nations will be directed towards increasing the development and stability of those nations for the benefit of their citizens.

Political cooperation around commercial competition: the challenges ahead

As we have seen, while other powers have been watching China's activities in Africa for lessons to apply to their own engagements, most, including those in the developing world, do not seek simply to replicate China's achievements, but to adapt them. The presence of so many other actors is a reminder that China is far from having an overwhelming grip on Africa. Approaches and strategies are still evolving on all sides. The challenge now for China is to develop ways of meeting its needs within a regulatory framework and as part of a rule-based environment, without having to partner 'pariah' states or shrinking from increasing its contribution to conflict-prevention measures. The test for Africa and the West will be to find ways to encourage China through this challenge and to verify any adjustments made, thereby helping to avoid a 'race to the bottom' by ensuring that other aspirant powers do not draw the wrong lessons from China's engagements in Africa.

While the major powers of East and West are already aware of some tensions between their respective interests in Africa, the shift towards multipolarity is only just beginning. Furthermore, the challenge posed by Chinese NOCs to the interests of the longer-established international oil companies on the continent can only grow as China gains experience, contacts and technical expertise. Increasing competition for resources in Africa is a reality. However, with governments exercising restraint and

222 | China's African Challenges

maintaining dialogue among themselves, this competition need not bring either excessive tension or conflict. An inclusive and comprehensive framework within which players can manage their commercial rivalries while contributing to Africa's development will aid the emergence of sustainable relations between all involved.

Among the key issues that this framework will need to address is transparency. Low levels of transparency fuel suspicion – in a game without rules, or without trust that the rules are commonly respected, all sides are apt to think that they are the ones losing out. The propensity of Chinese firms and state agencies to indulge and even encourage corrupt practices is also a crucial issue because of the damage corruption causes to Africa's development. Another important aspect of any framework will be functioning multilateral bodies for addressing issues of common concern. A way will need to be found, for example, to bring China into the International Energy Agency, both in order to better coordinate approaches to resolving common concerns about access to supplies, and to protect the smooth functioning of the global oil market.[73] Where appropriate and possible, China will need to be persuaded to play a role in supporting and developing existing codes of conduct, such as the Extractive Industries Transparency Initiative. Established Western actors in Africa would also do well to seek out opportunities to engage China and other emergent powers through multilateral institutions concerned with questions of development, such as the G8, the World Bank and the OECD. New agreements, mandates for action and partnerships will need to be negotiated, most obviously between members of the OECD's Development Assistance Committee and current non-members, which include China and India. Several agencies and initiatives are already in place that could contribute to the development of an overarching cooperative framework for development, among them the Chinese-initiated International Poverty Reduction Centre, the African-initiated Comprehensive Africa Agricultural Development Programme, the UN-initiated ISO 14000 Environmental Management Standard and the World Bank-brokered Equator Principles. The difficulties sub-Saharan African countries are experiencing in making progress against the targets set out in the UN's Millennium Development Goals also represent an opportunity for collaboration and coordinated action by the West, China and Africa.

In all these efforts, it will be important for states to remember that there is – at least at present – no strategic reason for conflict to result from China's increasing African interests. The CCP has shown no sign of having an active agenda of limiting the West's access to resources in Africa or curtailing its influence there. The pressures and challenges the Party faces at home, rather than any attempts at a grand redesign of the global order, are likely to remain its priority for some time to come. The course that China's development has taken over the past decade has demonstrated to the country's leadership the advantages of moving away from a position of comparative isolation and self-reliance towards greater interdependence.[74] This is not to say that China does not seek greater international influence, particularly closer to home in Asia. If China effectively tackles the many domestic difficulties it faces and succeeds in translating its burgeoning economic influence into greater political power, there may well be challenges ahead, for example for the US in maintaining its interests and military posture in Asia. Nevertheless, while China may seek greater freedom of action, it does not appear to view such freedom as necessarily coming at the expense of the West's security or development. There is no reason for China's pursuit of resources in Africa to become a zero-sum game with the West, or indeed to suppose that China would view it in this way. Smart, nuanced diplomacy by

Western powers that engages both China and Africa on these issues should ensure that this continues to be the case.

Engaging China on Africa

Some efforts are already under way to engage emerging powers, chiefly China, on developing a cooperative framework capable of managing the pursuit of commercial and strategic interests in support of development agendas. The need, identified above, for China to be engaged in institutions such as the UN, the World Bank and the G8 on codes of conduct and similar issues is beginning to be met, with China participating in some discussions on the development of reasonable rules and standards for commercial and political engagement with the world's poorest continent. In 2005, the US initiated a US–China 'sub-dialogue' on Africa as part of its wider bilateral strategic dialogue with Beijing. Held at the level of assistant secretary of state, the dialogue is presented by the US as an attempt to engage China as a partner in Africa's development and limit the potential for counterproductive political competition. In early 2008, the US was reportedly attempting to instigate a bilateral dialogue with China on development assistance, although by the end of the year, no official public meeting had yet taken place.[75] In a visit to Beijing in October 2008, US Assistant Secretary of State for African Affairs Jendayi Frazer gave further indications of the US's preparedness to cooperate with China on African development, highlighting infrastructure and the agriculture and health sectors as possible areas for cooperation.[76] Since the EU–China summit of 2006, the EU has operated a 'structured dialogue' with China on African peace, stability and sustainable development, though the dialogue is currently less developed than its US equivalent.[77] In October 2008, the European Commission proposed strengthening cooperation between the EU and China on Africa by creating a trilateral dialogue between the EU, China and Africa.[78] While China makes clear that it signed the OECD Development Assistance Committee's Paris Declaration on Aid Effectiveness as a recipient rather than a donor, it has also been involved in follow-up deliberations on this declaration, attending the Accra High-Level Forum on Aid Effectiveness in September 2008.

Many of these coordinating initiatives are in their early stages, still advancing mutual understanding of respective operations and approaches rather than delivering concrete examples of coordination and cooperation. There is a danger that while such meetings are convening far from Africa in Western and Eastern capitals, Chinese activities on the ground in Africa will continue to follow a pattern of engagement that exacts too high a price in terms of Africa's medium-term development, exacerbating Western concerns about the 'rise' of China instead of easing them. However, while the difficult task of negotiating collaboration and codes of conduct goes on, smaller-scale engagements in the form of targeted collaborative projects in particular sectors are helping to add some practical substance to the rhetoric of partnership on development assistance. Such projects should contribute to mutual understanding and coordination. In early 2009, the UK government pledged £250,000 to support the CABC's efforts to encourage the development of Chinese private-sector interests in Africa, and a further £250,000 to support a project to develop a sustainable and environmentally sound timber trade between China and East Africa.[79] Later in the year, China and the UK are to co-host a conference that will bring together international agricultural experts and African state officials to consider opportunities for developing Africa's agricultural sector as part of a programme of collaboration on food security.[80] Western diplomatic missions to China are increasingly engaging China on Africa not only when contentious issues emerge in the UN Security Council, but more generally, to coordinate aid programmes and share ideas on development. Such interactions are important, as they give the lie to the belief that the involvement of more actors in Africa necessarily bodes ill for traditional powers. Yet more could be done. For instance, hospitals and agricultural research centres could be staffed with experts from China working alongside those from the West.

As negotiations and initiatives progress, it will be crucial for the key powers with interests in Africa to maintain communication, not just in order to develop a more coordinated approach to Africa's problems, but also to aid mutual understanding on sensitive issues. In the context of globalisation and the accompanying rise of transnational threats, the interests of foreign actors in Africa can run the risk of colliding. Some of China's commercial interests on the continent have at times threatened to interfere with the US's more security-focused concerns. This is most obviously the case in Sudan, but there have also been concerns elsewhere, for example in relation to neighbouring Eritrea. The US is concerned about a potential terrorist threat from Somalia, and is working closely with Ethiopia there in order to manage what is effectively a failed state. Meanwhile, Eritrea is accused by the US of giving shelter to the Somali Islamist insurgency group al-Shabab, which is on the US State Department list of terrorist organisations and has ties to al-Qaeda.[81] The US has imposed an arms embargo on Eritrea, and revived its threat to add the country to its list of state sponsors of terrorism. In addition, despite a 2008 decision to withdraw UN peacekeeping troops, Eritrea's border tensions with Ethiopia remain unresolved, and skirmishes have taken place on its border with Djibouti, which hosts US and French military bases and provides Ethiopia with access to the sea.

Against this backdrop of difficult US–Eritrean relations, diplomatically isolated Eritrea is attempting to cultivate a resources-based relationship with China. However, while it is understood to have some petroleum and natural-gas deposits, as well as reserves of gold and industrial metals, in particular zinc and copper, Eritrea has yet to confirm any reserves of strategic importance. This should mean that, at least for the time being, Chinese responses to its overtures are likely to remain only moderately enthusiastic. Nevertheless, some engagements have begun. In 2007, Eritrea's Ministry of Mines granted licences to a Chinese company to prospect for iron and base metals and a Chinese–Eritrean joint venture to prospect for gold and base metals.[82] In November 2008, the Eritrean minister of mines gave a presentation on the mineral potential of his country to a mining conference in Beijing. In bilateral meetings at the conference, China's minister of land and natural resources promised to encourage Chinese companies to invest in Eritrea, noting that a committee had already been established to oversee such cooperation.[83] In the same month, the administrators of China's Xinjiang region and Eritrea's Gash Barka region signed a memorandum of understanding in what Eritrea hopes is a prelude to increased cooperation.[84] In March 2009, a Chinese delegation headed by CADF Vice President Lu Qingcheng visited Eritrea to explore potential investment opportunities and was greeted by an enthusiastic Eritrean President Isaias Afwerki.[85] In situations such as this, where there is potential for Chinese commercial interests to come into conflict with US security interests, dialogue between the two powers will be particularly important.

If communication on these and other issues can be kept up, China's relationship with Africa could represent an opportunity, not just for Africa's development, but also for the development of relations between China and the West. However, if the West wishes to encourage a China that is at ease within the mainstream of international diplomatic, security and economic cooperation, it needs to be clear about what the challenges are, and focus on them accordingly. Where there are problems over, for example, respect for democracy, good governance and the rule of law, Western nations and agencies need to say so, safe in the knowledge that if they do so consistently and fairly, this is likely to impact on China's thinking. Furthermore, while China will listen to what others say, it will balance this listening with watching what others do. Any inconsistencies between the West's diplomatic messages to China about Sino-African relations and its own activities on the ground in Africa will be taken as proof that the West is merely engaged in a politically motivated campaign against the CCP and is seeking to secure an advantage for Western companies. If such mistakes are avoided, there is a reasonable chance that dialogue will result in some concrete gains, as China's foreign policy, despite its purported ideological basis, is made pragmatically in accordance with Beijing's economic and strategic requirements, with adaptations and compromises made in response to consistently asserted key external interests.

As the West pursues this dialogue, drawing in a still-reluctant and sometimes sceptical China nervous of giving up its credentials as a stalwart alternative power in the face of the West, it should remember that such engagement is a means to an end, rather than an end in itself. The purpose of engaging with China in this way is to minimise the likelihood of it partnering states that challenge the present international system, while also demonstrating that there is scope within the system for a power that was not one of its initial designers to become a leading player. Any engagement strategies should be constantly evaluated against these goals.

In addition to ensuring that what they practise is consistent with what they preach and dispassionately evaluating their chosen approaches to engagement, Western powers also need to recognise that there can be no room for any crisis of confidence. The West must acknowledge its role in previous policy failures in Africa while resisting the temptation to overcorrect. The overly strict conditions attached in the past to loans from Western-influenced international financial institutions may have been counterproductive, but conditionality is a sound principle at heart. For instance, the World Bank was right to work with Chad to develop the Chad–Cameroon Pipeline, but it was also right to terminate its involvement in the project in mid 2008, following the failure of repeated attempts to persuade the Chadian government to honour its agreement to allocate a sizeable percentage of the pipeline's profits to poverty-reduction programmes.[86] Likewise, while there is certainly room for the West to increase the provision of more readily accessible aid on flexible terms in some circumstances, on the whole, the advocacy of long-term investment in a country's development sets the right tone for the future. Infrastructure undeniably matters, but so does investment in capacity-building to support the rule of law, respect for human rights and the development of civil society. Of course the West will not always have the right answers to the question of how best to ensure the promotion of sustainable business practice and democratic institutions and habits. Reflection and self-scrutiny will be important, but so will confidence in its own values and a willingness to speak up on issues that matter. Policymakers and commentators will need to trust that it is better to run the risk of occasionally being branded as hypocritical than to be defeated by the complexities of the issues involved and retreat to a superficially convenient position of moral indifference.

Nevertheless, as the West and likeminded African nations seek to defend and promote certain values, they would do well to take a strategic approach. Formulaic expressions of support for the promotion of good governance, respect for human rights and democracy in Africa might be appropriate for the consumption of Western and some African media, but they are less likely to engage China. A strategy of engagement that bears in mind the CCP's position at home and puts the emphasis less on the ideological content of a given approach and more on the possible gains to be had from greater stability in Africa might yet elicit more constructive responses from Beijing.

Engaging Africa

Having taken some time to fully recognise the value of liaising with China on African issues, the West now needs to be careful not to allow a preoccupation with the question of how to productively engage with China to distract attention from its own African diplomacy. As well as working with China on Africa, Western powers need to stop neglecting their direct engagements with Africa, and more actively nurture their African partnerships. There is a particular need to curtail the widespread tendency among Western nations to send an excessive proportion of their best diplomats to Asia, leaving embassies in Africa largely in the care of aid officials and counter-terrorist experts. The West's foreign ministries must now examine their own political and commercial engagements in Africa as critically as they do China's. Moreover, when considering issues of coordination and partnership, the West needs to be careful not to neglect non-Western states that have interests in Africa and that share a commitment to good governance, human rights and political freedom. Japan's restructured International Cooperation Agency is now one of the world's largest aid agencies, with an annual budget of more than $10bn.[87] South Korea, like Japan, is seeking to play a more global role, and will join the OECD Development Assistance Committee in 2010. India is another secular democracy with a growing interest in Africa, hoping to raise its profile in the international community. Such countries are partners-in-waiting for the US and the EU, who could themselves do more to improve coordination with one another on these issues and deepen mutual understanding of their respective dialogues with China on Africa.

China's engagements in Africa have made the continent a focal point in the debate about the values and principles that should govern the behaviour of a twenty-first-century global power. In this context, the West will wish to continue to press its liberal, inclusive, interventionist agenda with Africa as well as China. While it seems probable that the Chinese state and Chinese companies will come to appreciate that the development of transparent legal and regulatory frameworks in Africa with serious enforcement capacities serves Chinese as well as African interests, it is crucial to recognise that the momentum for progress must come from Africa itself. However, though African civil society may be starting to provide greater oversight of China's African ventures, there are still serious political, economic and capacitive constraints on its ability to influence Chinese investment strategies. Furthermore, as long as some African governments pay only lip service to ideas of good governance, transparency and the rule of law, Chinese businesses and agencies cannot be relied upon to buck the trend. Other investors and partners in Africa's development therefore have an important role to play in influencing the evolution of Sino-African relations, whether they be governments hoping to sponsor African development and encourage China to become a responsible supporter of a liberal multilateral system in the process, businesses seeking to compete in an environment that is not increasingly corrupt, or civil-society organisations pursuing greater protection for individual rights and freedoms.

Western governments and civil societies, working with like-minded partners, can help to build the capacity of African civil societies and governments to keep their concerns about Chinese activities in focus until these are more thoroughly addressed by improved regulation and monitoring, or by strategic adjustments made by China itself. Assistance, both financial and technical, can be given to African governments to support the development of improved governance capacity, a tighter regulatory environment and mechanisms to support the rule of law, all of which should help countries secure better terms from Chinese commercial engagements and ensure that these terms are observed. Assistance can be given to civil-society organisations in areas such as networking, finance and media access. Assistance can also be given to African businesses to seek more skills and technology transfer and training within joint ventures, as well as greater openness on the part of Africa's trading partners – including Western ones – to African goods beyond raw natural resources. This kind of broad-ranging, inclusive support should help to ensure that China is a factor in Africa's greater progress, and not its greater corruption.

A cooperative and collaborative approach by the West towards the development of Sino-African relations is the approach most conducive to the positive evolution of these relations, on the West's as well as on China's and Africa's terms. The development of an agreed framework for engagement will also set the terms under which other emerging powers will pursue their interests in Africa and elsewhere. The success of such cooperative action will have positive implications for China's relations with the West, as much as it will for those with Africa and the broader developing world.

Conclusion

For much of 2008, then-presidential candidate Barack Obama's campaigning slogan of 'change' seemed to permeate politics both in the US and beyond. China's leaders must have found it difficult to empathise with establishment politicians in the US competing to declare themselves agents of change, for theirs is almost the opposite task. For them, the goal is to present an image of continuity, emphasising the legitimacy and stability of the CCP and its system as the Party embarks on its seventh decade in power, while simultaneously working discreetly to effect the practical changes that are needed to ensure that it does indeed hold on to power. There is no doubt that China's various Party and governmental institutions have been learning from the country's African engagements and absorbing direct and indirect feedback as they consider how to refine their activities on the continent. China will not be encouraging external examination of the mistakes it has made in Africa or the lessons it has learned there but, as we have seen, there are signs of changes being made. So far, these changes have looked more like cautious steps in the direction of accommodating Chinese policy in Africa to Western norms than attempts at moving Africa towards Chinese norms and away from the influence of the West.

It has been said that changes in policy usually come through exposure to new ideas and circumstances, proactive national or civil leadership, or the advent of crisis.[88] The exposure of China's leadership to challenges in Africa, and its recognition of these challenges and improved responses to them, have created a basis from which the leadership can make the further changes needed for more sustainable relations. Ensuring that China avoids the scenario whereby it takes a crisis to force these changes is in the interest not just of the CCP, but probably of Africa and the West as well.

In the pursuit of positive dynamics in the trilateral relationship between China, Africa and the West, all those involved could benefit from displaying greater maturity in their diplomacy. The false dichotomy of China as a threat versus China as a partner does not serve Western diplomacy well. Similarly,

China's posturing as a champion of the developing world – anyway increasingly untenable – remains an obstacle to the development of positive trilateral relations. Faced with the complexities of diverse engagements at myriad political, economic, social and cultural levels, it is important that diplomacy on all sides avoids the temptation to generalise or overstate. Discipline will be needed to ensure that the facts of the various interactions dictate any theories about motivations or implications, rather than the other way round.

This book has argued that while China's trade with Africa has undergone dramatic development, the political framework within which this trade takes place is still being fashioned. Western states have a crucial interest in how this framework turns out, and good diplomacy, not just with China but with other actors as well, should enable them to have significant influence over the outcome. In the course of this diplomacy, there should not be vacillation on core issues such as sustainable development, good governance, or the promotion of individual and political freedoms. However, it must also be emphasised that there is no inherent conflict between China's interests in Africa and development, good governance and democracy on the continent. Indeed, stronger African partners would both offer a more stable environment for China's investments and help China to address any problems that emerged in the course of its African ventures far more satisfactorily and sustainably than weaker and more acquiescent ones.

Put bluntly, the West has little alternative but to seek to encourage and support China through the challenges it faces in Africa. It should offer its support willingly and with good grace, mindful that the PRC's economic development and political stability to date have come from its participation and integration in the international system, and that this is recognised by the Chinese authorities, who are as a result likely to see a future within this system. Burgeoning Sino-African relationships and international responses to them offer a further opportunity to encourage China's development as a player within the established world order, rather than as a more aloof and restless power that might eventually seek to pursue its own arrangements. The prospect of a relative eastward shift of power and influence within the international community following Asia's economic rise is often viewed apprehensively in the West and elsewhere, as a potential impediment to the flourishing of liberal democratic societies. Yet sophisticated, balanced and well-reasoned diplomacy on issues such as the development of China's relations with Africa should play an important part in ensuring that, if such a shift does take place, any rewriting of the rules on what constitutes responsible global authority will not be too uncomfortably revisionist.

NOTES

Introduction

1. For more details see Karen Harris, 'Not a Chinaman's Chance: Chinese Labour in South Africa and the United States of America', *Historia*, vol. 52, no. 2, November 2006, pp. 177–97. See also Persia Campbell, *Chinese Coolie Immigration to Countries within the British Empire* (London: Frank Cass, 1971), Chapter 4, 'The Transvaal Experiment'.

2. This is also mentioned in Philip Snow's history of Sino-African relations, *The Star Raft* (London: Weidenfeld and Nicolson, 1988), p. 50.

3. Questions in the House, 'Rand Mines Strikes – Employment of Imperial Forces', *Hansard*, 27 May 1907, vol. 174, cols 1308–1312.

4. See 'The Hopeless Continent', the *Economist*'s controversial cover story for its 13–19 May 2000 edition.

5. Something in the region of $500bn is a generally agreed (very) approximate figure. Thompson Ayodele, Franklin Cudjoe, Temba Nolutshungu and Charles Sunwabe, for example, put the sum at $500bn between 1960 and 1997 in 'African Perspectives on Aid: Foreign Assistance Will Not Pull Africa Out of Poverty', Cato Institute Economic Development Bulletin, no. 2, 14 September 2005. Though no analyst posits a lower amount, some estimates go higher. The Heritage Foundation has used the OECD's International Development Statistics to show that $543,461bn (in 2003 dollars) went to sub-Saharan Africa in overseas development assistance between 1960 and 2003. Brett Schaefer, 'Promoting Economic Prosperity Through the Millennium Challenge Account', Heritage Lecture no. 920, 13 January 2006. Dambisa Moyo goes substantially higher, suggesting an expenditure of $1 trillion over the past 50 years; see 'Aid Dependency Blights Africa: The Cure is in the Credit Crisis', *Independent*, 2 February 2009. The poverty-level figure comes from Shaohua Chen and Martin Ravallion, 'The Developing World is Poorer Than We Thought, But No Less Successful in the Fight Against Poverty', World Bank Policy Research Working Paper WPS4703, 1 August 2008. For an overview of this report's conclusions, see: http://siteresources.worldbank.

org/DEC/Resources/Poverty-Brief-in-English.pdf.

6   United Nations World Food Programme, 'Executive Brief: Democratic Republic of Congo Comprehensive Food Security and Vulnerability Analysis 2007–2008', July 2008.

7   World Bank, 'Regional Fact Sheet From the World Development Indicators 2008: Sub-Saharan Africa', http://siteresources.worldbank.org/DATASTATISTICS/Resources/ssa_wdi.pdf.

8   'Economic Report on Africa 2008: Africa and the Monterrey Consensus: Tracking Performance and Progress', United Nations Economic Commission for Africa and the African Union, March 2008.

9   The January 2009 update to the International Monetary Fund's world economic forecast showed growth slowing dramatically across all regions. Nevertheless, Africa was still expected to enjoy an average GDP growth rate of 3.4% in 2009. International Monetary Fund, 'World Economic Outlook: Update', 28 January 2009, http://www.imf.org/external/pubs/ft/weo/2009/update/01/pdf/0109.pdf.

10 Wen Jiabao, setting out Chinese policy in the region in an address to the China–ASEAN Business and Investment Summit, 7 October 2003.

11 Chinese customs statistics show Sino-Latin American trade totalling $102.61bn in 2007. Cited in 'China has a Steadily Developing Relationship with the American and Oceanian Area in the 30 Years of Reform and Opening Up', Chinese Ministry of Commerce website, 25 December 2008, http://english.mofcom.gov.cn/aarticle/todayupdates/200812/20081205974087.html.

12 Geoffrey York, 'PNG and China's New Empire', Globe and Mail, 2 January 2009.

13 Richard Hass, 'The Age of Nonpolarity', Foreign Affairs, vol. 87, no. 3, May–June 2008.

14 Final report of the Africa–China–US Trilateral Dialogue, co-sponsored by the Brenthurst Foundation, the Chinese Academy of Social Sciences, the Council on Foreign Relations and the Leon H. Sullivan Foundation, December 2007.

15 The status of the former Spanish colony of Western Sahara remains unresolved. For those recognising the claims to independence of the Sahrawi Arab Democratic Republic (SADR), there are 54 states in Africa. The African Union (AU) has 53 member states, of which Western Sahara (SADR) is one, with Morocco the only African country not a member, having withdrawn from the AU's predecessor, the Organisation of African Unity, in protest at the SADR's recognition.

16 See World Bank, 'New Data Show 1.4 Billion Live on Less than US$1.25 a Day, but Progress Against Poverty Remains Strong', press release, 26 August 2008, http://web.worldbank.org/TOTEUOV4E0. The GDP ratio is based on nominal GDP figures, rather than purchasing-power-parity-adjusted GDP.

Chapter One

1 'Chinese President's Africa Tour Gives Fresh Impetus to Traditional Friendship', Xinhua, 17 February 2009. The article itself is a good example of the kind of rhetoric that surrounds Chinese engagements with Africa. For one of many further examples of this rhetoric, see the remarks made by Xu Jinghu, director of the Department of African Affairs in China's Ministry of Foreign Affairs, in a speech in 2004: 'Despite the geographical distance, China and Africa enjoy a time-honoured friendship. For years, the Chinese and African people have trusted, respected, sympathised with and supported each other, forging a profound friendship.' 'Talking Points of Madame Xu Jinghu, Director General of the Department of African Affairs of the MFA at the Briefing of the Secretariat of the Chinese Follow-up Committee of the FOCAC', 14 July 2004, FOCAC, http://www.focac.org/eng/hxxd/jzgz/t157596.htm.

2 Snow, *The Star Raft*, p. 54.

3 Giles Mohan with Dinar Kale, 'The Invisible Hand of South–South Globalisation: Chinese Migrants in Africa', report for the Rockefeller Foundation by the Open University, Development Policy and Practice Department, October 2007, p. 8.

4 Ian Taylor, *China and Africa: Engagement and Compromise* (Oxford and New York: Routledge, 2006), p. 16, quoting from the New China News Agency, 5 June 1965.

5 The Bandung Conference was co-sponsored by the governments of Burma, India, Indonesia, Pakistan and Ceylon (Sri Lanka) and was attended by delegates from 29 countries in Asia, Africa and the Middle East. The conference laid the foundations for the Non-Aligned Movement, promoting economic and cultural cooperation between participants on the basis of the rejection of colonialism and imperialism.

6 'The Second Upsurge in the Establishment of Diplomatic Relations', Ministry of Foreign Affairs of the People's Republic of China, 17 November 2000, http://www.fmprc.gov.cn/eng/ziliao/3602/3604/t18056.htm.

7 These countries were Egypt (which recognised the PRC in 1956), Ethiopia (which took until 1970) and Liberia (which waited until 1977). South Africa, which was also effectively independent at the time (though it would not officially become a republic until 1961), also refused to recognise the PRC.

8 He also visited three Asian countries on the same tour.

9 Lin Biao, 'Long Live the Victory of People's War', Chapter 8, 'Defeat US Imperialism and its Lackeys by People's War', 3 September 1965. The essay can be read in translation at http://www.marxists.org/reference/archive/lin-biao/1965/09/peoples_war/index.htm.

10 Taylor, *China and Africa: Engagement and Compromise*, pp. 32–3.

11 *Ibid.*, p. 33.

12 UN General Assembly Resolution 2758, 25 October 1971. Text available at http://www.undemocracy.com/A-RES-2758(XXVI)/page_1/rect_485,223_914,684.

13 Deng Xiaoping made the claim that, no matter what happened, China

would never be a superpower in a speech to the United Nations in April 1974 expounding Mao's 'three worlds' theory. Deng Xiaoping, 'Chairman Mao Zedong's Theory on the Division of the Three Worlds and the Strategy of Forming an Alliance Against an Opponent', available from the Chinese Ministry of Foreign Affairs, http://www.fmprc.gov.cn/eng/ziliao/3602/3604/t18008.htm. The claim that China seeks neither international hegemony nor expansion has been consistently repeated since, featuring for example in Hu Jintao's report to the 17th National Congress of the CCP in 2007 and in Wen Jiabao's speech to the UN General Assembly in 2008.

[14] See, for example, Gerald Segal, 'China and Africa', *Annals of the American Academy of Political and Social Sciences*, vol. 519, no. 1, January 1992.

[15] Taylor, *China and Africa: Engagement and Compromise*, p. 37.

[16] Deborah Brautigam, *Chinese Aid and African Development: Exporting Green Revolution* (Basingstoke and New York: Macmillan and St Martin's Press, 1998), p. 4.

[17] Taylor, 'China's Foreign Policy Towards Africa in the 1990s', *Journal of Modern African Studies*, vol. 26, no. 3, September 1998, pp. 443–60.

[18] Taylor, *China and Africa: Engagement and Compromise*, p. 60. Taylor also cites a May 1985 *People's Daily* article criticising developing-world 'errors in policymaking' as a sign of the extent to which Beijing was distancing itself from Africa around this time.

[19] He Wenping, 'Moving Forward with the Time: The Evolution of China's Africa Policy', paper presented for 'China–Africa Relations: Engaging the International Discourse' workshop, Hong Kong University of Science and Technology, 11–12 November 2006, p. 7.

[20] Brautigam, 'China's African Aid: Transatlantic Challenges', report to the German Marshall Fund of the United States, April 2008, p. 11.

[21] Chris Alden and Ana Cristina Alves, 'History and Identity in the Construction of China's Africa Policy', *Review of African Political Economy*, vol. 35, no. 1, March 2008, p. 54.

[22] The full text of 'China's African Policy' can be found on the website of the Chinese government: http://www.gov.cn/misc/2006-01/12/content_156490.htm.

[23] 'Chinese President Delivers Keynote Speech on China–Africa Ties', Xinhua, 16 February 2009.

[24] Of course there are important differences between these diasporas and the Chinese population in Africa, not least the fact that most ethnic Chinese in Southeast Asia and the US will have taken citizenship or been born citizens in the countries in which they live. The Chinese diaspora is estimated to number between 35m and 40m globally.

[25] Notwithstanding these developments, air links between China and Africa still have considerable growth potential. While some routes are served by African airlines (if still mainly indirectly), at the end of 2008 there were still no Chinese airlines offering non-stop flights from China to any African cities. China Southern flew to Lagos via Dubai and to Monrovia via Urumqi and Paris, and Hainan Airlines flew to Luanda via Dubai.

[26] 'Sino-African Trade Passes $100 bln Mark in 2008', Xinhua, 27 January 2009.

27 Brautigam, 'China's African Aid: Transatlantic Challenges', p. 13.

28 According to Commerce Minister Chen Deming, quoted in 'China's Eight-Measure Economic Policy on Africa Well-Implemented', Xinhua, 20 January 2009.

29 'Angola China's Largest African Trade Partner', Xinhua, 19 January 2009.

30 The deal involved the China Railway Group, Asia's largest construction company, and Sinohydro Corporation. William Wallis, 'Congo Outlines $9bn China Deal', *Financial Times*, 9 May 2008.

31 Data from the governor of Katanga province, quoted in Simon Clark, Michael Smith and Franz Wild, 'China Lets Child Workers Die Digging in Congo Mines for Copper', Bloomberg, 23 July 2008.

32 Accusations from Western commentators that China is indulging in colonialist behaviour are too numerous to be listed. In December 2006, South African President Thabo Mbeki also uttered the 'c' word, in reference to what he saw as the dangers of Beijing's African engagements, reportedly prompting a severe reprimand on his next visit to Beijing. Billionaire financier George Soros made a similar accusation during a February 2008 visit to Senegal.

33 Chris Alden, 'China in Africa', *Survival*, vol. 47, no. 3, Autumn 2005, p. 151.

34 China's ambassador to Ghana, Yu Wenzhe, cited these figures and projects at the seventh-anniversary celebrations of the first meeting of FOCAC. 'China to Encourage Credible Investment in Ghana: Ambassador', report posted on the website of the Ghanaian government, 9 November 2007, http://www.ghana.gov.gh/ghana/ china_encourage_credible_investment _ghana_ambassador.jsp.

35 Vivien Foster, William Butterfield, Chuan Chen and Nataliya Pushak, 'Building Bridges: China's Growing Role as Infrastructure Financier for Sub-Saharan Africa', World Bank Report, July 2008, p. 8.

36 *Ibid.*, pp. vii–viii.

37 The implication that China has little interest in these countries' resources was rather disingenuous, however. Although not classically resource-rich, Tanzania and Mali do possess major gold deposits, and Senegal, which has iron-ore deposits, is also enjoying an increasing profile in the gold sector. Sinopec is prospecting for oil in northern Mali, while Chinese companies also have substantial interests in neighbouring landlocked Niger, giving China further reason to cultivate good relations with neighbouring transit countries.

38 Leni Wild and David Mepham (eds), 'The New Sinosphere: China in Africa', Institute for Public Policy Research, November 2006, p. 2.

39 As former US diplomat David Shinn noted in his written testimony to the US–China Economic and Security Review Commission of 21–22 July 2005, the PRC has an embassy on the Comoros Islands. The US does not; it manages its interests from Madagascar.

40 Hannah Edinger and Ruth Roberts, 'Premier Wen Jiabao's Seven-Nation Africa Tour', *China Monitor*, University of Stellenbosch Centre for Chinese Studies, July 2006.

41 As noted in the Introduction, the January 2009 update of the International Monetary Fund's World Economic Outlook predicted a growth

rate for Africa of 3.4% in 2009 (down from a prediction of 4.7% less than three months earlier). Sub-Saharan Africa was predicted to grow by 3.5%. The same update revised China's projected rate of growth in 2009 down to 6.7%, from 9% in October 2008. International Monetary Fund, 'World Economic Outlook: Update', 28 January 2009. Some commodities will be more recession-proof than others. For example, China's demand for copper should increase, as the government continues with its plans to expand the country's electricity-distribution network. The recession's impact on African countries will be uneven, and linked in part to the composition of each individual country's export basket. Such realities make any predictions of 'Africa's growth rate' somewhat meaningless.

42 Jeffrey Herbst and Greg Mills, 'Tough Lessons for Africa as Downturn Hits Home', *Business Day*, 8 January 2009.

43 'Beijing Says Global Crisis Risks China–Africa Trade', Reuters, 9 October 2008.

44 Wang Xing, 'China Union to Invest 2.6bn in Liberia's Iron Ore Mine', *China Daily*, 8 December 2008.

45 Li Xing, 'China Pledges to Increase Aid to Africa', *China Daily*, 13 February 2009.

46 Raphael Kaplinsky, Dorothy McCormick and Mike Morris, 'The Impact of China on Sub-Saharan Africa', Institute of Development Studies, Working Paper 291, November 2007, p. 14.

47 Foster, Butterfield, Chen and Pushak, 'Building Bridges: China's Growing Role as Infrastructure Financier for Sub-Saharan Africa', p. ix.

48 Two examples of Chinese interests in South African mining are the 2006 acquisition by Chinese goldmining company Zijin Mining of a 20% stake in South African platinum producer Ridge Mining, and Sinosteel's 2008 additional investment of $400m in the Sino-South African joint venture ASA Metals.

49 Figures from Trade Law Centre for Southern Africa's 2009 spreadsheet on 'Africa's Trading Relationship with China', based on data from Chinese customs. Accessible at http://www. tralac.org/cgi-bin/giga.cgi?cmd= cause_dir_news&cat=1044&cause_ id=1694.

50 Wallis, 'Drawing Contours of a New World Order', *Financial Times*, 24 January 2008.

51 David Zweig and Bi Jinhai, 'China's Global Hunt for Energy', *Foreign Affairs*, vol. 84, no. 5, September–October 2005, pp. 25–38.

52 Wang Jisi, 'Views on Devising International Strategy', published (in Chinese) in Shanghai newspaper *Dongfang Zaobao*, 10 January 2008.

53 'China's National Energy Strategy and Policy 2000–2020', Development Research Centre of the State Council, November 2003, p. 24. For the full original document see http://www.efchina. org/csepupfiles/report/2006102695218 495.5347708042717.pdf/Draft_Natl_E_ Plan0311.pdf. Also cited in Jonathan Holslag, Gustaaf Geeraerts, Jan Gorus and Stefan Smis, 'China's Resources and Energy Policy in Sub-Saharan Africa', report for the Development Committee of the European Parliament, 19 March 2007, p. 9.

54 Barry Sautman, 'Friends and Interests: China's Distinctive Links with Africa', Hong Kong University of Science and Technology, Centre on China's Transnational Relations, Working Paper no. 12, 2007, p. 7.

55 Foster, Butterfield, Chen and Pushak, 'Building Bridges: China's Growing Role as Infrastructure Financier for Sub-Saharan Africa', p. ix.

56 'CNOOC Seeks Expansion in Africa', *China Daily*, 20 July 2006.

57 Peter Goodman, 'China Invests Heavily in Sudan's Oil Industry', *Washington Post*, 23 December 2004, quoting Chen Fengying of the China Institute for Contemporary International Relations.

58 Holslag, Geeraerts, Gorus and Smis, 'China's Resources and Energy Policy in Sub-Saharan Africa', p. 36.

59 Foster, Butterfield, Chen and Pushak, 'Building Bridges: China's Growing Role as Infrastructure Financier for Sub-Saharan Africa', p. 18. The initial consortium broke up as a result of tensions between the firms, which culminated in CMEC and the Brazilian firm submitting separate bids. CMEC won with a more favourable bid, particularly with regard to infrastructure (it included 500km of new railway, rather than a 200km extension of an existing railway, financial guarantees, and a commitment to purchase the entire output), aided by the support of President Hu Jintao. 'China Given Monopoly to Work Gabon's Untapped Oil Resources', *Business Report*, 3 June 2006.

60 'China Firm to Develop Iron Ore Project in Africa', *China Daily*, 9 July 2008.

61 For more on this topic, see the website of the NGO International Rivers, under 'Belinga Dam, Gabon', http://www. internationalrivers.org/en/africa/ belinga-dam-gabon.

62 More than half of China's wheat and a third of its corn is grown on these plains. Michael Richardson, 'Water Crisis Plumbs New Depths', *Straits Times*, 14 August 2008. Still, China has enjoyed over 95% self-sufficiency in grain over the past ten years. 'China 95% Self-Sufficient in Grain Last Ten Years', Xinhua, 4 July 2008.

63 Jamil Anderlini, 'China Eyes Overseas Land in Food Push', *Financial Times*, 8 May 2008.

64 'The Sixth Senior Officials Meeting of the FOCAC is Held in Cairo', Chinese Ministry of Foreign Affairs website, 22 October 2008, http://www.fmprc.gov. cn/eng/zxxx/t518952.htm.

65 There is still some confusion over the nature of any deals agreed with the government of Mozambique, despite unconfirmed reports of a July 2007 memorandum of understanding to allow 3,000 Chinese settlers to run farms in Mozambique's Zambezia and Tete provinces. What is clear is that China is heavily engaged in a project to increase Mozambique's agricultural production, with more than a hundred Chinese experts present in the country, and an announcement in early 2008 that China would be helping to boost Mozambique's rice production fivefold over the next five years. For more details, see Loro Horta, 'The Zambezi Valley: China's First Agricultural Colony?', Centre for Strategic and International Studies, Africa Policy Forum (online), 9 June 2008.

66 It is not only Chinese firms that are interested in Angola's farming potential. The London-listed pan-African investment company Lonrho has announced an intention to acquire as much as 200,000 hectares of agricultural land in Africa. See Tom Burgis, 'Angola Launches US$6 Billion Agricultural Expansion', *Financial Times*, 4 October 2008.

67 Under a 1959 bilateral agreement with Sudan concluded in preparation for the construction of the Aswan Dam, Egypt lays claim to the great majority of the Nile's waters. An important flaw in the generally thorough 1959 agreement was the failure of the parties to include or even consult Ethiopia, with no water allotted for upstream use by any country except Sudan. If Ethiopia were, for example, to try to construct a dam across the Blue Nile to improve its own water access and agricultural potential, there could be serious political consequences.

68 Javier Blass and Andrew England, 'Foreign Fields: Rich States Look Beyond their Borders for Fertile Soil', *Financial Times*, 19 August 2008.

69 Foster, Butterfield, Chen and Pushak, 'Building Bridges: China's Growing Role as Infrastructure Financier for Sub-Saharan Africa', p. vi.

70 'Mozambique: China has Created over 11,000 Jobs since 1990', MacauHub, 5 May 2008.

71 While Africa supplies China with a third of its crude-oil imports, Africa accounts for only around 3% of China's export market.

72 For an example of this argument see Bill Durodie, 'China and Africa: A Rewarding Relationship', *The Times*, 16 July 2008. Durodie remarks that 'China's presence [in Africa] is a sign of its weakness, not its strength'.

73 As, for example, in the author's interview with a Chinese Academy of Social Sciences scholar, Beijing, 10 March 2008.

74 'China Interferes in 1st African Summit in Taiwan: Chen', *Asian Political News*, 15 September 2007.

75 Allen Whiting is one scholar who has highlighted the importance of Tiananmen in the reassessment of China's foreign relations. See his 'Chinese Foreign Policy Futures', in David Lampton and Alfred Wilhelm (eds), *United States and China Relations at a Crossroads* (Lanham, MD, and London: University Press of America, 1995), p. 59.

76 The US–Australia declaration can be read at http://www.shaps.hawaii.edu/fp/australia/us_au_joint_statement.html, and the US–Japan declaration at http://www.mofa.go.jp/region/n-america/us/security/security.html.

77 Bates Gill, *Rising Star: China's New Security Diplomacy* (Washington DC: Brookings Institution Press, 2007).

78 He Wenping, 'The Balancing Act of China's Africa Policy', *China Security*, vol. 3, no. 3, Summer 2007, p. 27.

79 Drew Thompson, 'Economic Growth and Soft Power: China's Africa Strategy', *China Brief*, vol. 4, no. 24, 7 December 2004.

80 Mark Leonard, 'China's New Intelligentsia', *Prospect*, March 2008.

81 He, 'The Balancing Act of China's Africa Policy', p. 27.

82 For an extension of this argument and comparative figures, see Firoze Manji, 'China Still a Small Player on the Continent', Pambazuka News, 27 March 2008.

83 Foster, Butterfield, Chen and Pushak, 'Building Bridges: China's Growing Role as Infrastructure Financier for Sub-Saharan Africa', p. ix.

84 Erica Downs, 'The Fact and Fiction of Sino-African Energy Relations', *China Security*, vol. 3, no. 3, Summer 2007, p. 45.

85 *Ibid.*, p. 44, quoting figures from Wood Mackenzie energy consultancy from March 2007.

86 'Hu Calls on China, South Korea to Strengthen Economic Cooperation',

Xinhua, 26 August 2008. My thanks to Chris Burke of the University of Stellenbosch Centre for Chinese Studies for drawing my attention to this point.

87 Joint UNCTAD and United Nations Development Programme report, 'Asian Foreign Direct Investment in Africa: Towards a New Era of Cooperation Among Developing Countries', UNCTAD Current Studies on FDI and Development, no. 3, 1 February 2007, p. 2.

88 International Energy Agency, 'World Energy Outlook 2007'. Highlights of this report are given in Fatih Birol, 'World Energy Outlook 2007: China and India Insights', on the website of the Climate Action Programme, 23 November 2007, http://www.climateactionprogramme.org/features/article/world_energy_outlook_2007_china_and_india_insights/.

89 Zhiming Zhao, Executive President of the China Petroleum and Petrochemical Industry Association. Wendell Roelf, 'China Wants 40 pct of Oil/Gas Imports from Africa', Reuters, 17 March 2008.

90 National Intelligence Council, 'External Relations and Africa', discussion paper (marked 'for discussion only, not representing views of US gov'), 16 March 2004, http://www.dni.gov/nic/PDF_GIF_2020_Support/2004_03_16_papers/external_relations.pdf.

91 Jean-Christophe Servant, 'China's Trade Safari in Africa', *Le Monde Diplomatique*, May 2005.

92 Harry Broadman, 'China and India Go to Africa', *Foreign Affairs,* vol. 87, no. 2, March–April 2008, p. 95.

93 'Remarks by Foreign Minister Yang Jiechi at the First Political Consultation Between the Foreign Ministers of China and African Countries', UN General Assembly, 26 September 2007, available on the website of the Permanent Mission of the PRC to the UN, http://www.fmprc.gov.cn/ce/ceun/eng/xw/t367082.htm.

94 Chen and Ravallion, 'The Developing World is Poorer than We Thought, But No Less Successful in the Fight Against Poverty', p. 25. China reduced the number of its citizens living below the poverty line from 835m in 1981 to 207m in 2005, while the number of Africans living below the poverty line increased from 200m in 1981 to 380m in 2005. The poor statistics on Africa are partly due to population increase.

95 For details of the centre's activities, see its website: http://www.iprcc.org.cn/index.php/en.

96 'Current Status of and Future Prospects for Sino-African Cooperation', report by Horizon Research Consultancy Group, September 2007.

97 Snow, *The Star Raft*, p. 154.

98 'Tazara on the Brink of Collapse', *Lusaka Times,* 29 October 2008.

99 'Save the "Uhuru Railway" from Collapse', *This Day,* 31 October 2008.

Chapter Two

1 For a more detailed look at CNPC's early activities abroad, see Downs, 'The Brookings Foreign Policy Studies Energy Security Series: China', Brookings Institution, December 2006, pp. 38–9.

2 See Garth Shelton, 'China, Africa and South Africa: Advancing South–South Co-operation', in Atilio Boron and Gladys Lechini (eds), *Politics and Social Movement in a Hegemonic World: Lessons from Africa, Asia, and Latin America* (Buenos Aires: Consejo Latinoamericano de Ciencias Sociales, June 2005), http://bibliotecavirtual. clacso.org.ar/ar/libros/sursur/politics/ Shelton, pp. 347–83.

3 Shelton, 'China and Africa: Building an Economic Partnership', *South African Journal of International Affairs*, vol. 8, no. 2, Winter 2001.

4 For historical detail on the evolving relationships between Chinese NOCs and the PRC, see Ma Xin and Philip Andrews-Speed, 'The Overseas Activities of China's National Oil Companies', *Minerals & Energy – Raw Materials Report*, vol. 21, no. 1, March 2006, pp. 17–30.

5 'PetroChina Becomes World's Largest Listed Company', Xinhua, 5 November 2007.

6 Deborah Orr and Scott DeCarlo, 'The Asian Fab 50', Forbes.com, 9 March 2008, http://www.forbes. com/2008/09/03/asian-fab-50-biz-asiafab08-cx_do_sd_0903fab50_land. html.

7 Jonathan Woetzel, 'Reassessing China's State-owned Enterprises', *McKinsey Quarterly*, July 2008. Huawei is officially a private company, but the connections of its founder, Ren Zhengfei, were enough to derail a proposed tie-up with US telecoms provider 3Com on grounds of US national security. Ren is a former low-ranking PLA officer. Huawei officially acknowledges the PLA as a client, but no more than that.

8 'Wired for Growth', *Africa-Asia Confidential*, July 2008, vol. 1, no. 9, p. 3. See also ZTE's website: http://wwwen. zte.com.cn/.

9 'China's African Policy'.

10 Report of the Secretariat of the Follow-up Committee on FOCAC, 2007.

11 In early 2009, the NDRC comprised 31 departments, bureaus, offices and administrations and employed around 1,000 staff.

12 Downs, 'The Brookings Foreign Policy Studies Energy Security Series: China', p. 40.

13 For more details, see SASAC's website: http://www.sasac.gov.cn/n1180/index. html.

14 See 'Current Status of and Future Prospects for Sino-African Cooperation', Horizon Research Consultancy Group report, September 2007.

15 China ExIm's 2006 annual report is available at http://english.eximbank. gov.cn/annual/2006.pdf.

16 One Chinese academic engaged in the study of China's energy security has suggested that the department has as few as 38 personnel. Interview, Singapore, 11 August 2008.

17 The 2009 target was cited by Commerce Minister Chen Deming in an interview with Xinhua. 'China's Eight-Measure Economic Policy on Africa Well-Implemented'.

18 For more on Chinese aid to Africa, see Dorothy McCormick, 'China and India

as Africa's New Donors: The Impact of Aid on Development', *Review of African Political Economy*, vol. 35, no. 1, March 2008, pp. 73–92; Martyn Davies, 'How China Delivers Development Assistance to Africa', University of Stellenbosch Centre for Chinese Studies, February 2008; Kaplinsky, McCormick and Morris, 'The Impact of China on Sub-Saharan Africa'; and Brautigam, 'China's African Aid: Transatlantic Challenges'.

19 Karby Leggett, 'China Flexes Economic Muscles Throughout Burgeoning Africa', *Wall Street Journal*, 29 March 2005, http://forums.yellowworld.org/showthread.phl?t=22911.

20 James Reilly and Wu Na, 'China's Corporate Engagement in Africa', in Marcel Kitissou (ed.), *Africa in China's Global Strategy* (London: Adonis and Abbey, July 2007), p. 132.

21 Bates Gill and James Reilly outline this juggernaut in 'The Tenuous Hold of China Inc. in Africa', *Washington Quarterly*, vol. 30, no. 3, Summer 2007.

22 Woetzel, 'Reassessing China's State-owned Enterprises'.

23 Interview, Beijing, 17 August 2008.

24 The Action Plan for FOCAC 2006 recognised a deficit of private Chinese commercial engagements in Africa, and stated the intention to 'strengthen cooperation among small and medium-sized enterprises'. See 'Forum for China–Africa Cooperation Action Plan', 16 November 2006, http://www.fmprc.gov.cn/zflt/eng/zyzl/hywj/t280369.htm.

25 'CPC Delegation Leaves for Visit to Three African Nations', International Department website, 18 July 2008, http://www.idcpc.org.cn/english/news/080718-4.htm.

26 There have been reports to suggest that Chinese military sales to Africa may now be picking up again. See Andrei Chang, 'China Expanding African Arms Sales', UPI Asia Online, 26 January 2009.

27 Details of these organisations can be found on the FOCAC website: http://english.focacsummit.org/2006-09/21/content_817.htm.

28 For details of the structures involved, see Peter Cheung and James Tang, 'The External Relations of China's Provinces', in David Lampton, *The Making of Chinese Foreign Policy and Security Policy in the Era of Reform* (Palo Alto, CA: Stanford University Press, 2000), pp. 91–123.

29 Broadman, *Africa's Silk Road: China and India's New Economic Frontier* (Washington DC: World Bank, 2007), p. 305.

30 Holslag, Geeraerts, Gorus and Smis, 'China's Resources and Energy Policy in Sub-Saharan Africa', p. 13.

31 The careful calibration of relations with provincial authorities and agencies is not a new challenge for Beijing. After 1978, when 'township and village enterprises' were first given the freedom to establish businesses without central-government approval, business successes quickly brought these enterprises considerable power. Since then, Beijing has been grappling with the task of negotiating the limits of provincial control.

32 China ExIm was one of the three original state 'policy banks'. Whereas one of these, CDB, is now transitioning to commercial status, China ExIm remains under full state control, though its long-term future probably lies in a similar transition.

33 Foster, Butterfield, Chen and Pushak, 'Building Bridges: China's Growing Role as Infrastructure Financier for Sub-Saharan Africa', p. x.

34 'Brief Introduction', http://english. eximbank.gov.cn/profile/introduction. jsp.

35 Standard and Poor, 'Export–Import Bank of China: Bank Credit Report', 10 August 2006.

36 'China Pledges US$20 Billion for Africa', *Financial Times*, 17 May 2007. ExIm's website has reported that loans to Africa accounted for around 20% of the bank's total loan book by June 2007. 'The Export–Import Bank of China Hosted a Symposium on Financing and Project Cooperation in Africa', press release, 24 July 2007, http:// english.eximbank.gov.cn/info/Article. jsp?a_no=2001&col_no=84. According to Martyn Davies, the proportion is closer to 40%. 'How China Delivers Development Assistance to Africa', p. 7.

37 Statement by CDB Vice Governor Gao Jian, 'China Approves China–Africa Development Fund', *China Daily*, 14 May 2007.

38 'China Development Bank, PTA Bank Sign 50 Mln USD Credit Agreement', Xinhua, 15 August 2008.

39 In late 2007, the CIC promised $20bn to help CDB become a more commercially oriented bank. The State Council approved the plan in March 2008. See Anderlini, 'Beijing Clears Way for CDB to Go Commercial', *Financial Times*, 3 March 2008.

40 Repayment periods can be extended to ten years. For detailed investment terms and conditions, see the fund's website: http://www.cadfund.com/en/ Column.asp?ColumnId=76.

41 Mao Lijun, 'Development Fund Signs First Deal in Africa', *China Daily*, 16 January 2008.

42 Commerce Minister Chen Deming, quoted in 'China's Eight-Measure Economic Policy on Africa Well-Implemented'.

43 Quoted in *Caijing* magazine, 26 July 2007, article reproduced on Africa-Invest.net, http://www.invest.net.cn/ en/News/ShowInfo2.aspx?ID=3094.

44 Anderlini, 'Beijing's Shadowy Pool for Buying up Best Assets', *Financial Times*, 12 September 2008.

45 Of the African countries recognising the PRC, only Somalia does not host a Chinese embassy.

46 Christopher Burke, Lucy Corkin and Nastasya Tay, 'China's Engagement of Africa: Preliminary Scoping of African Case Studies', University of Stellenbosch Centre for Chinese Studies, November 2007, p. 161.

47 Alec Russell and William Wallis, 'Efforts to Redress Bad-Boy Perceptions', *Financial Times*, 24 January 2008. South Africa alone has 11 official languages (Afrikaans, English, Ndebele, Northern Sotho, Southern Sotho, Swati, Tsonga, Tswana, Venda, Xhosa and Zulu).

48 Interview, Beijing, 22 November 2008. The interviewee expressing these views was talking about Zambia, where competition between Chinese businessmen engaged in the mining industry has become particularly fierce. Some have even referred to the groups competing for mineral rights as 'gangs'.

49 For details on these zones, see 'Construction of China–Africa Economic Cooperation Zones Proceeds Smoothly', *People's Daily*, 21 January 2009.

50 For details of the initial agreement, see 'Cabinet Decisions, 10 November 2006' on the website of the government of Mauritius, http://www.gov.mu.

51 Mikaili Sseppuya, 'Chinese Firm to Build Rakai Free Trade Zone', *New Vision*, 7 September 2008.

52 'Declaration of the Beijing Summit of the Forum on China–Africa Cooperation', 5 November 2006, http://www.bjreview.com.cn/document/txt/2006-12/14/content_50703.htm.

53 'Exclusive Interview Given by State Councillor Tang Jiaxuan to Xinhua News Agency', Xinhua, 23 October 2006, available at http://jm.china-embassy.org/eng/xw/t277496.htm.

54 Interview, Beijing, 13 August 2008.

55 Ana Cristina Alves, 'China's Economic Diplomacy in Africa: The Lusophone Strategy', in Chris Alden, Daniel Large and Ricardo Soares de Oliveira (eds), *China Returns to Africa: A Continent and a Superpower Embrace* (London: C. Hurst and Co., 2008), p. 76.

56 See 'Full Text of Joint Communiqué of Sino-African Ministerial Political Consultations', FOCAC website, 27 September 2007, http://www.focac.org/eng/zxxx/t367207.htm.

57 'China Shares Poverty Reduction Experience with Africa', Xinhua, 20 May 2008.

58 Liu Haifang, 'China–Africa Relations through the Prism of Culture: The Dynamics of Africa's Cultural Diplomacy', seminar paper, Institute of Social Studies (The Hague), 2008, p. 12.

59 Quoted in Nicolai Volland, 'Boss Hu and the Press', *The China Beat* (blog), 30 June 2008, http://thechinabeat.blogspot.com/2008/06/boss-hu-and-press.html.

60 Anderlini, 'Secretive Beijing Agency Uses Forex Reserves to Target Taiwan', *Financial Times*, 12 September 2008.

61 'Chinese President Delivers Keynote Speech on China–Africa Ties'.

62 'Costa Rica Gets Confucius Institute', *China Daily*, 19 November 2008.

63 Though there were already two Chinese cultural centres on the continent, established in 1988 in Benin and Mauritius.

64 According to an article in Xinhua, the Chinese government allocated more than $3m to establish 21 institutes in Africa by October 2008 (a target it missed), employ language teachers and purchase textbooks and audio programmes. 'Confucius Institutes Help Promote Exchange, Co-op Between China and African Countries, Educators', Xinhua, 8 October 2008. February 2009 figures from the Confucius Institute Online. For further details on the evolution of the Confucius Institutes in Africa, see Liu, 'China–Africa Relations through the Prism of Culture: The Dynamics of Africa's Cultural Diplomacy'.

65 Bjorn Brandtzaeg, He Wenping, Chibuzo Nwoke, Anna Eriksson and Osita Agbu, 'Common Cause, Different Approaches: China and Norway in Nigeria', report by Econ Pöyry, Chinese Academy of Social Sciences Institute of West Asian and African Affairs and the Nigerian Institute of International Affairs, 27 February 2008, p. 15.

66 Downs, 'The Brookings Foreign Policy Studies Energy Security Series: China', p. 39.

67 Wen Jiabao, address to the annual meeting of the African Development Bank, Shanghai, 16 May 2007, available on the Ministry of Foreign Affairs website, http://www.fmprc.gov.cn/eng/wjdt/zyjh/t320959.htm.

68 Kerry Brown, *Struggling Giant* (London and New York: Anthem Press, 2007), p. 50.

69 Presumably, Zhou's presence on the standing committee will have some effect on the committee's reflections on China's investments in Sudan and

their contribution to national energy security.

70 Illustrating his own ongoing interest in energy policy, in 2008 Jiang himself published a paper on the subject. Jiang Zemin, 'Reflections on Energy Issues in China', *Journal of Shanghai Jiaotong University*, vol. 13, no. 3, June 2008, pp. 254–74.

71 See the press release on China ExIm's website, 'The Export–Import Bank of China Hosted a Symposium on Financing and Project Cooperation in Africa'.

72 Interview, London, September 2007.

73 Interview, Beijing, 15 January 2008.

Chapter Three

1 Chris Alden calls FOCAC 2006 'the end of a decade-long effort of Chinese expansion into the continent' in *China in Africa* (London and New York: Zed Books, 2007), p. 120.

2 See for example the response of President Abdoulaye Wade of Senegal to US concerns about China expressed in 2006: 'Do you think we are children?' Cited in Abdoulaye Dukulé, 'Africa Between China and the West: The New War of Influence', *The Perspective*, 24 November 2006, http://www.theperspective.org/articles/1124200601.html.

3 Abdoulaye Wade, 'Time for the West to Practise What it Preaches', *Financial Times*, 23 January 2008.

4 Meles Zenawi, speaking shortly before the Beijing FOCAC meeting, 16 October 2006. Cited in Kenneth King, 'Aid Within the Wider China–Africa Partnership: A View from the Beijing Summit', paper presented to the China–Africa Links Workshop, Hong Kong University of Science and Technology, 11–12 November 2006, p. 4.

5 'KingJaja', in exchange with Guy de Jonquieres, 'First Drafts' (*Prospect* blog), 6 March 2008. http://blog.prospectblogs.com/2008/02/27/prospects-new-issue-how-china-thinks/.

6 Howard French, 'China in Africa: All Trade, with No Political Baggage', *New York Times*, 8 August 2004.

7 Philippe Maystadt, quoted in George Parker and Alan Beattie, 'EIB Accuses China of Unscrupulous Loans', *Financial Times*, 28 November 2006.

8 'Baseline Study of Labour Practices on Large Construction Sites in the Republic of Tanzania', International Labour Organisation, Sectoral Activities Programme, Working Paper 225, January 2005, p. 10.

9 See, for example, Shapi Shacinda, 'Workers Strike at Zambian Cobalt Producer, Chambishi', Reuters, 26 July 2007; Shacinda, 'Workers at Zambia's Chambishi Smelter Striking Over Pay', Reuters, 3 March 2008.

10 Interview with African journalist, Beijing, 21 November 2008.

11 Peter Bosshard, 'China's Environmental Footprint in Africa', South African Institute of International Affairs, China in Africa Policy Briefing no. 3, April 2008, p. 6, citing 'Expanding Cooperation with China on Investment Policies 2007–2008', OECD Directorate for Financial and Enterprise Affairs,

Investment Committee, 22 February 2007.

12 Gill and Reilly, 'The Tenuous Hold of China Inc. in Africa', p. 47.

13 'Companies Lacking Social Responsibility Criticized', Xinhua, 29 January 2007.

14 'Central SOEs Ordered to Play Leading Role in Fulfilling Duties', Xinhua, 9 January 2008.

15 Li Xing, 'Hu to Africa: Mutual Support Important', *China Daily*, 16 February 2009.

16 For details of members and their entry dates, see the 'Participants and Stakeholders' page of the compact's website, http://www.unglobalcompact.org/ParticipantsAndStakeholders/search_participant.html.

17 For an example of such allegations, see Roberta Cohen's letter to the *New York Times*, 'China Has Used Prison Labour in Africa', *New York Times*, 11 May 1991. For China's reply, see Chen Guoqing, 'China Doesn't Use Prison Labour in Africa', *New York Times*, 1 June 1991.

18 For example, 60% of Zambia's GDP comes from copper, yet only 60,000 people in a population of 12m are employed by the copper industry. See Burgis, 'Zambia's New President Pledges Boom', *Financial Times*, 2 November 2008.

19 David Shinn, in response to Taylor, 'Common Sense About China's Ties with Africa', Center for Strategic and International Studies Africa Policy Forum, 5 May 2008; both article and response available at http://forums.csis.org/africa/?p=102.

20 Lucy Corkin and Chris Burke, 'Constructive Engagement: An Overview of China's Role in Africa's Construction Industries', in Hannah Edinger et al. (eds), 'New Impulses from the South: China's Engagement of Africa', University of Stellenbosch Centre for Chinese Studies, May 2008, p. 48. These researchers, who focused only on the construction industry, concluded that 'with few exceptions ... local workers account[ed] for the vast majority' of those employed by Chinese contractors.

21 Stephanie Hanson, 'Angola's Political and Economic Development', Council on Foreign Relations Backgrounder, 21 July 2008, http://www.cfr.org/publication/16820/africas_oil_powerhouse.html.

22 Alec Russell, 'Jisco Takes Model Approach in S. Africa Project', *Financial Times*, 31 July 2008. The five Chinese are all managers.

23 Burke, Corkin and Tay, 'China's Engagement of Africa: Preliminary Scoping of African Case Studies', p. 190. For more detail, see the report's Uganda and Zambia case studies.

24 Meagan Dietz, Gordon Orr and Hane Xing, 'How Chinese Companies Can Succeed Abroad', *McKinsey Quarterly*, May 2008, p. 3. See also 'Promoting Local IT Progress', Huawei website, http://www.huawei.com/africa/en/catalog.do?id=542.

25 For a further indication of ZTE's more engaged approach, see its $400m investment in Angolan telecoms, which includes provision for the creation of a 'telecoms institute' for training Angolan staff, as well as a telecoms research laboratory. For details of this and ZTE's impressive expansion, see 'OECD Investment Policy Reviews: China 2008', OECD 2008, p. 99.

26 Corkin and Burke, 'China's Interest and Activity in Africa's Construction and Infrastructure Sectors', University of Stellenbosch Centre for Chinese Studies, November 2006, p. 79.

27 Broadman, 'China and India Go to Africa', p. 98.

28 Corkin and Burke, 'China's Interest and Activity in Africa's Construction and Infrastructure Sectors', p. 29.

29 'China, Zambia Sign MoU to Enhance Labour Law Abidance', *People's Daily*, 18 October 2006.

30 'Zambians Sacked Over China Attack', BBC News, 6 March 2008.

31 'No One Was Fired at Chambishi Mine', *Lusaka Times*, 7 March 2008.

32 '2 Chinese Strikers Die in Equatorial Guinea Clash', *China Daily*, 31 March 2008.

33 For more details, see 'Chinese Companies in Namibia Allegedly Receive Exemption From Affirmative Action', *The Namibian*, 1 July 2008.

34 Simon Clark, Michael Smith and Franz Wild, 'China Lets Child Workers Die Digging in Congo Mines for Copper', Bloomberg, 23 July 2008.

35 Interview, Beijing, 20 August 2008.

36 Russia came 22nd. Transparency International, 'Bribe Payers Index 2008', December 2008. The survey uses 2,742 respondents, with a minimum of 100 respondents per country. In addition to the 22 most influential economies, the survey also includes Australia, Brazil, India and South Africa for their regional roles (see p. 7 of the report). The full report is available at http://www.transparency.org/news_room/in_focus/2008/bpi_2008.

37 *Ibid.*, p. 8. Though the official categorisation was 'Africa and the Middle East', the countries surveyed were Egypt, Ghana, Morocco, Nigeria, Senegal and South Africa. Chinese firms came last in the other regional categorisations of Latin America, Europe and the Asia-Pacific.

38 Interview, Beijing, 23 November 2008.

39 Transparency International, 'Bribe Payers Index, 2008', p. 13. Sector analysis ranks public works and construction as the most bribery-prone sectors, with real estate and property development second, and oil and gas extraction third.

40 Richard Behar, 'Endgame: Hypocrisy, Blindness, and the Doomsday Scenario', *Fast Company*, 9 May 2008. See also a report of the meeting in which Li made the comment: Pamela Weaver, 'Strikingly Ridiculous', MyDigitalLife.co.za, http://www.mydigitallife.co.za/index.php?option=com_content&task=view&id=2057&Itemid=2.

41 See 'China, India, Korea, G8 Ministers Welcome EITI Implementation', EITI website, 19 June 2008, http://eitransparency.org/node/389.

42 See, for example, Margaret Lee, 'Uganda and China: Unleashing the Power of the Dragon', in Henning Melber (ed.), *China in Africa* (Uppsala: Nordic Africa Institute, 2007), Current African Issues no. 35, p. 37.

43 Emmanuel Uffot, 'The Rush for Chinese Products', *Newswatch*, 27 October 2008.

44 'FG-China to Sign Accord to Check Influx of Substandard Products', *Daily Trust*, 8 January 2009.

45 Russell, 'Infrastructure: Big Projects Fall Behind Schedule', *Financial Times*, 23 January 2008.

46 Efem Nkanga, 'Country's N40 Billion Satellite Missing From Orbit', *This Day*, 12 November 2008. Although the satellite was insured, and will be replaced by China's Great Wall Industries, the coverage of its failure in the Nigerian and foreign media will have served to further associate Chinese products with questions about quality in many minds. Lagos newspaper *This Day* reported soon after that this had been

the second Chinese satellite failure in two years. Nkanga, 'NigComSat is Second Chinese Satellite to Fail', *This Day*, 18 November 2008.

47 'Beijing's Spilled Milk', *Africa-Asia Confidential*, vol. 1, no. 11, September 2008, p. 1.

48 'The Water Margin', *Africa-Asia Confidential*, vol. 1, no. 4, February 2008, p. 5.

49 For information on the environmental and social issues surrounding the construction of the Mphanda Nkuwa Dam, see the website of NGO International Rivers: http://www.internationalrivers.org/en/africa/mphanda-nkuwa-dam-mozambique. For more on the issue of seismic activity in Mozambique, see 'Dam Safety in Southern Africa: Will the Walls Come Tumbling Down?', statement by Mozambican NGO Justica Ambiental in 2006, available on International Rivers website, http://internationalrivers.org/en/africa/dam-safety-southern-africa-will-walls-come-tumbling-down.

50 Burke, Corkin and Tay, 'China's Engagement of Africa: Preliminary Scoping of African Case Studies', p. 94.

51 'Zambia Closes Chinese-Run Mine Over Air Pollution', Agence France-Presse, 14 May 2007.

52 GlobalTimber.org.uk, 'China: Illegal Imports and Exports', 2006, http://www.globaltimber.org.uk/ChinaIllegalImpExp.htm.

53 See, for example, *ibid*.

54 'Sierra Leone Bans Timber Exports', Reuters, 14 January 2008.

55 Alden, *China in Africa*, p. 88.

56 Adina Matissof and Michelle Chan, 'The Green Evolution: Environmental Policies and Practises in China's Banking Sector', Friends of the Earth-US, November 2008, p. 18.

57 'China EPA, IFC to Develop Guidelines for Groundbreaking National Green Credit Policy', IFC website, 26 January 2008, http://www.ifc.org/ifcext/sustainability.nsf/content/Highlights_January2008_ChinaGreenCredit.

58 See Industrial Bank press release, 31 October 2008, http://www.equator-principles.com/documents/IB%20Press%20Release.pdf.

59 These were introduced in 2007 by the State Forestry Administration. Guidelines have also been issued to Chinese logging companies overseas. 'China Issues Rules for Logging Companies Overseas', Reuters, 29 August 2007.

60 See TRAFFIC, 'The State of Wildlife in China in 2007', accessible from http://www.traffic.org/home/2008/11/12/state-of-wildlife-trade-in-china-finds-consumption-rising-in.html. A national ivory-registration system was established in 2004. In the 2007 survey of China's wildlife trade cited above, TRAFFIC, an NGO that monitors the international trade in wildlife and wildlife products, noted that ivory consumption had been declining with 'increased enforcement of the regulations' (p. 6). However, the report also noted that wildlife consumption in China was increasing again, after a brief decline following the spread of the SARS virus in 2003 (p. 12). Elsewhere, TRAFFIC observes that 'while physical markets for endangered animal products are suffering as a result of improved law enforcement, the same trade is increasingly flourishing via the Chinese-language internet', 'Illegal Wildlife Trade Flourishing on the

Chinese-Language Internet', TRAFFIC, 28 January 2008, http://www.traffic. org/home/2008/1/28/illegal-wildlife-trade-flourishing-on-the-chinese-language-i.html.

61 Implementation of this policy proved problematic, with local governments reluctant to act against some of the worst offenders, who were also some of the most profitable companies in their regions. However, by February 2008, 12 companies had reportedly been banned from receiving loans. 'Efforts Needed on "Green Credit Policy"', Xinhua, 14 February 2008.

62 Xie Zhenhua, as reported in 'Officials Face Scrutiny for Failed "Green" Target', Xinhua, 29 November 2007.

63 For more on Indian complaints about Chinese gazumping, see 'India Outsmarted', *Financial Express*, 3 September 2005.

64 Corkin, 'China's Strategic Infrastructural Investments in Africa', in Dorothy-Grace Guerrero and Firoze Manji (eds), *China's New Role in Africa and the South* (Oxford: Fahamu, 2008), p. 140.

65 'China Forges Deep Alliances with War-torn Nations in Africa', *Sudan Tribune*, 30 March 2005, cited in Taylor's 'Unpacking China's Resources Diplomacy in Africa', Hong Kong University of Science and Technology, Center on China's Transnational Relations, Working Paper no. 19, p. 7.

66 Terence Creamer, 'Shock as Chinese Contractor Snaps up Big Water Contract', *Engineering News*, 26 January 2006, http://www.engineeringnews. co.za/article.php?a_id=80072.

67 For further details, see Adam Wolfe, 'Somalia Wishes it Had an Oil Problem', *On Political Risk* (blog), 20 March 2008, http://risk.typepad.com/blog/2008/03/somalia-wishes.html.

68 Though small Australian firm Range Resources has estimated on the basis of previous exploration reports that Puntland may hold between five and ten billion barrels of oil. The region does have proven gas reserves, but not in any quantity. *Ibid.*

69 The high-risk deal-making of Chinese SOEs is not confined to Africa. In 2007, China Metallurgical Group provided Afghanistan with the largest single foreign investment in its history when it agreed to invest $3.5bn in the development of the Aynak copper field, which included the construction of a power plant and a freight railway.

70 In 2008, China exported goods worth $50.84bn to Africa and imported goods worth $56bn, turning China's overall surplus in 2007 of $940m into a deficit of $5.16bn. 'China–Africa Trade Up 45% in 2008 to $107bln', *People's Daily*, 12 February 2009.

71 'Champions of Commerce', *Africa-Asia Confidential*, vol. 1, no. 12, October 2008, p. 1.

72 Zha Daojiong, 'China's Energy Security', paper presented to Regional Workshop on Energy and Non-Traditional Security, S. Rajaratnam School of International Studies, Singapore, 18 August 2008.

73 For a case study on worsening community relations among Chinese and local traders in Namibia, see the work done by Gregor Dobler on the town of Oshikango: 'Cheapness and Resentment: Chinese Traders and Local Society in Oshikango, Namibia', 'background reading' for paper given to a seminar at the African Studies Centre, Leiden, 27 March 2008. See also Brigitte Weidlich, 'Chinese Businesses "Kill" Local Retail Outlets', *The Namibian*, 21 October 2008.

74 Henry Umoru, 'FG Vows to Tackle China on Counterfeiting, Smuggling', *Vanguard*, 7 February 2009.

75 The Nigerian figure was 4.13% in 2008, according to the Nigerian National Bureau of Statistics, as reported in Jibrin Abubakar, 'Agric Biggest Contributor to GDP', *Daily Trust*, 17 February 2009. The figure for China hovers around the 40% mark. See, for example, Nouriel Roubini, 'Hard Landing in China?', *Forbes*, 11 June 2008.

76 Chinese Commerce Minister Chen Deming, quoted in 'China's Eight-Measure Economic Policy on Africa Well-Implemented'.

77 Macharia Kamau, 'Kenya Lobbies for Trade Relations with China', *The Standard*, 13 January 2009.

78 'China Mulls Zero-Tariff Expansion in Africa', Xinhua, 25 January 2009.

79 Nkosazana Dlamini-Zuma, address to a seminar to mark ten years of China–South Africa diplomatic relations, Beijing, 23 April 2008.

80 'Congo Shuts Chinese-run Mine Over Ore Export Ban', Reuters, 22 May 2008.

81 Tom Mackenzie and Mitch Moxley, 'China's "Little Africa" is Under Pressure', GlobalPost.com, 24 February 2009.

82 Pellet Kipela, 'IMF to Study Congo's China Deal Before any Accord', Reuters, 2 July 2008.

83 Barney Jopson, 'Donors Press Congo Over $9bn China Deal', *Financial Times*, 9 February 2009.

84 'Coal Mine Deaths Drop 15% in 2008', Xinhua, 28 January 2009. The official total number of deaths for the year was 3,215.

85 Alden, *China in Africa*, p. 131.

86 CAITEC, 'Guidelines on Corporate Social Responsibility Compliance for Foreign Invested Enterprises', draft for comments, August 2008, p. 3.

87 For more on the development of Chinese thinking on CSR, see the work of legal-service provider DLA Piper. DLA Piper Client Briefing, 'Corporate Social Responsibility Compliance for Foreign Invested Enterprises in China', 24 September 2008.

88 For more on the report, see 'Sinosteel Corporation Releases Sustainability Report on Africa', ChinaCSR.com, 27 October 2008, http://www.chinacsr.com/en/2008/10/27/3453-sinosteel-corporation-releases-sustainability-report-on-africa/.

89 For details and figures on the power shortage and on low coal reserves, see 'China Expects Power Shortages Amid Surging Demand', Xinhua, 2 June 2008.

90 Rujun Shen, 'As Small Chinese Mines Stay Closed, the Power Crisis in the Nation Grows', Reuters, 13 July 2008.

91 Interview, Beijing, 10 March 2008.

92 Interview, Beijing, 24 April 2008.

93 Interview, Geneva, 13 September 2008.

94 Alastair Fraser and John Lungu, 'For Whom the Windfalls? Winners and Losers in the Privatisation of Zambia's Copper Mines', Civil Society Trade Network of Zambia and the Catholic Commission for Justice, Development and Peace, January 2007, http://www.minewatchzambia.com/reports/report.pdf.

95 See remarks of the president of the Association of Chinese Corporations in Zambia, Tao Xinghu. Quoted in 'Chinese Investments Grow in Zambia', *Zambia African Safari* (blog), 20 January 2006, http://zambiasafari.blogspot.com/2006/01/chinese-investments-grows-in-zambia.html; also 'Zambia Calls on Chinese Ventures to Open

Processing Plants', *People's Daily*, 29 December 2005.

96   See Davies, 'How China Delivers Development Assistance to Africa', p. 47; also 'Zambian President Hails China–Zambia Cooperation', Xinhua, 19 December 2007.

97   'China Writes off Zambia's $211m Debt', *Business Day*, 10 November 2006.

98   Lewis Mwanangombe, 'Zambian President Sworn in, Opponents Protest', Associated Press, 11 February 2008.

99   'Chinese Investment Cheers ZCTU', *Times of Zambia*, 20 June 2008.

100   Brautigam, 'China's African Aid: Transatlantic Challenges', p. 18.

101   'Chinese to Build a New City in North West Province', *Lusaka Times*, 14 September 2008.

102   'Chambishi Copper Smelter to Begin Full Operations Next Month', *Lusaka Times*, 29 December 2008.

103   See Shacinda, 'Zambia Courts China to Help Boost Economy', Reuters, 23 October 2008.

104   Banda's victory may well have been greeted with sighs of relief in the West as well as in China, as Sata is a vociferous supporter of Zimbabwean President Robert Mugabe.

Chapter Four

1   Michael Ross, 'Blood Barrels: Why Oil Wealth Fuels Conflict', *Foreign Affairs*, vol. 87, no. 3, May–June 2008, pp. 2–3.

2   'Car Blast Near Nigeria Oil Port', BBC News, 30 April 2006.

3   '9 Chinese Oil Workers Killed in Ethiopia', *China Daily*, 24 April 2007.

4   'Darfur Rebels Say They Attacked Chinese-Run Oilfield in Sudan', Agence France-Presse, 11 December 2007. The Sudanese government has denied that this attack took place.

5   'Nine Chinese Oil Workers Kidnapped in Sudan', Reuters, 19 October 2008.

6   For example, in September 2008, a bulk carrier owned by Chinese shipping company Sinotrans was hijacked by pirates off the Somali coast on its way from Tunisia to India. Twenty-four of the 25 crew members were Chinese.

7   'Around 300,000 Killed in Darfur Violence since 2003 – UN', RIA Novosti, 23 April 2008.

8   The US imposed sanctions on government entities in both China and Pakistan in 1993, following the 1992 transfer of missile technology in violation of the Missile Technology Control Regime. Ed Scherr and Russell E. Dybvik, 'China, Pakistan Hit by US Sanctions for Missile Deal', United States Information Agency, http://www.fas.org/nuke/control/mtcr/news/930825-300647.htm. In April 1994, Premier Li Peng diverted a $1.5bn aircraft-construction contract that had been expected to go to Boeing to Airbus. For details of China's behaviour towards Boeing in this period, see David Sanger, 'Two Roads to China: Nice, and Not So Nice', *New York Times*, 9 June 1996.

9   The embargo on trade with China began in 1950. Restrictions imposed by US allies were lifted in 1957, but the US's own embargo continued

in full until 1969, when many of the restrictions were lifted.

10 The Malacca Strait is a 900km stretch of water between Indonesia and Malaysia that links the Indian and Pacific Oceans. More than 70% of China's energy imports are shipped through the channel, creating an obvious vulnerability to blockade. At its narrowest, the strait is only 1.5 nautical miles wide. In recent years, prompted by concerns about the risks of blockade, piracy and terrorism, China has been seeking to reduce its reliance on the strait by developing new supply lines, including from Sittwe port in Myanmar and Gwadar in Pakistan. For more details, see Graham Lees, 'China Seeks Burmese Route Around the Malacca Dilemma', *World Politics Review*, 20 February 2007. See also Ian Storey, 'New Energy Projects Help China Reduce its "Malacca Dilemma"', *OpinionAsia*, 14 May 2007.

11 For details of the agreements signed during the visit of Vice Premier Zeng Peiyang to Angola in 2005, see 'China, Angola Sign 9 Cooperation Agreements', Afrol News, 7 March 2005.

12 See Kenneth Lieberthal and Mikkal Herberg, 'China's Search for Energy Security: Implications for US Policy', NBR Analysis, vol. 17, no. 1, April 2006, p. 14; BP Group Vice President and Asia Regional President Gary Dirks, 'Energy Security: China and the World', address to International Symposium on Energy Security: China and the World, Beijing, 24 May 2006.

13 Richard McGregor, 'China's Diplomacy "Hijacked" by Big Companies', *Financial Times*, 16 March 2008.

14 Interview, Chinese academic working on energy security, Singapore, 29 August 2008.

15 International Crisis Group, 'China's Thirst for Oil', Asia Report no. 153, Executive Summary, 9 June 2008, p. 3.

16 'China's Energy Conditions and Policies', Chinese Government White Paper, 2007. See Chapter 4: 'Strengthening International Cooperation in the Field of Energy'.

17 Russell Hsiao, 'Energy Security the Centrepiece of China's Foreign Policy', *China Brief*, vol. 8, issue 16, 1 August 2008, pp. 1–2.

18 Zha, 'China's Energy Security: Puzzles in International Dialogue'.

19 For details of the problems caused by China's coal dependency, see Mao Yushi, Sheng Hong and Yang Fuqiang, 'The True Cost of Coal', report by Greenpeace, the Energy Foundation and the World Wildlife Fund, October 2008.

20 The International Crisis Group report cited above was among the external voices advocating the establishment of a consolidated energy ministry. International Crisis Group, 'China's Thirst for Oil'.

21 Wang Xu, 'New Statistics Bureau Chief Named', *China Daily*, 23 September 2008.

22 The perception of Dinka domination over other groups, for example, is one of a number of divisive issues that have the potential to cause conflict in southern Sudan.

23 'President Hu: Seize Favourable Opportunity on Darfur Issue', *People's Daily*, 19 July 2007.

24 The 1648 Treaty of Westphalia marked the beginning of a new political order in Europe founded on the principle of the sovereignty of the nation-state, based on territorial integrity and non-intervention.

25 For details, see Responsibility to Protect website, 'General Assembly – R2P Excerpt from Outcome Document', http://www.responsibilitytoprotect. org/index.php/united_nations/398? theme=alt1.

26 See 'About the Court' on the website of the International Criminal Court: http://www.icc-cpi.int/Menus/ICC/ About+the+Court/.

27 Samuel S. Kim, 'Chinese Foreign Policy Faces Globalization Challenges', in Alastair Iain Johnston and Robert S. Ross (eds), *New Directions in the Study of China's Foreign Policy* (Palo Alto, CA: Stanford University Press, 2006), p. 297.

28 Wang Jisi, 'Views on Devising International Strategy'.

29 As part of this process of reappraisal, in January 2008, the Ministry of Foreign Affairs hosted a meeting of foreign-policy experts to discuss the position of non-intervention in China's foreign policy.

30 Ellen Johnson-Sirleaf, 'Behold the New Africa', Sixth Annual Lecture, Nelson Mandela Foundation, Johannesburg, 12 July 2008. For the full speech, see http://www.nelsonmandela.org/index. php/news/article/the_sixth_annual_ lecture_address/.

31 See, for example, 'Botswanan President Criticises Mugabe', Agence France-Presse, 15 August 2008; Paul Simao, 'Kenyan PM Describes Mugabe as a Dictator', Reuters, 4 June 2008.

32 Li Xinfeng, editorial in the *People's Daily*, 14 January 2008. For a slightly more nuanced Chinese appraisal of the problems of democracy in Kenya, see He Wenping, 'Lessons to be Learnt From Kenya's "Democracy"', *China Daily*, 17 January 2008. 'Democracy', concludes He, 'is not a magic cure for all ills that works everywhere.'

33 Ken Kamoche, 'China Has to Play a Role in Divided Africa', *The Nation*, 24 February 2008.

34 John Reed, 'China Intervenes in Zambian Election', *Financial Times*, 5 September 2006.

35 'Russia, China Veto US-drafted Resolution on Zimbabwe', Xinhua, 12 July 2008, http://news.xinhuanet.com/ english/2008-07/12/content_8532135. htm.

36 Interview, Beijing, 16 November 2008. See also Patrick Wintour, Larry Elliot and Chris McGreal, 'Zimbabwe Sanctions Could Lead to Civil War, Mbeki Warns Leaders', *Guardian*, 8 July 2008.

37 Ian Evans, 'Robert Mugabe Forced into Talks with Opposition after China Told Him to "Behave"', *Daily Telegraph*, 26 July 2008.

38 For an illustration of this, see comments made by Chinese Ambassador to the UN Wang Guangya, as quoted in Andrew Woolford, 'China's Long Relationship with Africa', *Suite101. com*, 11 August 2008.

39 Jenny Booth, 'Zimbabwe Cholera Epidemic Could Hit 60,000', *Times*, 9 December 2008.

40 'Sinosteel Snaps up 67% in Zimbabwe Ferrochrome Producer', Xinhua, 21 December 2007.

41 Brian Heart, 'China Seals Chrome Mining Deal with Zim', *Zimbabwe Guardian*, 6 August 2008.

42 Shame Makoshori, 'Chinese Firm in US $400 Million Glass Project', *Financial Gazette*, 29 November 2008. This particular project had been in development for some time, with $160m invested by 2005. Makoshori, 'Chinese Company Invests in Glass Factory', *Daily Mirror* (Zimbabwe), 12 May 2005.

43 Makoshori, 'China Trade Hits US$500 Million Mark', *Financial Gazette*, 22 November 2008.

44 See Liu Guijin's comment that 'we have been playing the role of bridge … trying to give advice and persuade Sudan to be more flexible'. Quoted in 'China Urges Peacekeepers in Darfur', *China Daily*, 16 June 2007.

45 Quoted in Zhang Haizhou, 'Experts Debate China's Role in Somalia Mission', *China Daily*, 12 December 2008.

46 'China Decides to Send Navy Vessels to Fight Pirates off Somali Coast', Xinhua, 20 December 2008.

47 Thomas Christensen, 'Shaping China's Global Choices Through Diplomacy', statement to the US–China Economic and Security Review Commission, 18 March 2008, http://china.usc.edu/ShowArticle.aspx?articleID=1148.

48 Harvey Morris, 'China Defends Africa Aid Stance', *Financial Times*, 2 July 2008.

49 One example of the West's explicit linking of aid with good governance and democratic principles based on the rule of law is the Cotonou Agreement between the European Union and the 'ACP countries' (countries of Africa, the Caribbean and the Pacific), signed in Benin in 2000.

50 This is not the place to review the nature and depth of the PRC's historical suspicions about peacekeeping. For more on this see M. Taylor Ravel, 'China's Attitude toward UN Peace Keeping Operations since 1989', *Asian Survey*, vol. 36, no. 11, November 1996, pp. 1,102–22. Also Gill and Reilly, 'Sovereignty, Intervention and Peacekeeping: The View from Beijing', *Survival*, vol. 42, no. 3, Autumn 2000, pp. 41–55; Gill, *Rising Star: China's New Security Diplomacy*; Johnston and Ross (eds), *New Directions in the Study of China's Foreign Policy*; Drew Thompson, 'Beijing's Participation in UNPKO', *China Brief*, vol. 5, no. 11, 10 May 2005.

51 'Peace, Development and Cooperation: In Commemoration of the 35th Anniversary of Restoration of Lawful Seat of the People's Republic of China in the United Nations', Chinese Ministry of Foreign Affairs website, 2 November 2006, http://www.fmprc.gov.cn/eng/wjb/zzjg/gjs/gjsxw/t278484.htm.

52 Holslag, 'China's Diplomatic Victory in Darfur', Brussels Institute of Contemporary China Studies Asia Paper, vol. 2, no. 4, 15 August 2007, p. 3.

53 Zhang Ping, 'Remarks on the Chinese People's Liberation Army's Participation in UN Peacekeeping Operations', address to a conference on 'Multidimensional and Integrated Peace Operations: Trends and Challenges', Beijing, 26–27 March 2007, http://www.regjeringen.no/en/dep/ud/selected-topics/un/integratedmissions/seminars/beijing-presentations.html?id=477057.

54 Monthly summaries are available at http://www.un.org/Depts/dpko/dpko/contributors/.

55 By September 2008, this proportion had risen to 76%, with China's total troop contribution to missions worldwide up to 2,164.

56 See, for example, Robert Worth, 'Sudan Says it Will Accept UN–African Peace Force in Darfur', *New York Times*, 17 November 2006.

57 From 2000 to 2003, China ranked third as an arms supplier to Africa, behind Western European countries taken together and Russia. Raymond Copson, Kerry Dumbaugh and Michelle Lau, 'China and Sub-Saharan Africa', Con-

gressional Research Service Report no. RL33055, 29 August 2005, p. 7. According to one estimate, between 2000 and 2005, China's share of the sub-Saharan African arms market was 18%. David Shinn and Joshua Eisenman, 'Responding to China in Africa', American Foreign Policy Council, 30 June 2008, p. 3.

58 'Sudan: Stronger Arms Embargo Needed in Darfur – UN Experts', IRIN, 28 April 2006, http://www.irinnews. org/report.aspx?reportid=58870.

59 For greater detail, see 'Arms, Oil, and Darfur: The Evolution of Relations Between China and Sudan', *Small Arms Survey*, no. 7, July 2007. China was the source of approximately 90% of Sudan's small-arms purchases from 2004 to 2006 inclusive. Human Rights First, 'The Facts: China's Arms Sales to Sudan', factsheet, http://www. stoparmstosudan.org/pages.asp?id=22.

60 Eisenman, 'China's Post-Cold War Strategy in Africa', in Joshua Eisenman, Eric Heginbotham and Derek Mitchell (eds), *China and the Developing World: Beijing's Strategy for the Twenty-First Century* (New York: M.E. Sharpe, 2007), p. 49. Eisenman is quoting from 'China Ready to Step Up Military Cooperation with Sudan', Xinhua, 28 November 2005.

61 'Chinese, Sudanese Senior Military Leaders Hold Talks on Closer Ties', Xinhua, 4 April 2007.

62 The claim of self-sufficiency was made by Sudan's defence minister, Lt-Gen. Abdel-Rahim Mohamed Hussein. 'Sudan has Drones, is Pursuing Missiles – State Media', Reuters, 5 September 2007.

63 David Beresford, 'Chinese Ship Carries Arms Cargo to Mugabe Regime', *Guardian*, 18 April 2008.

64 At the time of this transaction, China was Zimbabwe's second-largest trading partner after South Africa.

65 See, for example, the comments made by Foreign Ministry Spokesperson Jiang Yu to a press conference on 22 April 2008, referring to the shipment as part of the 'normal arms trade between China and Zimbabwe' and calling on the US not to 'politicise' this trade. Available on the FOCAC website, http://www.focac.org/eng/ fyrth/t428243.htm. At a seminar to celebrate ten years of China–South Africa diplomatic relations co-hosted by CASS and the South African embassy in Beijing on 23 April 2008, Yang Guang, director of the Institute of West Asian and African Studies at CASS, responded to a question about the shipment by noting that Zimbabwe was not under UN arms embargo, and that the shipment was not illegal.

66 Gill, *Rising Star: China's New Security Diplomacy*, p. 75.

67 'Statement by Chinese Representative at UN Workshop on Small Arms and Light Weapons', Chinese Ministry of Foreign Affairs website, 19 April 2005, http://www.mfa.gov.cn/eng/wjb/zzjg/ jks/kjfywj/t195801.htm.

68 'China's National Defence in 2008', January 2009. Full text available at http://www.china.org.cn/government/ central_government/2009-01/20/ content_17155577.htm.

69 Wen Jiabao, 'Strengthen China–Africa Cooperation for Mutual Benefit', address to the opening ceremony of the High-Level Dialogue Between Chinese and African Leaders and Business Representatives and the Second Conference of Chinese and African Entrepreneurs, Beijing, 4 November

2006, http://new.fmprc.gov.cn/eng/wjdt/zyjh/t279849.htm.

70 This is not to belittle China's considerable contributions in these fields. Access to water is undoubtedly a problem in Darfur, and Chinese engineers are working to improve the situation. Nevertheless, though the list of such works undertaken by China is certainly impressive, it must be viewed in the broader context.

71 Yang Lihua, paper presented to seminar to celebrate ten years of China–South Africa diplomatic relations, Beijing, 23 April 2008.

72 Interview, Beijing, 21 November 2008.

73 'China's African Policy'.

74 'Chinese, African Trade Union Leaders Meet', Xinhua, 14 October 2008.

75 Interview with informal adviser to the Movement for Democratic Change, Geneva, 13 September 2008.

76 Interview, CASS official, Beijing, 15 January 2008.

77 'Save Darfur Coalition Urges Continued Chinese Engagement on Darfur Crisis', Save Darfur coalition press release, 9 July 2007, http://www.savedarfur.org/newsroom/releases/save_darfur_coalition_urges_continued_chinese_engagement_on_darfur_crisis/.

78 On the opening of the dam, see 'Sudanese President Inaugurates Merowe Dam on the Nile River', People's Daily, 3 March 2009.

79 There are considerable tensions over the question of resettlement, with most of the displaced communities trying to stay on in the surrounding area, while the Sudanese government seeks to relocate them further afield. For more on the Merowe Dam, see the website of NGO International Rivers: http://www.internationalrivers.org/en/node/350.

80 Ali Askouri, 'Sudanese Militia Kill Three People in Merowe Dam Area', Sudan Tribune, 22 April 2006.

81 Gill, Rising Star: China's New Security Diplomacy. The book charts China's changing approach to regional and global security diplomacy since the mid 1990s.

82 Susan Shirk, 'China's Multilateral Diplomacy in the Asia-Pacific', remarks to the US–China Economic and Security Review Commission hearing on 'China as an Emerging Regional and Technology Power: Implications for US Economic and Security Interests', La Jolla, California, 12–13 February 2004.

83 For example, in 2003 China donated $300,000 to the Peace Fund. In 2005, it donated a further $400,000 to the AU. Further contributions followed, including in 2007 and 2008.

84 'AUC Chair in Strategic Dialogue with Chinese Vice Minister', AUC News, no. 35, November 2008, http://www.africa-union.org/root/ua/Newsletter/Publication%2035%20Nov%202008.pdf.

85 Lesley Wroughton, 'China's Exim Bank, World Bank to Cooperate on Africa', Reuters, 21 May 2007.

86 'Meeting of Leaders of China, Japan and South Korea Issues an Action Plan on Cooperation', Chinese Ministry of Foreign Affairs website, 15 December 2008, http://www.fmprc.gov.cn/eng/zxxx/t526245.htm.

87 'NEPAD in Brief', NEPAD website, http://www.nepad.org/2005/files/inbrief.php.

88 Lynette Chen, paper presented to seminar to celebrate ten years of China–South Africa diplomatic relations, Beijing, 23 April 2008.

89 Gengezi Mgidlana, special adviser to the director of the NEPAD secretariat,

paper presented to seminar to celebrate ten years of China–South Africa diplomatic relations, Beijing, 23 April 2008.

90 The problem of poor coordination was acknowledged at the 18th NEPAD Heads of State and Government Implementation Committee Meeting in January 2008, where the decision to integrate the bodies was taken. But progress has been slow. In February, Jean Ping urged the integration process to be expedited. See 'Ping Calls for Faster Integration of NEPAD into AU', Bua News, 3 February 2009, http://www.pambazuka.org/aumonitor/comments/2158/.

91 Broadman, 'China and India Go to Africa', p. 103. There is some hope that Africa's business environment may be somewhat simplified by the free-trade agreement announced in October 2008 between members of the SADC, the East African Community and the Common Market for Eastern and Southern Africa. The agreement encompasses 26 countries with a combined GDP of $624bn.

92 'China, West Africa Initiate Trade Forum for Stronger Economic Ties', Xinhua, 23 September 2008. The 15 members of ECOWAS include São Tomé and Principe, with which the PRC does not currently have diplomatic relations. However, as with other issues, China tends to take a pragmatic approach to this. For example, in 2008, Sinopec began exploring for oil in the São Tomé–Nigerian Joint Development Zone in the Gulf of Guinea.

93 Edwin Musoni, 'China Donates Rwf55m to ICGLR', The New Times (Rwanda), 6 January 2009.

94 The US company Chevron had already abandoned its investments in Sudan's oilfields because of the country's instability by the time the US government called for this withdrawal.

95 Alden, China in Africa, p. 61.

96 US Energy Information Administration, 'Sudan', Country Analysis Brief, last updated April 2007, http://www.eia.doe.gov/emeu/cabs/Sudan/Full.html.

97 Figure calculated from Downs, 'The Fact and Fiction of Sino-African Energy Relations', p. 46. Downs's graph on equity oil shows China producing 217,000 b/d from Sudan in 2006, out of a total of 685,000 b/d from all its overseas equity-oil concerns. Of this 217,000 b/d, a maximum of 97,000 b/d was sent to China for consumption there. Only Kazakhstan was the site of greater Chinese equity-oil production, with Chinese companies producing 222,000 b/d there in 2006.

98 Servant, 'China's Trade Safari in Africa'.

99 'Investing in Tragedy: China's Money, Arms and Politics in Sudan', Human Rights First report, March 2008, p. i.

100 Estimates of the proportion vary. Peter Brookes has argued that Sudan has spent between 60 and 80% of its oil revenue on arms, with around half of this revenue coming from Chinese investment. In 2006, Sudanese oil revenue came to $4.7bn. Peter Brookes, 'Into Africa: China's Grab for Influence and Oil', Heritage Foundation Lecture no. 1006, delivered 9 February 2007.

101 'China Told Sudan to Adopt UN's Darfur Plan – Envoy', Sudan Tribune, 7 February 2007.

102 Downs, 'China's New Energy Administration', China Business Review, November–December 2008, p. 43.

103 Lydia Polgreen, 'China, in New Role, Uses Ties to Press Sudan on Troubled

Darfur', *International Herald Tribune*, 23 February 2008.

104 Interview, Beijing, 15 January 2008.

105 Liu Guijin, 'Darfur and Sino-African Relations', address to Royal Institute of International Affairs (Chatham House), London, 22 February 2008.

106 'China Signals It Will Not Introduce Resolution to Defer Bashir Indictment', *Sudan Tribune*, 3 November 2008.

107 For an example of China's official reaction to the issue of the arrest warrant, see the comments of Foreign Ministry spokesman Qin Gang in 'Mixed Reaction to Bashir Warrant', al-Jazeera.net, 5 March 2009.

108 'Hu Puts Forward Four-point Principle on Solving Darfur Issue', Xinhua, 3 February 2007; Alfred De Montesquiou, 'China's Hu Presses Sudan for Progress on Darfur', Associated Press, 3 February 2007.

109 'CNPC in Sudan', CNPC website, http://www.cnpc.com.cn/eng/cnpcworldwide/africa/Sudan/.

110 'Beijing Changes Stance on Darfur Issue', Press TV news network, 12 June 2008, http://www.presstv.ir/pop/print.aspx?id=59684.

111 'Sudan, China Sign Deals on Stronger Agricultural Co-op', Xinhua, 11 June 2008, http://english.sina.com/china/1/2008/0611/166369.html.

112 Zhongyuan Petroleum Exploration Bureau (owned by Sinopec) aided by BGP (the geophysical-services unit of CNPC). Benoit Faucon, 'China Discusses Darfur Oil-hunt Aid', *Wall Street Journal*, 9 July 2008. See also 'Sudan Talks to Chinese Firms for Help in Darfur Oil Exploration', *Sudan Tribune*, 9 July 2008.

113 Andrei Chang, 'Chinese Trainer Jets Tilt Military Balance for Sudan', United Press International, 17 September, 2008.

114 Chang, 'China Selling Advanced Weapons to Sudan', UPIAsia.com, 15 February 2008.

115 China had demanded key changes to early drafts of the resolution, such as the exclusion of the clause authorising peacekeepers to seize weapons from belligerents. Since the resolution passed, China has lent support to the regime in various ways, for example through its willingness to accept that certain delays in force deployment are due to 'technical difficulties', rather than to the regime's obstruction of the deployment.

116 Chen Xi, 'China's Follow-up Troop of Engineering Unit Arrives in Darfur', CRIEnglish.com, 18 July 2008.

Chapter Five

1 The Indian-owned Konkola Copper Mines firm in Zambia is one example of a non-Chinese developing-world firm that has been the focus of Western and African concerns over labour and environmental standards. See Abi Dymond, 'Undermining Development: Copper Mining in Zambia', Christian Aid, SCIAF and Action for Southern Africa, October 2007, Chapters 2 and 3.

2 Stephen Mihm, 'A Nation of Outlaws', *Boston Globe*, 26 August 2007.

3 Julia Kollewe, 'Absa Deal Makes Barclays Africa's Largest Lender', *Independent*, 10 May 2005. This disquiet was in part due to memories of Barclays's controversial involvement in South Africa under apartheid.

4 'Hundreds Protest Plans to Buy 70% of Ghana Telecom to Vodafone', Dow Jones Newswires, available at http://www.cellular-news.com/story/33010.php, posted to site on 12 August 2008. See also Ben Bland, 'Opposition Party Blocks £450m Vodafone Deal in Ghana', *Daily Telegraph*, 25 July 2008.

5 Polya Lesova, 'Anglo American Defends Investment in Zimbabwe', MarketWatch.com, Wall Street Journal Digital Network, 25 June 2008. See also Graeme Wearden, 'Mining Giant Defends Zimbabwe Investment', *Guardian*, 25 June 2008.

6 'Angola-gate', Economist Intelligence Unit Briefing, 19 November 2008.

7 Dorothy McCormick, 'China and India as Africa's New Donors: The Impact of Aid in Development', *Review of African Political Economy*, vol. 35, no. 1, March 2008, p. 80. In 1987, the World Bank estimated that tied aid reduced the value of assistance by around 25%.

8 *Ibid.* The OECD Development Assistance Committee formally recommended that aid to UN-designated Least Developed Countries be untied in 2001.

9 CIA World Factbook, 'Field Listing: Population Below Poverty Line', 2007 estimate, https://www.cia.gov/library/publications/the-world-factbook/fields/2046.htm.

10 Anderlini, 'Xinjiang Oil Boom Fuels Uighur Resentment', *Financial Times*, 28 August 2008.

11 Andrew Malone, 'How China's Taking Over Africa', *Daily Mail*, 18 July 2008.

12 See World Bank, 'New Financiers are Narrowing Africa's Infrastructure Deficit', press release 2009/017/EXC, 10 July 2008, http://web.worldbank.org/WBSITE/EXTERNAL/NEWS/0,,contentMDK:21836057~pagePK:34370~piPK:34424~theSitePK:4607,00.html.

13 This represents a substantial increase on previous years. From 2001 to 2003, China spent less than $1bn per year on infrastructure in Africa. Foster, Butterfield, Chen and Pushak, 'Building Bridges: China's Growing Role as Infrastructure Financier for Sub-Saharan Africa'.

14 'European Commission Launches an EU–Africa Partnership to Develop Trans-African Connections', EU press release, 13 July 2006, http://europa.eu/rapid/pressReleasesAction.do?reference=IP/06/986&format=HTML&aged=0&language=EN&guiLanguage=fr.

15 'The European Commission, the EIB and Nine Member States Launch the Infrastructure Trust Fund for Africa', EU press release, 23 April 2007, http://europa.eu/rapid/pressReleasesAction.do?reference=IP/07/538&format=HTML&aged.

16 Cole Mallard, 'Millennium Challenge Corporation Invests in African Infrastructure to Fight Rural Poverty', Voice of America News, 31 March 2008, http://www.voanews.com/english/archive/2008-03/2008-03-31-voa37.cfm?CFID=126782533&CFTOKEN=198061 09&jsessionid=88307d24eb87118eb2bd 1ec202424677521c.

17 Interview, Beijing, 16 January 2008.

18 The idea of a 'Beijing consensus' as an alternative model for development to rival the 'Washington consensus' was put forward by Joshua Ramo in 'The Beijing Consensus', Foreign Policy Centre report, May 2004. The term has since been widely adopted, although the precise features of the model are still debated and indeed its very existence disputed.

19 Stiglitz has repeatedly used the term 'market fundamentalism' to criticise what he sees as the doctrinal rigidity of the economic policies of the IMF and the World Bank. See, for example, Joseph Stiglitz, *Globalization and Its Discontents* (New York: Norton, 2002).

20 As quoted by Robert Zoellick, 'Changing Trends in Global Power and Conflict Resolution', Keynote Address to the IISS Global Strategic Review Conference, Geneva, 12 September 2008.

21 At the 2005 G8 summit at Gleneagles in Scotland, the OECD estimated that annual official development assistance from the G8 and other donors would increase by $50bn from 2004 levels by 2010, with half of this increase going to Africa. 'The Gleneagles Communiqué', 2005, points 27 and 28, p. 26, http://news.bbc.co.uk/1/shared/bsp/hi/pdfs/g8_gleneagles_communique.pdf. In April 2008, the OECD's Development Assistance Committee concluded that the promises made at Gleneagles and subsequent G8 summits implied that overall aid levels would rise to $130bn in 2010, from $80bn in 2004. 'Africa's Development: Promises and Prospects', Report of the Africa Progress Panel 2008, June 2008, p. 15, http://www.africaprogresspanel.org/pdf/2008%20 Report.pdf.

22 'Africa's Development: Promises and Prospects', p. 15.

23 *Ibid.*

24 On Sarkozy's visit to Africa, see Romy Chevallier, 'France Promotes New Relationship with Continent', AllAfrica.com, 3 March 2008, http://allafrica.com/stories/200803030014.html. For an example of Chinese rhetoric on this theme, see 'Talking Points of Madame Xu Jinghu, Director General of the Department of African Affairs of the MFA at the Briefing of the Secretariat of the Chinese Follow-up Committee of the FOCAC'.

25 See TICAD's promotional pamphlet, available at the Japanese Ministry of Foreign Affairs website: http://www.mofa.go.jp/region/africa/ticad/pamphlet.pdf.

26 Tony Blair, 'Africa: Choosing the Right Path', speech delivered at the University of South Africa, 31 May 2007. See 'In Full: Tony Blair's Africa Speech', BBC News, 31 May 2007.

27 In 2007, US imports from sub-Saharan Africa totalled $67bn, of which $53.6bn were oil imports. Figures from US Department of Commerce, Bureau of Census. See International Trade Administration, US Department of Commerce, 'US–African Trade Profile', http://www.agoa.gov/resources/US-African%20Trade%20Profile%20 2008%20-%20Final.pdf.

28 Danielle Langton, 'US Trade and Investment Relationship with Sub-Saharan Africa: The African Growth and Opportunity Act and Beyond', Congressional Research Service Report for Congress, RL31772, updated 28 October 2008, p. 7.

29 By mid 2008, 40 sub-Saharan countries had qualified for AGOA, with 27 of these also qualifying for important additional benefits on clothing trading.

30 Office of the United States Trade Representative, '2008 Comprehensive Report on US Trade and Investment Policy Toward Sub-Saharan Africa and Implementation of the African Growth and Opportunity Act', May 2008, p. 5, http://www.ustr.gov/assets/Trade_Development/Preference_Programs/AGOA/asset_upload_file203_14905.pdf.

31 In 2005, 89% of AGOA imports into the US came from Nigeria, Angola and Gabon. Langton, 'US Trade and Investment Relationship with Sub-Saharan Africa: The African Growth and Opportunity Act and Beyond', p. 25.

32 Office of the United States Trade Representative, '2008 Comprehensive Report on US Trade and Investment Policy Toward Sub-Saharan Africa and Implementation of the African Growth and Opportunity Act', p. 5.

33 US figure from the Office of the United States Trade Representative, '2008 Comprehensive Report on US Trade and Investment Policy Toward Sub-Saharan Africa and Implementation of the African Growth and Opportunity Act'. This figure is also cited in United Nations Conference on Trade and Development (UNCTAD), 'World Investment Report 2006: FDI from Developing and Transition Economies: Implications for Development', United Nations, 2006. The Chinese figure is taken from joint UNCTAD and United Nations Development Programme report 'Asian Foreign Direct Investment in Africa: Towards a New Era of Co-operation among Developing Countries'. The report also noted that on foreign direct investment, China came fourth among Asian investors in Africa, with Singapore, India and Malaysia leading the way. It also cited Sudan as the largest recipient of Chinese foreign direct investment worldwide.

34 Assistant to the President for National Security Affairs Stephen Hadley, 'Africa and Smart Development Policy', discussion meeting at Carnegie Endowment for International Peace, 5 February 2008, transcript available at http://www.carnegieendowment.org/files/0205_transcript_hadley.pdf.

35 For further details on PEPFAR, see PEPFAR website, http://www.pepfar.gov. Figure taken from 'PEPFAR Overview', updated January 2009, http://www.pepfar.gov/press/81352.htm. Regarding US action on malaria, in 2005, President Bush launched an initiative to reduce deaths from malaria by 50% in 15 of the worst-affected African countries. With funding of $1.2bn, by early 2008 the programme had reached an estimated 25m people.

36 With an integrated civilian and military staff of around 1,300, AFRICOM is projected to cost $4bn between 2010 and 2015. John Pendleton of the Government Accountability Office, 'AFRICOM: Rationales, Roles, and Progress on the Eve of Operations', testimony before a hearing of the Congressional Subcommittee on

National Security and Foreign Affairs on the progress of AFRICOM, 15 July 2008.

37 Some of this disquiet can be attributed to poor US public relations at the launch of the command, when it appears that little explanation of the reasons behind the command's creation was thought necessary. Attitudes in Africa are likely to soften as the command develops its outreach programmes, which include the provision of maritime training to improve local capacity to deal with smuggling, piracy, illegal fishing and the delivery of humanitarian aid in disaster situations.

38 'China in Africa: Implications for US Policy', hearing of the US Senate Committee on Foreign Relations, 4 June 2008, http://foreign.senate.gov/hearings/2008/hrg080604a.html.

39 Interviews, Beijing, 2008.

40 Though quotas on bananas, sugar and rice remained for a transitional period.

41 'European Commission Proposes New Strategy to Address EU Critical Needs for Raw Materials', EU press release IP/08/1628, 4 November 2008.

42 Resolution brought by Ana Maria Gomes, 'Chinese Policy and its Effects on Africa', INI/2007/2255, adopted 23 April 2008, http://www.europarl.europa.eu/oeil/file.jsp?id=5564762.

43 Lindsey Hilsum, 'China, Africa, and the G8 – Or Why Bob Geldof Needs to Wake Up', in Wild and Mepham (eds), 'The New Sinosphere: China in Africa', p. 5.

44 'Lisbon Declaration: EU–Africa Summit', 8–9 December 2007, http://www.eu2007.pt/NR/rdonlyres/BAC34848-05CC-45E9-8F1D-8E2663079609/0/20071208LISBONDeclaration_EN.pdf. For details on the EU–Africa partnership, see 'The Africa–EU Strategic Partnership: A Joint Africa–EU Strategy', December 2007, p. 1, http://www.eu2007.pt/NR/rdonlyres/D449546C-BF42-4CB3-B566-407591845C43/0/071206jsapenlogos_formatado.pdf.

45 International Energy Agency, 'World Energy Outlook 2007'.

46 Jairam Ramesh, a junior commerce minister, quoted in Jo Johnson, 'India Follows China's Path in Africa', Financial Times, 8 April 2008.

47 'India–Africa Trade to Reach US $70bn By 2014', TradeInvest Africa, 25 March 2009.

48 At a 2008 conclave meeting, 131 projects were discussed with a total value of more than $10bn. 'India–Africa Conclave to Discuss Projects Worth Over 10 Billion Dollars', Asian News International, 14 March 2008.

49 Sandeep Dikshit, 'India Doubles Credit to Africa', The Hindu, 9 April 2008.

50 The first phase of the project, which links India with 11 African countries, was officially inaugurated in February 2009. More countries are being connected to the network. 'India Launches Pan-African E-network Project', Indo-Asian News Service, 27 February 2009, http://www.hindustantimes.com/StoryPage/StoryPage.aspx?sectionName=HomePage&id=2daaa10a-927a-463c-8902-142dc3f3cf4e&Headline=India+launches+Pan-African+e-network+project.

51 Mohandas Gandhi, Harijan, 24 February 1946.

52 TICAD website, 'What is TICAD?', http://www.ticad.net/.

53 'Japan Vows to Double Aid to Africa by 2012', Associated Press, 28 May 2008. Other commitments included $4bn in soft loans for infrastructure and a fund of $2.5bn for the Japan Bank for

International Cooperation to support Japanese businesses in Africa.

54 See 'Joint Fact Sheet: US–Japan Cooperation on African Health and Food Security Challenges', White House press release, 8 July 2008, http://georgewbush-whitehouse.archives.gov/news/releases/2008/07/20080708-18.html.

55 'South Korea Weapons Sales Top $1bln for First Time', Reuters, 29 December 2008.

56 Song Jung-a, Christian Oliver and Tom Burgis, 'Daewoo to Cultivate Madagascar Land for Free', *Financial Times*, 19 November 2008.

57 Tom Burgis and Javier Blas, 'Madagascar Scraps Daewoo Farm Deal', *Financial Times*, 18 March 2009.

58 Figures from 'The Summit', page on the Turkey–Africa Cooperation Summit on Turkish Ministry of Foreign Affairs website, http://africa.mfa.gov.tr/the-summit.en.mfa.

59 'Brazil's Embrapa to Invest in African Countries Where China is Applying US$5 Billion', MacauHub, 7 May 2007.

60 See http://www.pambazuka.org/en/category/africa_china/.

61 Bernard Kihiyo, 'Consumers Protest on Sub-Standard Goods', Tanzania Consumer Advocacy Society blog, 15 April 2008, http://tanzaniaconsumer.blogspot.com/2008/04/message-of-tanzania-consumers-to.html.

62 'Niger Campaigners Call for More Details on Oil Deal with China', Agence France-Presse, 30 July 2008, http://www.energy-daily.com/reports/Niger_campaigners_call_for_more_details_on_oil_deal_with_China_999.html.

63 See Sanda Baboucar, 'A qui profitera le pétrole nigérien', *L'Action*, no. 37, 27 June 2008, p. 4, http://209.85.175.104/search?q=cache:1z_KDaNSPJUJ:www.nigerdiaspora.net/journaux/action.pdf+Niger+China+Diffa+oil+L%27Action&hl=en&ct=clnk&cd=1&gl=sg. On 26 January 2009, Niger member of parliament Mahaman Nomao Djika put a question to the president of Niger's legislative National Assembly on these issues. The text of his question is appended to the report: 'Parliamentarian Questions Assembly President on Mining Permits', Revenue Watch Institute, 5 February 2009, http://www.revenuewatch.org/news/020509.php.

64 Namibian Broadcasting Corporation Television, 31 July 2008.

65 Paul Kagame, 'Africa and Rwanda: From Crisis to Socioeconomic Development', public address hosted by the Lee Kuan Yew School of Public Policy, National University of Singapore, 22 May 2008.

66 For example, in 2007 the governor of the DRC's Katanga province experimented with a ban on exporting unprocessed ore from the province. Martin Creamer, 'Permanent Ban on All Raw Ore Export, DRC's Katanga Governor Decrees', *Mining Weekly*, 27 March 2007. A timber export ban was imposed by the government of Sierra Leone from January to June 2008 while rules on illegal logging were tightened. 'Sierra Leone', illegal-logging.info, http://www.illegal-logging.info/sub_approach.php?subApproach_id=165.

67 Whereas there were an estimated 600,000 child workers in Zambia in 1999, by 2006 the number had risen to 900,000. 'Zambia: Worker Headed for Decency, Prosperity Challenges', *Times of Zambia*, 1 May 2008, http://allafrica.com/stories/200805010349.html.

68 *Ibid.*

69 Dorothy Nakaweesi, 'Country's Labour Laws Now in Chinese', *The Monitor* (Uganda), 30 July 2008.

70 CAITEC, 'Guidelines on Corporate Social Responsibility Compliance by Foreign Invested Enterprises'.

71 Alec Russell and Matthew Green, 'Big Push to Be More Assertive', *Financial Times*, 24 January 2008.

72 The average developing country hosts in the region of 260 visits a year from donors. Zoellick, 'Changing Trends in Global Power and Conflict Resolution'.

73 For more on some of the problems here and Chinese attitudes to them, see Zhu Xiaolei, 'A Slippery Proposition', *Beijing Review*, no. 26, 26 June 2008, http://www.bjreview.com.cn/world/txt/2008-06/21/content_128598.htm.

74 One important moment in this move towards interdependence was China's joining the World Trade Organisation in December 2001.

75 Deputy Assistant Secretary of State for East Asian and Pacific Affairs Thomas Christensen mentioned this intention in 'Shaping China's Global Choices Through Diplomacy', his March 2008 statement to the US–China Economic and Security Review Commission. The 2008 annual report of the commission, published in November 2008, noted that no such meetings had yet taken place: '2008 Report to Congress of the US–China Economic and Security Review Commission', p. 249, http://www.uscc.gov/annual_report/2008/annual_report_full_08.pdf.

76 Daniel Schearf, 'US Seeks Cooperation with China in Africa', Voice of America, 15 October 2008.

77 The announcement of a 'structured dialogue' was made in the joint statement that emerged from the 2006 meeting. Joint Statement of the Ninth EU–China Summit, Helsinki, 9 September 2006, p. 4, see http://www.consilium.europa.eu/ueDocs/cms_Data/docs/pressData/en/er/90951.pdf.

78 European Commission, 'The EU, Africa and China: Towards Trilateral Dialogue and Cooperation', SEC(2008)2641, 17 October 2008, http://ec.europa.eu/development/icenter/repository/COMM_PDF_COM_2008_0654_F_COMMUNICATION_en.pdf.

79 Agreement between UK Prime Minister Gordon Brown and Chinese Premier Wen Jiabao during the UK–China Summit of January–February 2009, see 'UK–China Summit: Key Outcomes 2009', Downing Street website, 2 February 2009, http://www.number10.gov.uk/Page18214.

80 'UK and China – Partners for Africa's Development', in 'China and Africa', UK Department for International Development website, http://www.dfid.gov.uk/countries/asia/africa.asp.

81 In 2007, the UN accused Eritrea of funnelling 'huge quantities of arms' to al-Qaeda-linked groups in Somalia. Report of the Monitoring Group on Somalia Pursuant to Security Council Resolution 1724 (2006), S/2007/436, 18 July 2007.

82 'Eritrea Grants Two Mining Exploration Licenses', Reuters, 3 October 2007. Chinese exports to Eritrea increased 369% the previous year, but only to reach the comparatively low level of $37.7m.

83 'Delegation Participates in Chinese Mining Conference', Shabait.com, 13 November 2008. A high-level Chinese delegation also visited Asmara in July 2008 to investigate opportunities for cotton cultivation. 'Eritrea Courts China, Iran for Trade', Afrol News, 29 July 2008.

84 'Gash Barka Region and the [*sic*] China's Xinjiang Province Sign Memorandum of Understanding on Fostering Cooperation', Shabait.com, 5 November 2008.

85 'President Holds Talks with PRC Delegation', Shabait.com, 23 March 2009.

86 The World Bank initially provided financing for the pipeline project in 2001. After it became clear that the government of Chad was failing to uphold its commitment to use the revenue generated by the pipeline to support poverty reduction, a new memorandum of understanding was signed in July 2006, committing the government to spending 70% of the 2007 revenue from the project on poverty-reduction programmes. In 2008, the World Bank terminated its involvement in the project in protest at the ongoing failure to uphold revenue spending agreements. The government of Chad duly paid back the World Bank for its pipeline-related financing. World Bank, 'World Bank Statement on Chad–Cameroon Pipeline', press release 2009/073/AFR, 9 September 2008.

87 For more information on the Japan International Cooperation Agency and for budget comparisons with other major donor agencies, see 'Facts and Figures' on the organisation's website, http://www.jica.go.jp/english/news/field/2008/pdf/081003.pdf.

88 Dino Patti Djalal, spokesperson for the president of Indonesia, 'Transforming Indonesia: Implications for the Region and the World', public address hosted by IISS-Asia, Singapore, 7 October 2008.

Adelphi books are published eight times a year by Routledge Journals, an imprint of Taylor & Francis, 4 Park Square, Milton Park, Abingdon, Oxfordshire OX14 4RN, UK.

A subscription to the institution print edition, ISSN 0567-932X, includes free access for any number of concurrent users across a local area network to the online edition, ISSN 1478-5145.

2009 Annual Adelphi Subscription Rates		
Institution	£381	$669 USD
Individual	£222	$378 USD
Online only	£361	$636 USD

Dollar rates apply to subscribers in all countries except the UK and the Republic of Ireland where the pound sterling price applies. All subscriptions are payable in advance and all rates include postage. Journals are sent by air to the USA, Canada, Mexico, India, Japan and Australasia. Subscriptions are entered on an annual basis, i.e. January to December. Payment may be made by sterling cheque, dollar cheque, international money order, National Giro, or credit card (Amex, Visa, Mastercard).

For more information, visit our website: **http://www.informaworld.com/ adelphipapers.**

For a complete and up-to-date guide to Taylor & Francis journals and books publishing programmes, and details of advertising in our journals, visit our website: **http://www.informaworld.com.**

Ordering information:
USA/Canada: Taylor & Francis Inc., Journals Department, 325 Chestnut Street, 8th Floor, Philadelphia, PA 19106, USA. **UK/Europe/Rest of World:** Routledge Journals, T&F Customer Services, T&F Informa UK Ltd., Sheepen Place, Colchester, Essex, CO3 3LP, UK.

Advertising enquiries to:
USA/Canada: The Advertising Manager, Taylor & Francis Inc., 325 Chestnut Street, 8th Floor, Philadelphia, PA 19106, USA. Tel: +1 (800) 354 1420. Fax: +1 (215) 625 2940.

UK/Europe/Rest of World: The Advertising Manager, Routledge Journals, Taylor & Francis, 4 Park Square, Milton Park, Abingdon, Oxfordshire OX14 4RN, UK. Tel: +44 (0) 20 7017 6000. Fax: +44 (0) 20 7017 6336.

The print edition of this journal is printed on ANSI conforming acid-free paper by Bell & Bain, Glasgow, UK.

1944-5571(2009)49:1;1-O

The Evolution of Strategic Thought

Classic Adelphis

The Adelphis book series is the Institute's principal contribution to policy-relevant, original academic research. Collected on the occasion of the Institute's 50th anniversary, the twelve Adelphis in this volume represent some of the finest examples of writing on strategic issues. They offer insights into the changing security landscape of the past half-century and glimpses of some of the most significant security events and trends of our times, from the Cold War nuclear arms race, through the oil crisis of 1973, to the contemporary challenge of asymmetric war in Iraq and Afghanistan.

Published April 2008; 704 pp.

Bookpoint Ltd. 130 Milton Park, Abingdon, Oxon OX14 4SB, UK
Tel: +44 (0)1235 400524, Fax: +44 (0)1235 400525
Customer orders: book.orders@tandf.co.uk
Bookshops, wholesalers and agents:
Email (UK): uktrade@tandf.co.uk,
email (international): international@tandf.co.uk

Routledge
Taylor & Francis Group

THE INTERNATIONAL INSTITUTE FOR STRATEGIC STUDIES

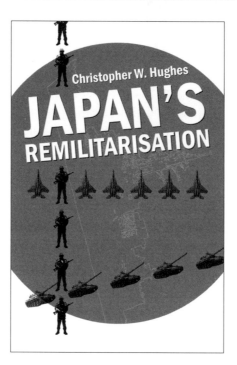

China's relations with African nations have changed dramatically over the past decade. African oil now accounts for more than 30% of China's oil imports, and China is Africa's second-largest single-country trading partner, as well as a leading lender and infrastructure investor on the continent.

Yet these developments are bringing challenges, not only for Africa and the West, but for China as well. This book examines these challenges, considering Africa as a testing ground, both for Chinese companies 'going global' and for a Chinese government that is increasingly having to deal with issues beyond its shores and immediate control. What does China need to do to protect and develop its African engagements, against a backdrop of mounting African expectations, concerns from Western actors in Africa, and the rival presence of other emerging actors? How sustainable is the momentum that China has established in its African ventures?

China's adaptations to the challenges it is facing in Africa are examined and assessed, as are the implications of these changes for China, Africa and the West. China's African engagements are certainly changing Africa, but could they also be changing China?

Sarah Raine is a Research Associate at the International Institute for Strategic Studies (IISS). Before joining the IISS, she worked at the British Foreign and Commonwealth Office.

ASIAN POLITICS/AFRICAN POLITICS/
INTERNATIONAL RELATIONS
www.iiss.org

ISBN 978-0-415-55693-4

Routledge
Taylor & Francis Group

IISS